LOCALITY AND IDENTITY: ENVIRONMENTAL ISSUES IN LAW AND SOCIETY

To Sam and Gus

Issues in Law and Society
General Editor: Michael Freeman

Titles in the Series:

Children's Rights: A Comparative Perspective
Edited by Michael Freeman

Divorce: Where Next?
Edited by Michael Freeman

Exploring the Boundaries of Contract
Edited by Roger Halson

Law as Communication
Edited by David Nelken

Iraqgate: The Constitutional Implications of the Matrix-Churchill Affair
Edited by Rodney Austin

Positivism Today
Edited by Stephen Guest

Governing Childhood
Edited by Anne McGillivray

Legislation and the Courts
Edited by Michael Freeman

Locality and Identity: Environmental Issues in Law and Society
Edited by Jane Holder and Donald McGillivray

Overcoming Child Abuse
Edited by Michael Freeman

Science in Court
Edited by Michael Freeman and Helen Reece

Law, Culture, Tradition and Children's Rights in Eastern and Southern Africa
Edited by Welshman Ncube

Locality and Identity: Environmental Issues in Law and Society

Edited by
JANE HOLDER and DONALD McGILLIVRAY

Routledge
Taylor & Francis Group
LONDON AND NEW YORK

First published 1999 by Dartmouth and Ashgate Publishing

Reissued 2018 by Routledge
2 Park Square, Milton Park, Abingdon, Oxon OX14 4RN
711 Third Avenue, New York, NY 10017, USA

Routledge is an imprint of the Taylor & Francis Group, an informa business

Copyright © Jane Holder and Donald McGillivray 1999

All rights reserved. No part of this book may be reprinted or reproduced or utilised in any form or by any electronic, mechanical, or other means, now known or hereafter invented, including photocopying and recording, or in any information storage or retrieval system, without permission in writing from the publishers.

Notice:
Product or corporate names may be trademarks or registered trademarks, and are used only for identification and explanation without intent to infringe.

Publisher's Note
The publisher has gone to great lengths to ensure the quality of this reprint but points out that some imperfections in the original copies may be apparent.

Disclaimer
The publisher has made every effort to trace copyright holders and welcomes correspondence from those they have been unable to contact.

A Library of Congress record exists under LC control number: 98049092

Typeset by Manton Typesetters, 5–7 Eastfield Road, Louth, Lincs, LN11 7AJ, UK.

ISBN 13: 978-1-138-32630-9 (hbk)
ISBN 13: 978-1-138-32631-6 (pbk)
ISBN 13: 978-0-429-44992-5 (ebk)

Contents

Acknowledgements	vii
Preface	ix
Foreword by Kevin Gray	xi
List of Contributors	xiii

Introduction   1
Jane Holder and Donald McGillivray

PART I   Moral and Market Boundaries

1 Using Environmental Ethics to Create Ecological Law   17
 David Wilkinson
2 Challenging the Ethos of the European Union
 A Green Perspective on European Union Policies and
 Programmes for Rural Development and the Environment   51
 David Wood

PART II   Nature and Identity

3 Capturing Values for Nature: Ecological, Economic and Cultural
 Perspectives   85
 Carolyn Harrison, Jacquelin Burgess and Judy Clark
4 Private Country? Hunting, Land and Judicial Interventions   111
 Davina Cooper
5 Hedgerows, Laws and Cultural Landscape   133
 Jane Holder

PART III Environmental Justice

6 The Grassroots at Risk: Local Perceptions and Environmental Injustice   151
   Angela C. Halfacre and Albert R. Matheny
7 Environmental Justice: The American Experience and its Possible Application to the United Kingdom   169
   Antonia Layard

PART IV Legal Mechanisms and Social Practices

8 Save as you Spend: Consumer Protection of the Environment and Local Social Cohesion   197
   Françoise Jarvis
9 Common Property and Private Trusts   223
   Paul Kohler

Acknowledgements

We would like to thank many colleagues and friends for their help and support in bringing this collection of papers together. First, our thanks go to Michael Freeman, the 'Issues in Law and Society' series editor, for encouraging us to work on a book on environmental issues. Our main thanks are to the contributors who, as well as producing thoughtful and interesting work, were also remarkably patient with the editing process. We would also like to thank Ian Bache, William Howarth, Joanne Scott and John Wightman for their insightful comments and advice on the collection, as well as Ashgate for their speed and professionalism in seeing the collection through to publication. Finally, our thanks go to the Research Committee of the Faculty of Laws, University College London, for their funding of the seminar which triggered this collection.

Preface

This book arose from a seminar with the enticingly broad title 'Environmental Issues in Law and Society', which was held on the notable date of 2 May 1997 at University College London. Papers were given by lawyers, geographers and those working in environmental studies, most of whom had 'stayed up for Portillo' earlier that morning. Although the papers were diverse in subject matter and born from different academic disciplines, the two main themes of locality and identity emerged. These have come to form the focus of this book. Undeniably abstract, they nevertheless offer a way in to thinking about important issues relating to the environment – of globalisation, sustainable development, ethics, participation in decisions about the environment and the valuation of nature.

The book is not directed at a particular readership. Its strength is its diversity of subject matter – appealing hopefully to those interested in environmental law, but also beyond. Where there is some overlap of subject areas – landscapes (physical and cultural), valuation of environmental resources, land use planning – these are seen from different disciplinary and theoretical perspectives, so that networks of understanding might be built around a particular issue or problem.

The seminar began a process of exchange of ideas and views between the contributors, the contributors and editors, and the editors themselves. It is this which has made the editing process a stimulating one, and this is hopefully reflected in the collection.

Foreword

One suspects that the great environmentalist John Muir did not have much time for lawyers and their dusty books, although his Scots origins would have implanted a certain respect for any true learning which those books concealed. Well over a century ago Muir recorded, in a strangely haunting journal entry, that one day he 'only went for a walk, and finally concluded to stay out till sundown, for going out, I found, was really going in'.

This radical reversal of perspective ought, in so many ways, to have a forceful contemporary resonance. There is still a tendency – a strong popular instinct – to regard those engaged with environmental issues as being, in some significant sense, on the outside, somehow distanced from the current reality of law and politics. Admittedly there is also, nowadays, a reluctant realisation that environmental questions press upon us all as never before; there is an incipient recognition that these questions will not simply go away. Yet, so far, there is no deep general perception that environmental concerns are absolutely central and crucial, as distinct from annoyingly peripheral, to the contemporary business of law, politics and community life. Beguiled by the fragile technological and other advances so evident in modern western society, we remain largely unmindful that the *real* world is the raw external physical world which, indeed, so few of us actually enter or understand. The only truly critical area of engagement may turn out to have been the one sphere from which so many – not least lawyers – have remained arrogantly aloof. In secular terms the earth is all we really have – all that really matters – and, as that other great American naturalist and visionary, Henry Thoreau, once put it, 'in Wildness is the preservation of the World'.

This book of essays contributes significantly towards the reorientation of perspective which is needed to underscore the primacy of environmental law and policy as central concerns of all who care about our future. Its message, particularly for lawyers, is a *bouleversement* of traditional priorities of interest and direction. It is, above all, a deeply thoughtful book which, in a manner profoundly informed by legal analysis and technique, explores the construction of a modern value system for the physical environment. Even in its title, *Locality and Identity*, the book reinforces a perception of external landscape as the counterpart of a vital inner landscape of the mind, in which the formation of a coherent and disciplined relationship with the natural environment is ultimately self-identifying and self-constituting. The book poses, without doubt, some difficult questions – the reader is not asked to agree with every viewpoint or argument expressed – but each of the essays contained in this collection provides, in its own way, a remarkably valuable, vivid and stimulating point of entry to the world that matters.

Kevin Gray

List of Contributors

Jacquelin Burgess, Environment and Society Research Unit, Department of Geography, University College London

Judy Clark, Environment and Society Research Unit, Department of Geography, University College London

Davina Cooper, School of Law, University of Keele

Kevin Gray, Faculty of Law, University of Cambridge

Angela C. Halfacre, Department of Political Science, University of Charleston

Carolyn Harrison, Environment and Society Research Unit, Department of Geography, University College London

Jane Holder, Faculty of Laws, University College London

Françoise Jarvis, Faculty of Law, University of Aberystwyth

Paul Kohler, Faculty of Laws, University College London

Antonia Layard, Bartlett School of Planning, University College London

Albert R. Matheny, Department of Political Science, University of Florida

Donald McGillivray, Kent Law School, University of Kent

David Wilkinson, Department of Environmental Social Sciences, University of Keele

David Wood, Centre for Rural Economy, Department of Agricultural Economics and Food Marketing, University of Newcastle upon Tyne

Introduction

Jane Holder and Donald McGillivray

In this collection the relationship between humans and the environment is explored through questions of locality and identity. We adopt this approach because, as researchers working in the socio-legal area, our concern is that geographic, economic and moral boundaries have been drawn around particular ways of understanding this relationship, leading to the partial defining of environmental problems and the marginalisation of particular groups in decisions about the state of the environment. Law has played an important part in drawing such boundaries, for example, by narrowly defining 'the environment' as air, water and land, and by generally dividing up matters of conservation, land use and landscape protection for separate treatment. Law's traditional preoccupation with jurisdiction compounds this state of affairs: environmental problems are conceived of, and contested, in terms of international, European Community and national law, often with little appreciation of the operation of complex and often contradictory 'laws of nature' – of cross-media, transboundary and cumulative environmental effects. A further legal boundary is drawn between that which is privately owned and that which is 'common', with law having traditionally upheld private property rights at the expense of common ownership. This creates some doubts about the capacity of law to protect the environment as 'commons' via individualised legal mechanisms. Much of the law relating to the environment may therefore be characterised by spatial, theoretical and disciplinary closure.

While strides have been taken in geography, philosophy and other disciplines in understanding and valuing the environment, with regard to the categorisation and regulation of the natural environment law is both inward looking and limited: law has failed to recognise critical developments in other disciplines and has failed to develop its own critical strains. Debates within environmental law have often been about drawing the margins of the discipline. Instead, our concern here is how issues of identity and locality – globalisation and ethics, valuing the environment, environmental justice and the use of traditional and new legal forms – cross disciplines. This approach lends itself to a diversity which is reflected in the chapters which follow. The aim of this collection is therefore to explore and, in some cases, to confront the limitations of law where they prevent recognition of the relationship between humans and nature.

Marking Out the Boundaries

Part I of the book marks out the moral, market and political boundaries which typify the treatment of environmental issues in law and society. David Wilkinson's chapter on environmental ethics considers how far purely environmental interests might be enhanced in law, so as to create 'ecological law' which stresses the interrelation of human activities and the natural environment. This represents a departure from more traditional analyses which assume that law relating to the environment can be identified as a discipline in its own right and, by implication, that environmental problems can be resolved by the direct legal regulation of human activities. Taking two key areas of environmental law – pollution control and nature conservation – as his focus, he asserts that law and legal structures need to be based on biocentric and ecocentric environmental ethics which, coupled with principles taken from Deep Ecology, are less concerned either with physical or human-made boundaries and more attuned to bringing the non-human into the community of interests. For example, law based on ecocentric principles ought to accord greatest considerability to the conservation over time of ecosystems than to species, and to species rather than their individual component organisms.

This approach, applied generally to legal regulation, poses nothing less than a full-scale assault on the classical liberal-democratic theory underpinning modern law. All entities (human and non-human) with moral considerability must be seen as individuals with interests and rights to be upheld through law, while Deep Ecology clearly has a strong view of what the good life entails. But more importantly, the ideology of individualism which underpins liberalism is, as Wilkinson observes, 'in particular conflict with Deep Ecology's prescription of self-realisation through increasing identification with others as part of an inter-related holistic natural world'. Such identification requires far greater rights of public participation in the legal process, and measures such as the constitutional entrenchment of ecological values and improved ecological education.

The market, as opposed to moral, boundaries of ecological understanding are discussed by David Wood in a chapter which challenges both 'sustainable development' and the role of public participation in its realisation. The case study taken is the response of the European Community (EC) to geographic inequalities of wealth – principally via the Structural funds – set against the background of the enshrining into the EC Treaty of the principle of 'subsidiarity' and, following the Amsterdam Treaty, inclusion of the promotion of a 'harmonious, balanced and sustainable development of economic activities' amongst the Community's aims. Against the background of a critique of globalisation, and the broader and deeper reach of capitalist industrialism, Wood presents a sceptical view of sustainable development that, by failing to challenge the orthodoxies of late modern capitalism, translates into practice as little more than 'business as usual' and fails to work towards either the achievement of the genuine sustainability of natural systems or local empowerment. Informed by political ecology, he criticises these initiatives as failing to confront the impact of globalisation on local people and communities, or to offer a radical vision of sustainability. Thus, although no formal definition of sustainable development is given, he argues that legal meaning is imparted via the practice of key actors – the Community institutions, governments and transnational enterprises – with most reason to resist change. Moreover, the institution of the 'partnership' principle in Structural funding – partnership between the Commission, national governments, and economic and social partners – is motivated primarily by concerns to ensure that funding is used efficiently on the ground. And while forthcoming reforms to the funds may secure the greater inclusion of environmental interests, problems in securing genuine participation remain; there is little to suggest that the scope for challenge to the received, top-down, vision of sustainable development will be widened. Similar criticisms are made of the LEADER initiative and of the Common Agricultural Policy.

Wood's chapter therefore identifies a use of law both participatory but, for him, unresponsive, wedded to the market and an adjunct to globalisation. This is nowhere better reflected than in the work of the European Court of Justice (ECJ), seen as keen to strengthen the corporate bias of the Community and to secure better legislative implementation, but much less keen to stretch the Treaty to give legal voice to the interests of individuals, local groups or environmental associations against Community action. EC law, and the ECJ, therefore stand accused of furthering the integration of the European market, in the interest of ensuring European competitiveness in the global economy, at the expense of market regulation in the interests of disadvantaged communities and of the environment. And moves to weave sustainable development into EC law seem beset by the same forces and factors which led to law being used to reinforce global market liberalism at the time of the Brundtland Report (World Commission on Environment and Development 1987) rather than create a radical and challenging vision of sustainability.

Both chapters illustrate a more general trend in law towards greater scope for participation. But political structures at local level remain ill-equipped to deal with the consequences of globalisation for popular participation and may often be used to facilitate existing views of the good life. Within law, and more generally, this has led to a restriction on the extent to which ethical and cross-disciplinary issues of the kind raised in both chapters may meaningfully be debated.

Nature and Identity

Debates about participation necessarily centre around how the environment is valued and specifically how a community's identity may be bound up with different locales and their familiar features – a river, hedgerow, or forest. In Part II, the contributors question whether law can purposefully shape this process of identification or whether it merely draws lines, be they protective or exploitative, around existing identities. In particular, the chapters by Carolyn Harrison, Jacquelin Burgess and Judy Clark, and by Jane Holder, question the premise that the social and cultural importance of the environment is best quantified in quasi-objective and quantifiable terms, an approach which fits well with the current dominance of economistic approaches to environmental valuation (see, for example, Pearce 1995).

Together with Wilkinson, who for ethical reasons is also critical of such economism, Harrison, Burgess and Clark discuss the limitations of current economic valuation techniques such as contingent valuation which assume that individuals, living in a society dominated by the market, will pursue their interests with little sense of community or common purpose. Instead they advance the development of more discursive and participatory valuation techniques which attempt to give greater weight to concerns such as typicalness, distinctiveness, setting and context and to capturing the 'common good'. In particular, they explore an approach to valuation premised on values not being something to be argued from but reasoned towards, and which are therefore distinct from the more transient preferences which form the basis of 'willingness to pay' surveys. Revealingly, their 'Stakeholder Group', through dialogue, works towards 'science' and 'common good' approaches to valuing nature, rather than approaches based on private rights or individual use-values. Their study shows how attention to process can capture the less tangible values associated with the cultural and social significance of natural attributes in what appears, at least in their case study, to be a seemingly non-contentious way.

The valuation of such 'environmental capital' marks an ambitious turning-point towards common good approaches to valuing nature, and one which has found favour with the Environment Agency. Indeed, it may be seen as inclusionary not merely in recognising the importance attached by residents of particular localities to their interaction with the natural world but also, through the valuation process, contributing to the strengthening of local communities. Yet two key difficulties remain. First, the Agency's duty to have regard to likely costs and benefits (including environmental costs and benefits)[1] does not prescribe any particular methodology by which these are to be valued. Statutory guidance notes the use of economistic approaches, but is silent about the use of more participatory and discursive approaches. But a second key issue is what follows from the drawing of the boundaries of Local Environment Agency Plans (LEAPs). While these are not legally provided for, the use of riverine catchment management boundaries in environmental planning may unduly restrict or predetermine the community of interest. With all bar the scientific approach to valuation, boundary questions intrude. *Whose* view, or use-value preference, counts can then become a more important determinant in decision making than the weight attached to such a view or preference, as the considerable publicity surrounding the use of economic valuation in a recent English water abstraction appeal so well illustrates (ENDS Report 1998). Where environmental features are of more than local interest, *where* to draw the line around the community of those with legitimate interests in decision making will always be problematic, but all too often is drawn narrowly.[2] A similar point is made by Wood in his discussion of the implementation of the EC's Structural Funding Regulation and the concept of partnership, where national governments may keep a tight hold on determining the composition of partnership groups to ensure that national policy objectives are met.

The valuation of natural resources in objective terms is further discussed by Jane Holder in a chapter on the role of law both in constituting the landscape via hedgerows to mark out property following enclosure, and also the more recent use of law in attempting to conserve landscape through hedgerow protection. In particular, she observes how the Enclosure Acts helped shape not merely the natural world but also a broader landscape composed of physical forms and human perception. However, recent legislative attempts at hedgerow protection have failed to capture this richer, extended vision of landscape. Instead, as well as having numerous practical and procedural shortcomings, the law has ignored or avoided any attempt to capture the social and cultural importance of hedgerows for particular localities. Rather, what might be considered a relatively crude approach to valuing the importance of hedgerows through such techniques as the counting of species and features is used. Doubtless one reason for this is the practical inability for law to capture the importance of such incalculable concerns using legal methods which are sufficiently objective to be workable, but what is really at stake is a legal indifference to the creation of nature by culture.

6 Locality and Identity

The cultural importance of landscape and countryside activity is further explored by Davina Cooper in a chapter which examines the tension between the idyllic forms of the local – the rural village and the urban neighbourhood (and between public and private) – in the context of hunting law. For Cooper, what is of interest in hunting law is the connection between its private and public faces, in particular the role the private domain (equated here with the rural) performs in the reproduction and maintenance of public activity. The legal treatment of hunting must be seen in the context of the wider defence of the racialised, cultural reproduction associated with the countryside which, through protecting natural and cultural work, makes possible the collective identity that urban life and nation, in turn, rely upon. Hunting therefore becomes a matter of both public and private concern, but its key feature is in its articulation to the land, embedded in the very conception of countryside and soil, and thus as an ingredient in the reproduction of nationhood. But in contrast to the urban, the rural appears to reproduce national identity non-juridically, that is, relatively spontaneously through the ties and affection that develop between people and land rather than by legal controls. What is at issue is national identity as this is shaped through the counterpoising of urban multiculturalism with the white, Christian, Anglo-Saxon way of life of which hunting forms a part. Necessarily, however, upholding at local level activities deemed to be culturally significant in this respect will be exclusionary, not merely of urban interests but of those within rural hunting communities. For example, the Somerset councillors trying to ban deer hunting on council land in the Quantock Hills found their political viewpoints dismissed as private opinions by courts which take as their starting point the value of hunting as a social practice.

Both the case studies on hedgerow protection and hunting illustrate how some of the more odious political projects have used images of nature and landscape in their support,[3] and provide some evidence that the state[4] may seek to find legitimacy by supporting national identity through its defining environmental images. Yet this may be at the expense of the protection of the cultural building blocks that go to make up this wider community. Holder's chapter in particular shows that while law has played an important role in the construction of the rural landscape, for reasons connected with its need for certainty, objectivity and generalisability, it is less able to perform this role in its protection, to the detriment of local communities. Cooper's point, however, is that regardless of the *origins* of hunting and other rural practices as private, a considerable degree of legal intervention is required if hunting's public functions are to be *maintained*.

Environmental Justice

Whereas the chapters in Part II of the book are primarily concerned with the issue of identification in valuing and representing nature, those in Part III address issues of locality, specifically the siting of locally undesirable projects and land uses. Both the chapters by Angela Halfacre and Albert Matheny, and by Antonia Layard, are concerned with the overlaps between social and environmental injustice, that is, how and why adverse environmental consequences bear on particular communities. This is not least because of the usual spatial dissonance between the (often) localised costs and wider social benefits of hazardous activities, costs generally falling on those communities least capable of resistance. Harsh political reality, rather than hard 'science', may therefore tend to dictate the location of hazardous enterprises, making informed community participation in the regulatory process essential if local communities are to participate alongside experts and organised interests. These chapters suggest that regulatory law is neither universal nor uniform, but rather is capable of being used to structure environmental inequalities.[5] It is telling, therefore, that the research that Halfacre and Matheny draw upon – the findings of focus group research with under-represented citizens living in the shadow of nuclear installations – indicate that local interests need not take a NIMBYist form but are capable of articulating wider communitarian ideals. More particularly, these ideals play a part in the everyday lives of these non-activists as much as they emerge through the social processes of grassroots activists.

By contrast, the chapter by Layard combines theory and practice in probing the ethical underpinning of the US Environmental Justice Executive Order and the accompanying Strategy of the Environmental Protection Agency. These, initially, identify and prioritise the entitlement in being free of pollution and, if this cannot be achieved, the equitable distribution of risks. Layard then looks at how these interests might be protected in the context of pollution control in the UK. Specifically, she considers the two key approaches taken in the US to distributing locally undesirable land uses – the use of the market and of regulatory law – in the pursuit of inter-community justice. As the examples drawn from the US indicate, however, market-based approaches are problematic, not least in relation to potential inequality of bargaining power and issues of intra-community justice. Yet regulatory law may also tend towards many of the characteristics, not least negotiation and bargaining, associated with marketplace decisions. In the UK, for example, planning obligations may be used to extract, both *ex ante* and *ex post*, community benefits from developers in a way which attempts to integrate equity and entitlement. But issues of intra-community justice persist, issues which may only be addressed seriously by a more precautionary approach towards environmental protection.

Legal and Social Mechanisms for Change

Many of the chapters discussed above are concerned with existing social and legal practices. Following the approach adopted by Layard, Part IV of the book is forward looking, focusing on legal and societal mechanisms for change. Whereas the chapter by Wood considers a range of mechanisms by which local communities might resist globalisation and the economisation of everyday life, the chapter by Françoise Jarvis looks in more detail at the legal underpinning of some of these mechanisms. The main question addressed is whether it is possible to foster forms of 'green consumerism' rather than consumerism more generally. On whether regulation alone will suffice, Jarvis is sceptical, highlighting for example the inevitable difficulties of regulating product claims such as 'easy on the environment' and the difficulties individual consumers face in gaining knowledge of how traded goods are produced, let alone the environmental impact this may have had. By contrast, Jarvis is more optimistic about the possibility of using 'parallel' or 'alternative' forms of exchange not merely to allow for more effective green consumerism but, as importantly, to constitute local communities through the shared social practice of green consumer behaviour, most tellingly through practices such as LETS schemes and cooperatives. These act as catalysts for alternative and regional economies and may contribute to 'local environmental democracy'.

At least in the case of LETS schemes, perhaps because of their relative novelty, formal legal regulation seems to intrude only in relation to taxation. Although it is not clear how, for example, contract or criminal law would be used against those who might abuse the system, it is notable that the potential for such abuse appears not to have been realised, with seemingly strong bonds of trust between members. But, as Jarvis recognises, further work may be needed to determine the extent to which such ties, and thus the generation of 'community' through such schemes, can be attributable to participation in the schemes themselves or demonstrates only pre-existing shared perspectives and values amongst participants. It may therefore be that the practice of local trading schemes not only illustrates the neglect of formal legal structures in grounding exchange relations within local communities but also serves to highlight the limits of law in creating stable market institutions (see, for example, Gray 1994: 27).

In a similar vein, Paul Kohler explores the possibility of constituting and empowering local communities through trust law. As the chapters by

Wilkinson and Cooper indicate, the scope for local communities to pursue environmental objectives under local government law may be restricted in the pursuit of national objectives. Building on discussion of the nature of common property Kohler sees in judicial dicta the scope for trusts to be enforced by a broader category of beneficiary in the interests of common ownership. In such dicta, therefore, may lie the germ of a fully-fledged public trust doctrine. A key issue would then be where the boundaries of the community are drawn, that is, *which* individuals would have sufficient legal standing to enforce the trust. What advantages such an approach would have over public regulatory techniques is obviously important; it might be argued, for example, that the use of 'community' trusts would inevitably divert attention away from the pursuit of legitimate environmental regulation at local or national level. In reply, there may be merit in the opportunistic, yet strategic, use of private legal forms of law as a supplement or irritant to public regulation (see generally Conaghan and Mansell 1993; Harlow and Rawlings 1992; for a strong view of this thesis, see McGillivray and Wightman 1997).

Cross-boundary Issues

Several important and common issues are raised by this collection – meanings of community, the convergence of social and environmental justice and questions of legal form and development. In considering meanings of community, a central tenet of environmentalism (and more so of ecologism)[6] has been the two-fold importance of community in social relations. First, that local communities are 'closer to nature' and thus best placed to understand and appreciate the importance of local features and environmental interests (for example, through preservation of local knowledge). This finds legal expression in the Rio Declaration,[7] and permeates Agenda 21. But a further reason is that 'nature' is itself seen as constitutive of local communities and identity. Thus, as Harvey writes, 'Decentralisation and community empowerment, coupled with a certain degree of bioregionalism, is then seen as the only effective solution to an alienated relation to nature and alienation in social relationships' (1996: 181).[8] There is, however, a tendency for local knowledge and values to be idealised by the green movement and mainstream political parties alike, and for large-scale organisations and enterprises to be demonised. And where the barriers between people and nature are broken down such that conservation is seen not as an attitude adopted towards nature but rather 'a way of life, a state of being', local communities, especially those post-colonially defined 'indigenous peoples', may ironically be enslaved to their natural environments at the very moment their struggle for acknowledgement in law is recognised (Wilder 1997).[9]

With these perspectives in mind, the question arises whether law can help to express community bonds and values, or respond to 'community' and community-type action, given that the forms of action available in modern law traditionally tend towards the individualised, liberal and generalised. Indeed, there must be a dialectical relation between law and community, for law (alongside other social practices and forms) both responds to community and simultaneously generates notions of 'community', and communities themselves. In particular, can (and ought) law generate and respond to the forms either of environmental community or, more strongly, of ecological communities?

Arguably, glimpses of Wilkinsons' expansive vision of an ecological law can already be seen. In European Community law, for example, certain habitats and species have been recognised as forming part of the 'common heritage of the Community',[10] while certain EC environmental directives may have the effect of giving individual citizens rights in clean air and water, thus reordering traditional notions of property rights (see Chapter 9). However, developments in other fields, most notably international environmental law, suggest that movement towards 'common heritage' approaches to environmental conservation have been headed off by a reassertion of the interests of nation states and of property rights. In addressing the issue of community, however, any discussion must now recognise the sheer diversity of groups and communities within society which might share a locality but, equally, experiences, functions, or needs (Cotterrell 1995: 336). For example, much of this book is taken up with discussing the development of environmental or ecological communities, not just in the obvious sense of groups such as the Centre for Alternative Technology, but also apparently looser groupings of consumers, trust beneficiaries and those affected by a nuclear installation or chemical works.

Diversity, though, extends beyond overlapping communities of interests. As Wilkinson observes, autonomous, bounded bodies of knowledge are anathema to thinking ecologically; underlying environmental problems are interconnected activities, states and substances, the nature of which jars with the formal boundaries of disciplines, literatures and specific methodologies. As discussed above, much of the legal writing on the environment has been taken up with justifying environmental law as a discipline and is therefore frequently introspective. But as the chapters in Part III of the book show, certain social, predominantly 'community health', issues may be translated into, or are presented as, 'environmental' issues, representing some convergence of environmental and social justice (Di Chiro 1996).

Finally, several contributors prompt an approach to law which emphasises geographical as much as historical concerns, space as much as time (see further Blomley 1994). Nevertheless, there is much to be taken to support recent work on the historical development of law, for example the emergence of reflexive law and legal structures and the theory of legal autopoiesis[11] and the fragmentation of law (Cotterrell 1992: 409). As regards the former, this concern with process and participation, and with communication between and learning from other disciplines and social substructures, chime with the development of common research methods between law, science and political geography which this collection describes. But there remain significant barriers preventing law from learning the critical lessons of other disciplines, for example, geography. The present collection therefore suggests both the possibilities, and limits, of interdisciplinarity, but does not in itself offer a theoretical explanation of such variance. It should be noted, however, that while there is much to be taken from this collection to support the emergence of new forms of law, this is not to accept such developments uncritically. As many of the contributors argue, much is to be gained by looking closely both at process and at forms of participation, and at the links both with substantive law and substantive outcomes. In addition, the concern of others is, implicitly, that developmental theories, be they legal or economic, are not a refuge for pessimism and passivity.

What general lessons, then, are we to draw from the present collection of essays in relation to law, environment, identity and locality? First, law must be able to respond to many terrains, not merely the geographical, which individuals and communities inhabit. But we now live in many communities, both of choice and circumstance, and thus any discussion of 'community' requires careful handling. Second, we need to explore critically the relations between nature and locality, avoiding simplistic naturalistic fallacies whilst at the same time recognising the importance of 'environment', amongst many other arenas, where human meaning is to be found and expressed. Third, we need to pay greater attention to the legal mechanisms through which 'rootedness' within such communities can be achieved and maintained. This may involve enhanced participatory structures in regulatory law, or the novel use of existing private law actions or education. But it also extends to positing forms of environmental valuation and substantive legal provisions which move away from reliance on economism and scientism and take local concerns, perceptions and meaning, as well as interdisciplinarity, seriously.

Notes

1 Section 39 of the Environment Act 1995 charges the Environment Agency with taking into account the likely costs and benefits of its actions (or inaction), unless unreasonable to do so or where the Agency is bound to comply with other obligations.

2. See the contrasting judgments in *R v. North Somerset District Council and Pioneer Aggregates (UK) Ltd ex p Garnett and Pierssene* [1997] JPL 1015 and *R v. Somerset County Council and ARC Southern Limited ex p Dixon* [1997] JPL 1030.
3. Though, as Harvey (1996: 171) rightly remarks, 'the point ... is not to see all ideas about "moral community", bioregionalism or place-bound thinking ... as necessarily exclusionary or neo-Nazi' (see also Barns 1996).
4. It might be more appropriate here to refer to the 'hollowed-out state' (see Rhodes 1997: Ch. 3). This would recognise that with globalisation has come a rethinking of boundaries both outwards and upwards, to the international community, and inwards and downwards towards the local, contributing to the 'hollowing-out' of the nation state, though leaving the nation state with the important role of distributing and making accountable powers of governance to the supra- and sub-national levels (Hirst and Thompson 1995).
5. In doing so, of course, regulation often does little more than the law of private nuisance which, through the locality rule in amenity nuisance cases, can equally be charged with replicating existing structural inequalities.
6. The distinction between environmentalism and ecologism may be seen as that between a 'managerial' and 'radical' agenda to the relationship between humanity and the natural environment; where environmentalism incorporates environmental thinking into existing discourses and ideologies, ecologism stands as a challenge to other political ideologies, and to industrialism, demanding the wholesale adoption of an ecocentric, anti-growth, approach. See, for example, Dobson 1995: Ch. 1.
7. 'Indigenous people and their communities, and other local communities, have a vital role in environmental management and development because of their knowledge and traditional practices. States should recognize and duly support their identity, culture and interests and enable their effective participation in the achievement of sustainable development' (Principle 22, *Declaration of the UN Conference on Environment and Development*, Rio de Janeiro, June 1992). See also WCED 1987: 114–115.
8. Bioregionalism seeks to identify localities with bounded natural areas, based on physical geography and biological characteristics, emphasising local self-sufficiency and co-dependency with natural resources (Sale 1997; see also Wood, in this volume).
9. For Wilder, the interplay of the global and local may lead to the return of the Noble Savage as a mediating force at a time of uncertainty about our relationship with nature.
10. Case C-44/95, *R v. Secretary of State for the Environment, ex parte Royal Society for the Protection of Birds* ('Lappel Bank') [1996] 3 CMLR 411, para. 24.
11. Reflexive law is seen as a response to modern legal formalism and autonomy which, as Teubner (1983: 250) points out, is not simply to be equated with notions of the rematerialisation of formal law, though it certainly includes elements of substantive rationality. Rather, it encompasses also 'the "reflexive" rationality of the process-oriented structuring of institutions and organizing of participation' (Teubner 1983: 251), typified by setting in place the conditions for regulated autonomy, regulating more indirectly through attention to communication between subsystems than direct regulation.

References

Barns, I. (1996) 'Environment, Democracy and Community', *Environmental Politics*, 4: 101.

Blomley, N.K. (1994) *Law, Space and the Geographies of Power* (New York: Guilford Press).
Conaghan, J. and Mansell, W. (1993) *The Wrongs of Tort* (London: Pluto).
Cotterrell, R. (1992) 'Law's Community: Legal Theory and the Image of Legality', *Journal of Law and Society*, 19: 405.
Cotterrell, R. (1995) *Law's Community: Legal Theory in Sociological Perspective* (Oxford: Clarendon Press).
Di Chiro, G. (1996) 'Nature as Community: The Convergence of Environmental and Social Justice', in Cronon, W. (ed.) *Uncommon Ground: Rethinking the Human Place in Nature* (London: W.W. Norton).
Dobson, A. (1995) *Green Political Thought* 2nd edn (London: Routledge).
ENDS Report (1998) 'Water abstraction decision deals savage blow to cost-benefit analysis', *ENDS Report*, 278, March: 16.
Gray, J. (1994) *The Undoing of Conservatism* (London: Social Market Foundation).
Harlow, C. and Rawlings, R. (1992) *Pressure Through Law* (London: Routledge).
Harvey, D. (1996) *Justice, Nature and the Geography of Difference* (London: Blackwell).
Hirst, P. and Thompson, G. (1995) 'Globalization and the future of the nation state', *Economy and Society*, 24: 408.
McGillivray, D. and Wightman, J. (1997) 'Private Rights and Environmental Protection', in Ireland, P. and Laleng, P. (eds) *The Critical Lawyers' Handbook 2* (London: Pluto).
Pearce, D. (1995) *Blueprint 4: Capturing Global Environmental Value* (London: Earthscan).
Rhodes, R.A.W. (1997) *Understanding Governance: Policy Networks, Governance, Reflexivity and Accountability* (Buckingham: Open University Press).
Sale, K. (1997) 'Mother of All: An Introduction to Bioregionalism', in Hannum, H. (ed.) *People, Land and Community* (New Haven/London: Yale University Press).
Teubner, G. (1983) 'Substantive and Reflexive Elements in Modern Law', *Law and Society Review*, 17(2): 239.
Wilder, L. (1997) 'Local futures? From denunciation to revalorization of the indigenous other', in Teubner, G. (ed.) *Global Law Without a State* (Aldershot: Dartmouth).
World Commission on Environment and Development (1987), *Our Common Future* (Oxford: Oxford University Press).

PART I
MORAL AND MARKET BOUNDARIES

1 Using Environmental Ethics to Create Ecological Law

David Wilkinson

> *Do we want a civilisation that will move towards some more intimate relation with the natural world, or do we want one that will continue to detach and isolate itself from both a dependence upon and a sympathy with that community of which we were originally part?*
>
> Krutch (1956)

Introduction

It is increasingly common to find arguments to the effect that in order to secure a proper relationship between humans and nature, environmental law should evolve to follow the principles of environmental *ethics* (for example, Stone 1972; Emmenegger and Tschentscher 1994). This chapter surveys some of the key theories of environmental ethics and considers the role of environmental ethics generally in environmental law. It concludes that biocentric and ecocentric environmental ethics, together with the principles of the Deep Ecology movement, although not currently reflected by environmental law, could provide a rational and proper basis for human–nature relations. It further concludes that a body of law which did adequately reflect these ethical principles – which in this chapter will be referred to as 'ecological law' – would be in a state of considerable tension with classical liberal-democratic theory.

Specifically, ecological law would conflict with liberalism's demands for freedom from state interference and, without further safeguards, be inconsistent with democracy's claim that the people should be free to choose legislative ends. It is therefore suggested that the institution of democracy is only compatible with a body of ecological law if ecological values are protected from democratic subversion. This protection could be provided by entrenchment of ecological values in pre-democratic (constitutional) measures and by improved education in ecological values. Ecological law could itself play an important part in this educative process by contributing to the development of personal ecological values – both through dissemination of knowledge of ecological law's content and, importantly, through participation in the process of environmental justice. The compatibility of ecological law and democratic theory thus depends, in part, on a sufficiency of rights of standing and opportunities for personal involvement in the legal process.

The Evolution of Environmental Ethics

Theories of environmental ethics have developed over time from views which took the environment to be nothing more than a resource for human exploitation (*anthropocentric* ethics), through theories attaching moral considerability to individual animals and plants (*biocentric* ethics), to comprehensive environmental ethics which locate ethical considerability in every kind of natural living entity (*ecocentric* ethics).

Anthropocentric Ethics

Historically, nature was conceived of as a God-given body of resources to be manipulated to produce benefits for humans (Thomas 1984). Writers have attributed this anthropocentric view of nature variously to the Greek stoics (Passmore 1974; Hargrove, 1989), Christianity (White 1967), capitalism (Moncrief 1974; Marx 1993) and technology (Moncrief 1974; Anonymous 1997). Whatever its origins, there can be little doubt that this conception of nature has contributed greatly to the process of ecological devastation.

There have been attempts to modify the basic anthropocentric position in ways that give meaning to nature other than merely as an instrument for the satisfaction of human wants. One way to do this is to adopt a theological ethic of *stewardship* – a duty to God to care for nature (Montefiore 1970; Attfield 1983, 1991; Hargrove 1986; McDonagh 1986). We find an interesting example of judicial endorsement of the religious doctrine of stewardship in the views of the seventeenth-century Chief Justice, Sir Matthew Hale: 'The end of man's creation was, that he should be the viceroy of the Great God of heaven and earth in this inferior world; his steward, *vicillus*, bailiff or farmer of this goodly farm of the lower world' (1677: 370).

Fortunately, it is not necessary to assume a position of subservience to the Deity to reach a more environmentally benign position. Indeed, most intra-human ethics can be extended in ways beneficial to the environment. More enlightened versions of utilitarianism, for example, will have regard to the long-term human benefits of biodiversity (Wilson 1994) as well as the more immediate pleasures derivable from nature contemplation (Mill 1848). The anthropocentric basis for environmental protection is made more credible if future persons are taken into account (Sikora and Barry 1978).

Enlightened anthropocentric ethics all depend on consideration of human interests and are, therefore, subject to the same central criticism: the contingency of nature's value. If humans cease to regard nature or some aspect of nature as worthy of respect, or overlook its potential to fulfil human needs, then it becomes relegated to the status of inert material, 'resource', to be treated with moral indifference.

Biocentric Ethics

One way to avoid the moral dependency of nature on human concern is to treat plants and animals as objects of moral concern *per se*. A leading example of this genre of environmental ethic is Regan's (1983) argument for animal rights. Regan asserts that all normal mammals of one year or more of age – a sub-category of animals which he refers to as 'subjects of a life' – have a moral right to life, since, he argues, subjects of a life are morally indistinguishable from mentally enfeebled human beings who are themselves generally accepted to possess such a right.

Although Regan's ethic is limited to a sub-category of sentient animals, more inclusive biocentric ethics have been developed. According to Van De Veer (1979), all organisms possess equal moral *considerability* (see Goodpaster 1978), but not equal moral *weight*; the moral weight to be afforded to any given organism being a function of (a) the type of interest that is at stake and (b) the organism's psychological capacities. Taylor (1986) has developed a more egalitarian ethic based on *species egalitarianism* – the view that all species, including *Homo sapiens*, are morally equal. Taylor posits that all organisms are moral subjects because all organisms have 'inherent worth'. A sufficient and necessary condition for possession of inherent worth by organisms is that they have *a good of their own*, that is, it is possible to imagine the world from their standpoint, to make judgements about what would be a good or bad thing to happen to them, and to treat them in such a way as to help or hinder them. For example, one can consider that although a tree does not feel pain when it is chopped down, it is nevertheless a bad thing to happen to the tree as it prevents the tree from fulfilling its potential life progression. Taylor maintains that to accept these premises leads one to adopt an attitude of *respect for nature* which, in turn, implies the acceptance of a number of specific duties towards all natural organisms.[1]

Ecocentric Ethics

Whilst biocentric ethics take us some considerable distance beyond the narrow anthropocentric position, all suffer from one weakness: they have no place for 'wholes' such as ecosystems and species. Ethics which focus on ecosystems and species are generally referred to as *ecocentric* ethics.

One of the problems of developing convincing ecocentric ethics is meeting criticisms of the concepts of 'species' and 'ecosystem' that are the object of moral concern. If holistic concepts such as 'ecosystem' and 'species' have no validity, no basis in reality, then there is no reason to incorporate them in an environmental ethic.

The concept of the 'ecosystem' – now ubiquitous in ecological writing – developed in reaction to the earlier concept of the 'biotic community' which originated in the work of the American plant ecologist F.E. Clements and his principal 'apostle' John Phillips (Phillips 1931, 1934, 1935). The Clements/Phillips model of plant communities had three main elements. First, plants are organised into 'biotic communities'. Secondly, such biotic communities develop through predictable stages – a process known as *succession* – until a stable '*climax*' stage is reached. Thirdly, and most controversially, Clements and Phillips asserted that biotic communities are real organisms:

> The developmental study of vegetation necessarily rests upon the assumption that the unit or climax formation is an organic entity ... As an organism the formation arises, grows, matures, and dies ... Furthermore, each climax formation is able to reproduce itself, repeating with essential fidelity the stages of its development. The life history of a formation is a complex but definite process, comparable in its chief features with the life-history of an individual plant. (Clements 1928: 3)

In 1935 the British ecologist Arthur Tansley published an influential article, 'The Use and Abuse of Vegetational Concepts and Terms' (Tansley 1935) challenging the Clements/Phillips organismic view of nature. Specifically, Tansley denied that biological associations are *in fact* organisms, opposed the view that nature is organised into 'communities', and doubted the extent to which such communities proceed through succession to reach stable climaxes. He maintained that although individual plants and animals may properly be referred to as organisms, in their interactive constituencies plants and animals form collections too diverse to warrant that title. Furthermore, Tansley considered that the concept of a 'system', which carries no purposive or teleological connotations, would be better fitted to describe the relationships between organisms in the context of their whole physical environment. Thus the concept of the 'ecosystem' was born.

Tansley's 1935 paper was well received and the concept of the ecosystem thereafter largely replaced that of the 'biotic community' although, ironically, the substance of the Clements/Phillips model remained relatively undisturbed. Ecologists continued to believe ecosystems to be formed by *succession*. Eugene Odum – one of the foremost post-war ecologists – added influential support to this view through his theory of succession. This maintained that rapidly-reproducing pioneer species are replaced by long-lived, slower-reproducing 'K-species' resulting in increased ecosystem stability (Odum 1969). Although ecologists now accept that ecosystem development may be unpredictable or chaotic (Drury and Nisbet 1973; Connell and Slayter 1977), that certain ecosystems never reach equilibrium and that others require intermediate-level disturbances for their long-term maintenance (Connell 1978; Pickett and White 1985), succession is still the basic model of ecosystem development.

The organismic element in the Clements/Phillips model of nature has similarly refused to disappear. It is, for example, central to Lovelock's Gaia theory. This postulates that life on earth, together with abiotic components, is a superorganism, Gaia, which maintains the conditions which are required for life to persist (Lovelock 1988, 1995; Goldsmith 1988). Superorganism theory has also recently been controversially revived as part of evolutionary theory (Wilson 1994; Sober 1984; Schindler 1987).

Except for a small minority (for example, Cahen 1995), most ecologists accept that ecosystems, 'the circulation, transformation, and accumulation of energy and matter through the medium of living things and their activities' (Evans 1956), are the 'basic units of nature' (Evans 1956) and the most important concept in ecology (Cherrett 1989). Likewise, in the main (cf. Schindler 1987), environmental philosophers accept that ecosystems are real entities and, as such, appropriate objects of ethical concern (cf. Cahen 1995). Species, the other main 'whole' which environmentalists consider deserving of ethical consideration, are usually defined as 'Groups of interbreeding natural populations that are reproductively isolated from other such groups' (Mayr 1969).

Barriers to breeding may take many forms, for example, geographic isolation, infertility and behavioural incompatibility. Such barriers provide genetic isolation which, over time, usually leads to morphological distinctions that enable the visual recognition of distinct species (Wilson 1994). However, care is needed in relating morphological distinctness to species taxonomy. Sometimes reproductive barriers, which taxonomically create species, do not lead to morphological variation, as is the case in many species of the fruit fly Drosphila which are indistinguishable in form (Grant 1994). Conversely, unusual forms – the objects of great pleasure and interest for naturalists – are often 'mere' varieties of the same species. For example, the Northern spotted owl, long the object of legal conservation efforts in the United States, interbreeds with and is therefore a variant of the more prevalent Californian spotted owl (Grierson 1992).

There are some difficulties with the biological species concept. First, it is possible to refuse to accept that species exist at all: preferring to maintain that nature consists only of individuals (Grant 1981). This ontological objection, which cannot be fully explored here, is similar to the question of whether the human body exists, or only the organs and cells of which it is comprised. This objection is considered by Cahen (1995). Then there is the problem of *semi-species*: distinct groups of individuals whose members only occasionally interbreed. Sometimes individuals in group A can interbreed with those in group B, but not with those in group C, although individuals in group B can interbreed with those in group C: are these individuals all one species or several sub-species? Individuals in two groups may be interfertile but also intersterile (such as the horse and donkey, producing the infertile mule). Some biologists reject the standard, biological, definition of species, on the grounds that species comprise those individuals with close genetic matches (Masters and Spencer 1989) or other shared characteristics (Regenmortel 1992). Organisms that engage in asexual reproduction – some lizards, insects and crustaceans as well as most bacteria – cannot be fitted into any particular closed gene pool: each individual is its own closed gene set and, in effect, species line.

Despite these difficulties, the biological species concept works for the vast majority of larger or more evolutionary sophisticated organisms. In those organisms that do engage in sexual reproduction, the existence of barriers to sexual reproduction is the principal cause of long-term morphological and genetic distinctions between individuals. Species are, therefore, the basic units of evolution and speciation is the method by which evolution progresses. Since evolution is the parent of advanced life on earth, most environmental ethicists feel that it is justifiable to adopt species as objects of moral concern.

Many environmental philosophers have argued for the moral considerability of species and ecosystems (Callicott 1980; Wenz 1988; McLaughlin 1993). One of the earliest ecocentric ethics is Leopold's Land Ethic. Aldo Leopold, game manager turned environmental philosopher, set out an ethic based on reintegrating humans into a community with the land (where 'land' is to be understood as 'soils, waters, plants, and animals ... collectively') pithily summarised in two sentences: 'A thing is right when it tends to preserve the integrity,stability, and beauty of the biotic community. It is wrong when it tends otherwise' (Leopold 1966: 224–225).

In the Land Ethic, although both the individual organism and the biotic community are worthy of respect, the individual is ultimately subordinate to the community. The ethic demands not that no animals, plants or habitat ever be destroyed but that such destruction be avoided where it would damage the beauty, stability and diversity of the ecosystem as a whole (Callicott 1994).

The primacy afforded to community over individual in the Land Ethic has led some to charge Leopold, and implicitly other ecocentric ethicists, with a form of 'environmental fascism' and totalitarianism (Regan 1983; Kheel 1985). Such fears are probably unfounded except in the most extreme types of holism, since positing moral concern for wholes does not imply abandoning moral concern for individuals (Marietta 1988). Furthermore, the Land Ethic is designed as a guide to human–nature, not intra-human, relations and so cannot be criticised for endorsing unethical treatment of humans (Freyfogle 1990).

Representative of more recent and philosophically sophisticated work is Rolston's (1988) combined biocentric and ecocentric ethic. Rolston's ethic is constructed on the premise that natural organisms and wholes possess 'intrinsic value', that is, value independent of their usefulness for human purposes.

In relation to individual organisms, Rolston ranks intrinsic value according to neural or phylogenetic complexity (humans above elks, elks above plants, plants above microbes and so on). Human individuals are, generally, ethically superior to non-human individuals, but human conduct towards other sentient animals should accord to a principle of non-addition of suffering and should avoid ecologically pointless suffering. Thus, hunting with a rifle for food is probably ethically justifiable since the death pain is not greater than the suffering involved in natural deaths (but not if the animals are killed for fur coats since this is ecologically pointless).

In relation to non-sentient animals and plants, Rolston proposes a principle of *non-loss of goods*. Thus using plants for human needs is permissible where the good that accrues to humans outweighs or equals the good lost in destruction of the plants. Eating plants for food or cutting timber to make housing would count as ethically permissible on this view.

Species are valued in Rolston's ethic because they are:

> ... dynamic natural units, if not corporate individuals. A species is a coherent, ongoing form of life expressed in organisms, encoded in gene flow, and shaped by the environment ... The individual represents (re-presents) a species in each new generation. It is the token of a type, and the type is more important than the token. (Rolston 1995: 65–67)

In general, duties to species outweigh those owed to individuals because the species line is the more fundamental living system, of which individual organisms are the essential parts. Accordingly, the obligation to advance the interests of human individuals will not always outweigh those of species. It may be preferable not to bring into being a million unconceived and unborn humans than to lose certain endangered species or habitats.

It also follows from this general elevation of species over individuals that predation on individuals is good since it serves the species:

> Predation on individual elk conserves and improves the species *Cervuc canadensis*. The species survives by its individual elk being eaten. When a wolf is tearing up an elk, the individual elk is in distress, but the species is in no distress. The species is being improved, as is shown by the fact that wolves will subsequently find elk harder to catch. If the predators are removed and the carrying capacity is exceeded wildlife managers may have to benefit a species by culling half its individual members. (Rolston 1988: 147)

Although ecosystems are not, for Rolston, 'superorganisms', they are nevertheless kinds of vital 'field' which capture value, providing a heading for species diversification, support and richness (1988: 175). Ecosystems tend to maximise individuality and have, over evolutionary time, maximised species diversity. Superimposed on this increase in quantitative diversity is an increase in the quality or value of the individual lives that ecosystems facilitate. Ecosystems which originally consisted of one-celled organisms have evolved, over aeons, into ecosystems that contain diverse higher beings including sentient intelligent animals (1988: 184). This process of producing individuals of high intrinsic value causes ecosystems to have what Rolston terms *systemic* value.

Rolston holds that ethics of ecosystems, species and individuals are interrelated since loss of individuals causes loss of species, and loss of individuals and species generally both imply damage to ecosystems. However, ecosystems have axiological priority to species since species only exist as 'species in ecosystems'; and it is the species in the system that we desire to protect. Ecosystems are likewise ethically prior to individuals since individuals cannot exist except through the support of the overall system (1988: 183). It is this priority of ecosystems over species, and species over individuals, that permits wildlife managers, ethically, to allow forest fires to burn, to refuse to treat diseased animals in national parks and to cull deer that have lost their natural top predators. There is no place in Rolston's ethic for misguided sentimentality.

The Deep Ecology Movement

Associated with the biocentric and ecocentric environmental ethics is the Deep Ecology movement. The aim of Deep Ecology is to alter consciousness, hence behaviour, towards the natural world, rather than to offer a single logically unassailable argument for environmental protection. The name 'Deep Ecology' derives from distinctions made by Naess and other practitioners between 'shallow' and 'deep' environmental policies (Naess 1973, 1989). Shallow policies are concerned primarily with averting the worst excesses of pollution and resource depletion in order to safeguard the health and affluence of people in developed countries. Deep Ecology is based on more radical principles:

1. The well-being of non-human life on Earth has value in itself. This value is independent of any instrumental usefulness for limited human purposes.
2. Richness and diversity of life forms contribute to this value and is a further value in itself. Richness here is used for what some others call 'abundance'. The maintenance of richness has to do with the maintenance of habitats and the number of individuals (size of populations). No exact count is implied. The main point is that life on Earth may be excessively interfered with even if complete diversity is upheld.
3. Humans have no right to interfere destructively with non-human life except for the purposes of satisfying vital human needs.
4. Present interference is excessive and detrimental.
5. Present policies must therefore be changed.
6. The necessary policy changes affect basic economic and ideological structures and will be the more drastic the longer it takes before significant change is started.
7. The ideological change is mainly that of appreciating life quality (dwelling in situations of intrinsic value) rather than adhering to a high standard of living.
8. The flourishing of human life and cultures is compatible with a substantial decrease of the human population. The flourishing of human life requires such a decrease.
9. Rejection of the man-in-environment image in favour of the relational, total-field image, i.e. organisms as knots in the field of intrinsic relations.
10. Those who subscribe to the foregoing points have an obligation directly or indirectly to try to implement the necessary changes. (Naess 1984: 266 and 1989: 29–30)

Deep Ecology, it will be noted, pays attention to the value of richness or abundance: thus a world which is largely wild nature is better than one which is largely human-made, even if both contain the same number of species and types of ecosystem. Furthermore, Deep Ecology provides a prescription for living in nature rather than apart from nature. In part this arises from its emphasis on the importance of *Self-realisation*. In this context 'Self' is not an egoistic individual but is, rather, equivalent to Ghandi's *atman*, the universal Self, the supreme being (Naess 1989). Self-realisation involves identification with nature and concern for community, allowing the individual to see nature conservation not as a matter of sacrifice, but as the fulfilment of the potentialities of all life forms (Naess 1995). This, in turn, requires 'dwelling in situations of intrinsic value'. Thus Deep Ecology does not advocate the isolation of humans from nature, but rather the sensitive rehabilitation of humankind into wild settings (Naess 1984: 270).

Ethical Conclusions

A number of conclusions can be drawn from the above overview of environmental ethics. The traditional narrow anthropocentric world-view is no longer an acceptable basis for human–nature relations, hence environmental law. Enlightened anthropocentric ethics have something to offer but are inevitably weakened by their tendency to arrogate human interests above those of the environment itself. Biocentric ethics take us a little further, providing a basis for proper treatment of individual organisms, but these cannot provide proper justification for the preservation of wholes such as species and ecosystems. We need, therefore, to adopt a combination of biocentric and ecocentric ethics as the proper basis for environmental protection. The biocentric and ecocentric normative positions are best advanced and best understood within the Deep Ecological framework which stresses the interrelatedness of all life and which calls for radical changes in societal institutions.

The Ethical Content of Environmental Law

It is not possible in this contribution to provide a full and detailed critique of the ways in which environmental law at all levels – national, regional and international – falls short of the standards of ecocentric ethics and Deep Ecology. However, a few examples taken from environmental legislation and case law will illustrate the view that a major revision of environmental law is necessary if environmental law is to support the intrinsic value in nature, at individual and holistic levels, identified by environmental ethics.

Pollution Legislation

Pollution legislation is generally anthropocentric, technocentric and overly concerned with criteria of efficiency. Ostensibly, pollution control legislation is designed to protect the environment. In practice, pollution standards are usually generated by reference to the predicted effects of a very limited range of substances on human populations, not plants or animals. In water, for instance, strict standards have been legislated for only a very few (17) out of the 50,000 or so substances in common usage in the European Union due to disagreements over selection criteria (ENDS 1992). Such mandatory maximum permissible levels for substances as do exist are usually calculated by reference to toxic effects on individual organisms, not by reference to the effects on species or ecosystems. Cumulative, synergistic or long-term effects of toxic substances which are most likely to damage ecosystems are rarely part of the assessment process. Amongst the few notable exceptions to this approach is the European Union's Draft Framework Directive on Water Resources (Commission of the European Communities 1997). However, the effectiveness of even this measure is reduced by the discretionary nature of its obligations.

Pollution legislation is underpinned by a philosophy of *technocentrism* – the optimistic belief that human progress and scientific knowledge can develop technological solutions to all environmental problems and that, therefore, key environmental decisions should be taken by technical or scientific 'experts' rather than formulated through the political expression of ethical standards (O'Riordan 1981). Concrete environmental standards are reserved as matters for central government and/or environmental regulatory agencies (as, for instance, the process of formulating statutory water quality objectives under the Water Resources Act 1991). Staff in regulatory agencies may, and probably do, impose their unconscious professional ideologies and values without reference to the values of biocentric or ecocentric ethics. There is no requirement to provide any ethical justification for decisions to permit pollution levels which are harmful to nature. Pollution law's technocentric mode of operation is illustrated by the legal treatment of Best Practicable Environmental Option (BPEO) under the Environmental Protection Act 1990. The Royal Commission for Environmental Pollution in its 1988 report on the concept of BPEO acknowledged the importance of local consultations in determining BPEO: 'There must be appropriate and timely consultation with people and organisations directly affected. The circle of those involved in taking decisions must be appropriately wide' (Royal Commission on Environmental Pollution 1988: 9).

Furthermore, at least in difficult cases, 'The selection of a BPEO cannot be left to scientists, industrialists and regulatory experts alone. Public involvement is needed so that the *public values* underlying the choice of BPEO are identified and clearly understood' (Royal Commission on Environmental Pollution 1988: 18, emphasis added).

The Environmental Protection Act 1990 gives effect to a very weakened concept of BPEO. BPEO was not defined by the 1990 Act but left to Her Majesty's Inspectorate of Pollution (HMIP), now the Environment Agency, to elaborate. The formulation of BPEO by HMIP resulted in a complex formula which attempts to compare mathematically, across media, the ratios of released substances to legal maximum allowable concentrations for those media and to combine these into one numerical 'integrated environmental index'. Determination of BPEO in this manner is certainly not, as it could be, 'a step towards comprehensive environmental planning, in which the social, economic and political impacts of a proposed activity are evaluated within an environmental framework' (UKELA 1987: 15). Less still does it approximate the 'comprehensive environmental planning' recommended by the World Conservation Strategy (IUCN 1980: sec.10). Furthermore, this BPEO methodology pays only lip service to analysis of the *actual effect* of those substances on affected wildlife which, as Guruswamy and Tromans have observed, casts doubt on the usefulness of the whole process (1986: 655). Predictably, in conformity with its technocentric ideology, the Environment Agency's BPEO methodology involves no ethical justification of the damage caused, or any requirement for the elucidation of public values through consultation as emphasised by the Royal Commission on Environmental Pollution.

Technocentrism is itself dangerously preoccupied with *efficiency*, usually expressed by inclusion of a requirement for cost-benefit analysis (CBA) or some other formula which takes costs, rather than ethical propriety, as the principal criterion of action. The ethical poverty of using costs rather than values as a determinant criterion of environmental protection is itself well documented (for example, Sagoff 1988; Wenz 1988). The central criticism of CBA methodology is that it uses monetary measures of consumer preference, such as 'willingness to pay' or 'willingness to be compensated', to evaluate the acceptability of environmental damage or protection (Winpenny 1991). Surveys which obtain such measurements force respondents to behave towards the environment as 'consumers' rather than 'citizens', thereby replacing values with preferences (Sagoff 1988). Research reveals that people reject the denigration of the environment intrinsic to this approach, preferring the view that nature should be thought of as having rights to continued existence independent of the monetary costs/benefits involved (Hanley and Milne 1996). We do not (yet) allocate law and order resources or medical treatment according to the 'value' attached to individuals by other individuals. By analogy, legal protection or remediation for species and ecosystems cannot be properly determined by economic criteria.

The problem of CBA in pollution legislation is marked in the United States where obsession with efficiency has, in certain cases, undermined the substantive goals of environmental legislation. For example, the requirement of the Clean Air Act of 1970 that the United States' Environmental Protection Agency set primary National Ambient Air Quality Standards adequate 'to protect public health' with 'a margin of safety' was undermined by a later Executive Order prohibiting action by federal regulators except where the benefits exceed the cost (Berne 1990).

In the UK, a shift towards CBA is insidiously taking place. Cost benefit analysis was implicit in the notion of Best Practicable Means (BPM) and is now present in the requirement to adopt the Best Available Techniques Not Entailing Excessive Cost (BATNEEC) for processes which come within the integrated pollution control regime of the Environmental Protection Act 1990. CBA now has a more general legal effect: section 4(1) of the Environment Act 1995 requires the Environment Agency to take into account any likely costs in discharging its functions and section 39 of that Act provides that, in considering whether to exercise any of its powers, the Environment Agency shall, unless it is unreasonable for it to do so, take into account the likely costs and benefits of the exercise or non-exercise of that power.

Perhaps the most fundamental disjunction between pollution laws, in their common form, and biocentric or ecocentric ethics derives from the reactionary and legitimating function of this genre of law. As we have observed any genuine substantiation of the Deep ecocentric position requires, at minimum, a recognition that society's basic orientation towards ceaseless economic growth must change. No congruence between environmental law and ethics can emerge whilst society fashions pollution controls which provide the minimum degree of protection necessary to continue maximum economic growth and material consumption:

> Environmental protection legislation ... is misnamed: in the intent, protection is quite secondary. The desire to facilitate development by keeping environmental degradation within 'tolerable' limits – usually expressed as 'maximum permissible levels' of contaminants – is paramount. The legislation is utilitarian not utopian. It lacks vision. Pollution is rationalised and, after the necessary permit is issued, legalised. (Edmond 1984: 340)

This 'business as usual' approach, implicit in the concept of sustainable development, 'reflects the dominant paradigm of exploitation rather than harmony' and is 'arguably of little value in the struggle to save our planet' (Conaghan and Mansell 1993: 126).

These problems indicate that pollution legislation lacks both the transformative character demanded by Deep Ecology and the moral content of ecocentric environmental ethics. Its concern is the well-being and health of human populations and not the preservation of species and ecosystems.

Conservation Legislation

Conservation legislation is ostensibly designed to secure the protection of plants, animals and habitats. As such it is, to a degree, necessarily biocentric and ecocentric in effect. However, closer examination of the priorities and objectives of most conservation instruments reveals *purposes* concerned with the provision of human benefits – aesthetic, contemplative, biological, economic, etc. Only a small minority of more progressive conservation instruments aim to protect wildlife for its own sake based on nature's intrinsic value.

Fundamentally anthropocentric conservation legislation is not difficult to find. Examples in international law include the Declaration for the Protection of Birds Useful to Agriculture 1875 – the title of which speaks for itself – and the International Convention for the Regulation of Whaling 1946. The preamble of the latter treaty begins by recognising 'the interest of the nations of the world in safeguarding for future generations the great natural resources represented by the whalestocks'; terminology, which, applied to great whales, is ethically offensive from the biocentric perspective, and certainly demonstrates a lack of consideration of the ethical status of whales as such. Likewise, parties to the Convention on International Trade in Endangered Species of Wild Flora and Fauna 1973 (CITES) declare that 'wild fauna and flora in their many beautiful and varied forms are an irreplaceable part of the natural systems of the earth which must be protected *for this and the generations to come*' (emphasis added) and record their awareness of 'the ever-growing value of wild fauna and flora from aesthetic, scientific, cultural, recreational and economic points of view'.

Anthropocentricism is also apparent in national conservation legislation. An instructive example is the provisions of the National Parks and Access to the Countryside Act 1949, now found with modifications in the Wildlife and Countryside Act 1981. The report of the Wildlife Conservation Special Committee, on which the conservation provisions of the 1949 Act was based, expressed the view that: 'The concept of nature conservation, broadly interpreted, embraces several more or less distinct purposes ... biological survey and research; experiment; education; and amenity' (1947: 14).

Chief amongst these human-focused concerns was scientific study, and the system of National Nature Reserves and Sites of Special Scientific Interest (SSSIs) were envisaged as 'living laboratories' (Evans 1992: 7). The purpose of conservation in this Act was *not* to protect the intrinsic value of wild nature. Because of its essentially anthropocentric approach, the 1949 Act introduced a 'representativist' system of nature protection, relying on small sites, oases in seas of urban and agricultural development. The Special Committee's report likened the proposed system of SSSIs and Nature

Reserves to a national museum, implying a need to include only token or representative examples of the range of habitats and species in England and, accordingly, endorsed the view that the aim of the ensuing legislation should be to 'give the most balanced result possible within the smallest overall area of land' (Wildlife Conservation Special Committee 1947: 16). Protection of nature through the establishment of protected sites, in principle, may be congruent with the principles of ecocentric ethics, in so far as such an approach has the potential to protect a high proportion of species and habitat types. When, however, combined with a 'Noah's ark' philosophy, such a policy inevitably fails in that task, principally through its disregard of the values of *richness* or *abundance*. The demands of ecocentric ethics are not met by a stamp collection approach to nature protection. As Naess observes, 'life on Earth may be excessively interfered with even if complete diversity is upheld' (1989: 30).

Since the 1970s, it has been common for conservation laws to contain multiple, contradictory, justificatory appeals to anthropocentric, biocentric and ecocentric perspectives. The Convention on Wetlands of International Importance especially as Waterfowl Habitat 1971 (the 'Ramsar' convention), for instance, opens with recognition of the interdependence of humans and their environment and points out that 'wetlands constitute a resource of great economic, cultural, scientific, and recreational value' but simultaneously notes 'the fundamental ecological functions of wetlands as regulators of water regimes and as habitats supporting a characteristic flora and fauna, especially waterfowl'. No mention is made of the tension between treating wetlands as economic resources and as ecological regulators. Likewise the parties to the Convention on Biological Diversity 1992, declare their consciousness of *both* the intrinsic value of biological diversity *and* the ecological, genetic, social, economic, scientific, educational, cultural, recreational and aesthetic values of biological diversity and its components. It is doubtful that the content of these instruments substantially reflects the standards of environmental ethics; these are principally rhetorical statements included to appease the global environmental lobby and to give the appearance of ethical progress.

Several features of a programme of conservation legislation which would be consistent with ecocentric ethics can be suggested.

Nature should be respected as a priority and exploitation permitted only as the exception to this general rule Rather than legislating for narrow categories of protected sites and lists of protected species, environmental law informed by the principles of ecocentric ethics and Deep Ecology would afford protection to all components of nature, whether or not teetering on the edge of extinction. Destruction of nature would be legally proscribed except where the basic needs of human populations failed to be satisfied, and permanent ecosystem or species damage would not ensue ('Basic', here, referring to a lower (material/consumption) standard of living than presently obtains – society should seek to recapture a life 'simple in means, rich in ends').

There are some examples of legal instruments which come close to this formulation (see Emmenegger and Tschentscher 1994). Perhaps the most ethically advanced 'soft' law instrument is United Nations General Assembly Resolution 37/7: the World Charter for Nature. The preference for the term 'nature' rather than 'environment' in the title of this instrument itself reveals a shift towards an ecological perspective by relinquishing the relational view which places humankind as the locus of ethical concern. The Charter begins, significantly, by noting that 'every form of life is unique, warranting respect regardless of its worth to man, and, to accord other organisms such recognition, man must be guided by a moral code of action'. 'Hard' law instruments with a more acceptable ethical content include the moratorium on whaling established under the 1946 International Convention for the Regulation of Whaling and the European Union Habitats Directive[2] which, through the 'Natura 2000' programme, is concerned to protect species in their context of natural ecosystems, not merely as isolated pockets of rare kinds.

Legislation should not only seek to protect endangered species but should contain measures designed to prevent common species and habitats from becoming endangered With a few notable examples (for example, the CITES convention), conservation law focuses on species that have declined beyond the point of effective preservation. Species that are in decline but which have not reached fragile or endangered populations tend to be ignored (Kunich 1994). Whilst this approach may be necessitated by 'triage' principles[3] in a world fundamentally oriented towards material and economic growth, conservation law informed by Deep Ecology's emphasis on the structural causes of environmental problems would insist on affording effective protection to those species and ecosystems that are not yet endangered. This would require a greater emphasis on abundance and the maintenance of large populations of flora and fauna.

Legislation should place special value on wild nature Wilderness in the sense of a complete absence of anthropogenic substances or influences exists nowhere on earth, but many environments are relatively close to wilderness. Wilderness demands size, abundance and relative non-interference. Rather than choosing multifarious small sites to manage as islands of inherent value in a sea of human domination, ecological conservation law would emphasise the need to set aside large areas of land where nature is allowed to take its course. The total area required is indeterminate, but clearly much greater than is currently protected. The protection and recreation of wilderness areas would not necessarily guarantee the preservation of all endangered species but evolution and speciation would continue which would ensure that, in the long term, biodiversity would be maintained.

Such a policy would be advanced by creation of true national parks, where human habitation is minimal or absent, without major roads and private cars. Clearly, given present population distribution and travel arrangements, such a policy would take time to achieve, but it is possible. Concomitant reductions in population levels need to be expressed in governmental policy and given effect through tax laws or other legal instruments such as improved health/welfare provision and compulsory birth control education (Ehrlich 1970: Prologue; Hardaway 1996). This does not mean that nature should be rid of humans – on the contrary, Deep Ecology assumes rather that the human condition is greatly in need of contact with nature. Ecological law can resolve the tension between the need to develop areas of relatively unmolested nature and the need for greater human contact with wild nature by ensuring that humans 'step lightly on the earth'. In ecological law, activities that re-engage more environmentally benign styles of life – hiking, camping, skiing, canoeing, riding, fishing – would be encouraged.

Management of nature would be de-emphasised. Deep Ecology places little faith in the ability of humans to second-guess nature and to sit at the control panel of 'spaceship earth' (Devall and Sessions 1984). Priority would be given to Commoner's 'rule' of ecology that 'nature knows best' (1971: 37) except where intervention is necessary to restore excessively anthropomorphised environments to a wild or semi-wild condition.

Case Law

Analyses of 'fit' between the common law and environmental ethics reveals that, historically, the common law has been hostile to the incorporation of environmental values (Thompson 1985; Alder 1996). Has this changed? An examination of case law demonstrates that the judiciary are ambivalent about allowing principles of environmental ethics to invade the sanctity of legal reasoning, or the reasoning of public institutions. A striking example of this is the United States Supreme Court decision in *Sierra Club* v. *Morton*.[4] Here the petitioner sought judicial review of a federal decision to grant a permit allowing the construction of a ski resort in the Mineral King Valley in the Sequoia National Park. Before the case was heard by the Supreme Court, Professor Christopher Stone wrote his influential article, 'Should Trees Have Standing?' (Stone 1972) in which he argued that the natural environment should be considered as having both moral and legal rights in relation to its own well-being and, as a consequence, should be granted *locus standi* in its own right to bring actions for judicial review through representative environmental groups.

By a majority the Supreme Court denied the Sierra Club's claim on the basis that 'the injury in fact' test of standing requires the party seeking the review to be amongst the injured. The possibility for judicial acceptance of environmental ethics is revealed in the dissenting judgments. Justice Douglas, who had read proofs of Stone's article, commented:

> The critical question of 'standing' would be simplified and also put neatly in focus if we ... allowed environmental issues to be litigated ... in the name of the inanimate object about to be despoiled, defaced, or invaded by roads and bulldozers and where the injury is the subject of public outrage. (p. 741)

In explaining his radical position, Justice Douglas referred to Leopold's Land Ethic:

> [T]hose who hike the Appalachian trail into Sunfish Pond, New Jersey and camp or sleep there ... or climb the guadalupes in West Texas, or who canoe and portage the quetico superior in Minnesota, certainly should have the standing to defend those natural wonders before courts or agencies ... Then there will be assurances that all the forms of life which it represents will stand before the court ... the pileated woodpecker as well as the coyote and bear, the lemmings as well as the trout in the streams. Those inarticulate members of the ecological community cannot speak. But those people who have so frequented the place as to know of its values and wonders will be able to speak for the entire ecological community. Ecology reflects the land ethic; and Aldo Leopold wrote in *A Sand County Almanac* (1949), 'The Land Ethic simply enlarges the boundaries of the community to include soils, waters, plants and animals, or collectively, the Land.' That, as I see it, is the issue of 'standing' in the present case and controversy. (p. 744)

It is unfortunate that the majority rejected this reasoning by appealing to conventional legal reasoning on *locus standi*.

In English law, judicial consideration of environmental ethics has arisen explicitly in a number of cases. A leading case is *R* v. *Somerset County Council, ex parte Fewings and Others*[5] in which the applicants, representing the Quantock Stag Hounds, sought judicial review of a decision by Somerset County Council to ban deer hunting on County Council-owned land. The case is instructive both in terms of judicial attitudes towards cognisance of environmental ethics by public bodies and for its substantive ethical content (see also Chapter 4).

The applicants argued that the Council had wrongly based their decision on moral criteria, specifically the alleged cruelty of deer hunting. The case turned on interpretation of section 120(1)(b) of the Local Government Act 1972 which empowers local authorities to acquire and manage land for the 'benefit, improvement or development of their area'. Laws J concluded that:

> Section 120(1)(b) [of the 1972 Act] confers no entitlement on a local authority to impose its opinions about the morals of hunting on the neighbourhood. In the present state of the law those opinions, however sincerely felt, have their proper place only in the private conscience of those who entertain them. The council has been given no authority by Parliament to translate such views into public action.

In the Court of Appeal this decision was upheld, although on narrower grounds, with Sir Thomas Bingham MR and Simon Brown LJ taking the view that it could not be said that considerations of cruelty were irrelevant in determining what was for the 'benefit of the area'. Simon Brown LJ went further and commented, *obiter dicta*: 'The cruelty argument, as well as the countervailing ethical considerations, were necessarily relevant to the decision. Had they been ignored I believe that the council would have been open to criticism.'

This acknowledgement of the legitimacy of ethical reasoning in decision-making processes of public bodies is to be welcomed. Arguably, in contentious environmental decisions involving ethical dilemmas, public bodies should be legally bound to give reasons[6] and more specifically a duty to give reasons which demonstrate that the decision has been taken after consideration of the 'ethical dimension'. Statements of reasons should be in the form of public documents, which would enable concerned citizens and environmental action groups to challenge decisions based on patently unreasonable ethical grounds or decisions which do not take ethical dimensions into account. In this way, the legal process, and the action for judicial review in particular, would form part of a surrogate political process for the expression and challenge of societal values (Feldman 1992).

The substantive ethics of the *Fewings* decision show how biocentric and ecocentric ethical reasoning can come into conflict. Somerset County Council had prepared a report in 1986 on the matter of stag hunting which concluded:

> It is the existence of the hunt which leads many local farmers and landowners to tolerate crop damage from the deer ... The majority of local farmers are sympathetic towards the deer. Many people maintain that the disappearance of hunting would eventually lead to the loss of that sympathy and a steady increase in shooting, possibly resulting in the extinction of the red deer in the hills.

The Council's Planning and Transportation Committee considered the matter in 1986 and noted that:

(a) [I]f the hunt is wholly banned ... and hunting consequently ceases, the deer herd will very soon be decimated and then irrevocably reduced by;
(b) indiscriminate shooting especially with shotguns, which will involve as great suffering as with hunting, and possibly even greater; and
(c) a significant increase in poaching, very probably on a commercial scale;
– all these leading in a very few years to the extinction of the red deer herd.

The only argument in favour of banning the hunt, that had emerged at this stage, was the environmental destruction and nuisance caused by vehicles following the hunt, a problem that seemed to have been largely resolved by 1993.

The full Council met on 4 August 1993 to consider a resolution to continue to permit hunting over an area of Council-owned land, Stowey Common. At that meeting an 'amendment' to the resolution was put forward reversing its effect. The truncated notes of the meeting show that supporters of the amendment spoke of hunting using phrases such as 'unnecessary and cruel', 'cruel, barbaric, sickening', 'people enjoy blood lust' and 'pleasure torturing animals now unthinkable e.g. slavery'. This moral language swayed the Council and the amended motion, banning hunting, was passed.

What are the ethical dimensions of this type of reasoning? Clearly the Council had, for some time, been persuaded of the ecocentric value of hunting. In ecocentric ethics, as we have seen, the species, ecosystem or group takes priority over the individual. Predation is part of all food webs. Thus, where, as in the United Kingdom, natural top predators (wolves and bears) have become extinct through human activity, it is ethically justifiable for humans to hunt to replace that natural function. In contrast the Council's amended resolution was clearly motivated not by ecocentric ethics but by a mixture of biocentric ethics and virtue ethics. The preceding account of biocentric ethics indicates that this is an ethical genre in which the individual takes priority over the species or ecosystem. It would be quite in order, from the biocentric perspective, to limit deer hunting to rifle culling if death by hounds was determined to be more painful than death by bullet (taking account of incidental pain in both cases such as pain caused to escaping and wounded animals) or if deer were considered to have a right to freedom from the distressing pursuit of the hounds. From the perspective of virtue ethics (Hill 1983), deer hunting with dogs might justifiably be banned in order to reduce, in the longer term, the propensity to engage in 'cruel' or 'barbaric' sports, thus preventing depravity.

Often it will be possible to combine ecocentric and biocentric ethics by adopting the most humane and rights-respecting means to effect the *greatest* ecosystem and species protection. But occasionally these two maximal desiderata will be mutually exclusive. But what should public bodies do when faced with apparently irreconcilable biocentric and ecocentric ethical arguments? The first section of this chapter indicates that in such cases ecocentric ethics provide a firmer basis for *environmental* policies (rather than animal welfare policies) than biocentric ethics and should, therefore, generally be preferred. What is important is that public bodies create legal instruments and take decisions only after full and balanced consideration of relevant ethical factors and that the preference for one rather than another ethical theory is made evident on the face of the decision.

Environmental Law and Ethics

Analyses of 'environmental law' usually assume that a body of law specific to the environment can be identified as a discipline or bounded area of law in its own right. This in turn suggests that environmental problems can be resolved by the application of a discrete body of regulation to some fraction of human activities (generally assumed to be direct acts of pollution and direct acts of nature degradation). It is this flawed assumption that lies at the root of the weakness of environmental law. Deep Ecology and ecocentric ethics stress the total interrelatedness of all activities, states and substance. It is not the freakish, malicious, or extreme forms of human behaviour which threaten the environment, but the everyday patterns of life of the global population, especially those in the developed North.

Law which embodies ecocentric ethics and the principles of Deep Ecology – 'Ecological law' – would deal with the fundamental or institutional aspects of human–nature relations, and regulate areas of life usually considered to be outside law's proper domain. This would include (but not be limited to) challenges to:

- unlimited mobility through private motorised transport;
- use of large amounts of energy and the underlying reliance on fossil fuels;
- high consumption consumer lifestyles;
- destruction of landscapes in the name of 'development';
- freedom of international trade, and
- reproduction of an unlimited number of children.

38 Locality and Identity

In this section I wish to consider whether, were such a body of ecological law to emerge, it could retain its justification in liberal-democratic theory. This question is of importance because failure to achieve this or some other jurisprudential justification may delay the evolution of ecological law

In addressing this question it is necessary, first, to distinguish the claims of liberalism from those of democracy. The central tenets of *liberalism* are freedom from state interference (Mill 1972) and neutrality amongst conceptions of the good life (Dworkin 1978; Rawls 1972; Sagoff 1995). Democracy's central claim, on the other hand, is that decisions should be made by the population, the *demos*, and not by some individual, monarch, committee or philosopher king. Liberalism does not necessarily imply democracy or vice versa. There have existed dictatorships, monarchies and forms of communism which have adhered to liberal norms as well as democracies in which liberty has been greatly reduced by popular demand for security, order, etc.

Ecological Law and Liberal Theory

The dominant view in modern Western jurisprudence is that law is, or should be, based on the tenets of liberalism and that law should not, therefore, interfere with matters of personal morality. The grounds for this position are varied but include: the purported supreme self-knowledge of individuals in matters of happiness (Mill 1972); denial of the necessity of a fixed morality for the existence of society (Hart 1963); the repugnance and baseness of common moral opinion (Hart 1977), and the difficulty of ascertaining public morality or the feelings of 'right-minded people' (Hughes 1962; Dworkin 1966).

Non-liberals have responded that society has the right to enforce morality in order to ensure its own continued existence (Devlin 1968); that morals must be enforced for their own sake (Stephen 1967); that the law must draw a line between what is acceptable in a civilised society and what is not;[7] that law cannot, in fact, remain morally neutral (Mitchell 1967); and that law which fails to reflect a growing body of moral opinion will lead to the population taking matters into their own hands (Dworkin 1966). The latter reason is of considerable importance as environmental activists and 'eco-warriors', dissatisfied with the paltry, reactionary and piecemeal environmental law project, have shown that they are prepared to act on their moral beliefs and public sense of outrage by taking the law into their own hands (Foreman 1991; List 1993).

In his examination of the relationship between environmentalism and liberalism, Sagoff has concluded that environmentalists can be liberals, implying that environmental law is consistent with, and justified by, the tenets of liberalism. The key to Sagoff's conclusion is his assumption that few if any existing environmental laws transgress liberalism's basic demand for a core of private behaviour and beliefs:

> Environmental decisions, by and large, have to do with what goes on out of doors not indoors; they concern the character and quality of the public household not of the private home ... Thus the content of environmental policy rarely becomes relevant to the kind of neutrality essential to liberalism. (Sagoff 1995: 183)

What I wish to emphasise here is that this optimistic conclusion is based on an unusually weak conception of liberalism in which legal intervention is to be considered *generally* legitimate, except in private matters such as choice of friends, sexual practices and religion. This, of course, provides a much broader mandate for legal intervention in private affairs than liberals will normally admit to.

Whilst it is possible that *environmental* law may be compatible with this weak form of liberalism, there are a number of reasons why *ecological* law is not. First, ecological law makes nonsense of liberalism's proscription of interference except on grounds of harm to others. Ecocentric ethics, as we have seen, demonstrate that plants, animals, species and ecosystems are morally considerable bearers of intrinsic value. These entities must, therefore, assume the status of 'individuals' in determinations of the limits of legal or state intervention. Since all nature consists of organismic or communitarian 'individuals', and since *all* human activity has some detrimental environmental consequences, liberalism's claim to rope off a safe area of private 'law-free' behaviour is misguided.

Secondly, the Deep Ecology movement, unlike liberalism, is not neutral between competing conceptions of the good. Rather, it seeks to alter our fundamental perceptions of human–nature relations such that we are able, over time, to empathise with and care for the environment. Ecological law, by definition, would have to prefer and advance a conception of the good life which engenders and nurtures this attitude. Ecological law is, in the Platonic sense, 'republican' since it seeks to further moral virtues necessary for a sustainable society of humans and nature.

There is a further, perhaps more profound, reason why ecological law cannot draw on liberal theory for justificatory support. As critics have often observed, liberalism is underlain by the ideology of *individualism*: a model of the human psyche which is in considerable tension, not to say conflict, with environmental ethics that take groups or wholes as their subject matter. Communitarians reject this conception of the human condition, maintaining that humans are not self-creating uninfluenced selves (MacIntyre 1985) and point out that ethical life requires adoption of social roles. Recovery from alienation, they point out, requires a reversal of the decay in the locatedness that individuals once received from the institutional fabric: a locatedness lost through technology, industrialisation, bureaucracy, urbanisation, population growth and by the treatment of nature as *other*. Individualism is, therefore, in particular conflict with Deep Ecology's prescription of self-realisation through increasing identification with others as part of an interrelated, holistic natural world. Ecological law must, therefore, be built on *public* recognition of ecocentric and biocentric values. Environmental harm is a matter for the community requiring communal decision making, not 'individual consumers expressing personal wants' (Freyfogle 1994: 843).

If ecological law is inconsistent with classical liberal theory, then other, non-liberal, theories will have to provide its jurisprudential underpinnings. 'Natural law' theories appear, appropriately, to hold considerable promise in this matter. The notion that human affairs are properly ordered when they accord to an underlying and pre-existing 'natural' order is one which appeals to many environmentalists. On this view we should order our affairs with nature according to 'ecological practicable reasonableness' (after Finnis 1980). On this view the preservation of the planetary life-support system, the reduction of the global human population, the strict control of human eco-destructive activities, the legal embodiment of inherent ecological values, would all properly be considered to be goals which any coherent and effective body of law must strive to achieve. Natural law jurisprudence would imply that laws should 'be chosen according *to an ideal goal or good*, rather than represent the haphazard implementation of voters' preferences, be they popular, or those of specific interest groups' (Westra 1993). In this jurisprudence we would expect to see an increase in judicial activism (Dias 1994) and the development of new legal principles[8] to guide the evolution of the law in novel matters and statutory interpretation; areas of law in which, unhappily, the UK judiciary seem thus far to be unimaginative.[9]

Ecological Law and Democratic Theory

The desirability of democratic participation in the formulation and enforcement of environmental law is usually taken as a given by environmentalists. However, we should not assume that democracy is implicit in and can be derived from environmental ethics: this would be to confuse theories of value (about nature) with theories of agency (how to act politically) (Goodin 1992). Ethics are determined not by what is popular, but by what is good, right or virtuous (Regan 1983). Popular support, especially local support, for policies that are environmentally destructive but which provide tangible short-term benefits is to be expected in a world of self-interested individuals

(Hardin 1977). Democracy cannot, therefore, be identified as a green 'good' to be ranked alongside other green values (Saward 1993).

The tendency of democracy to favour the selection of short-term environmentally destructive policies may be countered by the entrenchment of 'pre-democratic' rights (Harrison 1993) and education (Mill 1848; Hargrove 1989: 207; Westra 1993: 128) providing, respectively, barriers against the selection of immoral policies, and encouragement towards the common good through enlightened leadership. The first of these – pre-democratic entrenchment of ecological values – may be achieved either by adopting an environmental Bill of Rights and/or by embedding ecological values in constitutional law. Either would elevate ecological law to take precedence over other legal and policy choices. It is encouraging to see that both of these methods of entrenching ecological values are now being used (Muldoon 1988; Rabie 1991; Verschuuren 1993; Orie 1995; Schmelz and Brandl 1996).

The second technique, education, is essential to the initial acceptability of ecological law: 'Public education programmes may be required both before and after the law comes into force to help the public understand and support it' (IUCN 1980: para 11.9). Education is, in this context, to be used not only as information *about* environmental ethics but also to induce the production of those values in a wide proportion of the population. We may expect that, in the future, education in ecological values will be included in mainstream education programmes. Education in environmental ethics will be especially important for all those who may hold positions of political power since, both in theory and practice, legislators behave as intellectually independent representatives, not mere delegates (Mill 1912) often giving the population only options of form, not substance, on key issues (Plamenatz 1973). Empirical evidence encouragingly suggests that government officials who deal with the negotiation of environmental instruments often hold quite deep personal ecological values (Craig and Glasser 1993).

In attempting to assess the likelihood of widespread and successful education in ecological values, one should not overlook ecological law's own educative function. This derives both from increasing dissemination and knowledge of the substantive content of environmental law and from increasing opportunities to become actively involved in the machinery of environmental law. Psychological theories of moral development suggest that knowledge of laws and acting from a sense of legal obligation are important intermediate stages in the path to higher stages of personal ethical development (Kohlberg 1969, 1984). Just as the knowledge that murder is *illegal* and severely punishable adds to our moral understanding that murder is *wrong*, so too knowledge of the content of ecological law would contribute to the development of personal ethical values that favour environmental protection. Furthermore, recent 'narrative' studies of moral development stress the importance of contextual and cultural influences, especially language, in the development of moral thinking (Day and Tappan 1996; Tappan 1997). So, just as the ordinary meanings of so-called legal terms (for example, 'infant', 'corporation') influence their judicial interpretation (Stone 1972: 488), so too the language of law ('legal right', 'trust', 'duty of care', 'offence', etc.) forms part of the narrative of right living in individuals. Ecological law would, in proclaiming the 'rights' of nature and duties to avoid nature destruction, act to transform personal values.

As noted above, part of ecological law's educative role resides in its provision of opportunities for individuals and pressure groups to become involved in the process of environmental governance. Pressure groups have recently gained wider rights of *locus standi* and are increasingly seen, even by the judiciary, as legitimate protectors of environmental interests (Robinson 1993; Robinson and Dunkley 1995; Krämer 1996). Participation in the process of environmental governance is important, because through such activities people define themselves as ecological citizens and become educated about the problems involved (Dryzeck 1987; Young 1990, Dryzeck 1992; Robinson 1993). Increased participation in legal decision making and in the enforcement of environmental law facilitates the transformation of individuals from '"self-regarding" individuals to "other-regarding" citizens with an appreciation of their common (environmental) interests and compassion for non-human nature' (Hayward 1995: 221). The benefits of this educational/transformative function accrue not only to the participants, but to the society as a whole through the dissemination of law reports and media coverage of disputed environmental issues.

Conclusion

We have seen environmental ethics locate intrinsic value in all living organisms, species and ecosystems, and rank humans as of only relative importance. Unlike the vast majority of human ethics, in cases of priority or competition between individuals (for example, plants and animals) and groups (for example, species or ecosystems) ecocentric environmental ethics generally favour the protection of groups or systems. Most human ethics are content to deal in matters of justice, rights and duties – matters which, being largely concerned with distribution of goods and bads, have little to say about the basic growth-oriented technological basis of society. In contrast, environmental ethics, informed by the principles of Deep Ecology, demand radical changes to our basic patterns of life.

This chapter seeks to demonstrate that, in its current form, environmental law generally fails to demonstrate any firm commitment to these principles. Much environmental law is 'anthropocentric'. Little if any environmental law is concerned with protection of ecosystems and biotic communities as such: that which is tends to adopt a 'Noah's Ark' policy of preserving the minimum possible. Environmental law as a whole tends towards maintenance of the status quo in terms of economic development and offers little challenge to the 'deep' or basic causes of environmental destruction.

Legal programmes at international, regional and national level need not exhibit these characteristics. It is possible for environmental law's ethical content to be revised creating a new body of 'ecological law'. It is to this aim that environmental lawyers and practitioners should be directed. It ought to be openly recognised, at a jurisprudential level, that ecological law cannot draw on liberal political theory for its basic justification, since it requires greater sacrifices of personal liberty than that body of political theory will allow. This loss would be more than compensated by a strong basis in environmental ethics. We should also recognise that, if it is to retain its compatibility with democratic theory, ecological law requires entrenchment in constitutional and overarching law forms as well as extensive public education in environmental values; a function partly undertaken by law itself. Ecological law would itself challenge democratic theory; first, by requiring a narrowing of the range of goods or ends for which legal prescription or proscription might be sought; second, by demanding a broadening of access to environmental legal machinery by NGOs and citizens. The relationship between ecological law and democracy could, in time, be partly self-supporting since law would act as an educator and originator of personal ethical values. A body of ecological law would, by that means, become an instrument for determining ourselves both personally and as part of a wider community with nature.

Notes

1 These include: *the duty of non-maleficence* (a duty not to do harm to any entity in the natural environment which has a good of its own); *the duty of non-interference* (a requirement for a 'hands-off' policy in relation to whole biotic communities); *the duty of fidelity* (a duty not to break trust that a wild animal has placed in us in a situation of our making); and *the principle of restitutive justice* (a duty to restore the balance of justice between a moral agent and a moral subject when the subject has been wronged by the agent).
2 Directive 92/43/EEC on the conservation of natural habitats and wild fauna and flora OJ 1992 L 206/7, 21.5.1992.
3 'Triage' refers to the system developed by French military medics during the Napoleonic wars. The wounded were divided into three groups: those who would probably die, even if treated; those who would probably live even if not treated, and those who

would probably die if not treated but who would probably live if treated. Medical supplies, being in short supply, were reserved for the wounded in the last group.
4 405 U.S. 727 (1972).
5 [1995] 1 All ER 513, 92 LGR 674.
6 'Where the question is whether the life of a ten-year-old child might be saved by however a slim chance, the responsible authority ... must do more than toll the bell of tight resources ... They must explain the priorities that have led them to decline to fund the treatment' (*R* v. *Cambridge Health Authority* [1995] 2 All ER 129, per Laws J, at 137).
7 See *R* v. *Brown* [1994] 1 AC 212, and *Laskey, Jaggard and Brown* v. *United Kingdom*, 24 EHRR 39, 19 February 1997.
8 For an early example see the principles of environmental law advanced by the World Commission on Environment and Development (1987) *Our Common Future* (Oxford: Oxford University Press).
9 *R* v. *Secretary of State for Trade and Industry, ex p. Duddridge and Others* [1994] Env. LR 1.

References

Alder, J. (1996) 'Legal Values and Environmental Values: Towards a Regulatory Framework' in Rodgers C.P. (ed.), *Nature Conservation and Countryside Law* (Aberystwyth: University of Wales Press).

Anonymous (1997) The Unabomber's Manifesto, http://www.soci.niu.edu/~critcrim/uni/uni.html

Attfield, R. (1983) 'Christian Attitudes to Nature', *Journal of the History of Ideas*, 44: 369–386.

Attfield, R. (1991) *The Ethics of Environmental Concern*, 2nd edn (Athens and London: University of Georgia Press).

Berne, M. (1990) 'Government Regulation and the Development of Environmental Ethics under the Clean Air Act', *Ecology Law Quarterly* 17: 539–580.

Bookchin, M. (1980) *Towards an Ecological Society* (Montreal: Rose Black Books).

Bowden, P. (1995) 'Citizen Suits – Can we Afford Them and Do we Need Them Anyway?' in Robinson and Dunkley (1995).

Cahen, H. (1995) 'Against the Moral Considerability of Ecosystems' in Pierce and Van De Veer (1995).

Callicott, J.B. (1980) 'Animal Liberation: A Triangular Affair', *Environmental Ethics*, 2: 311–338.

Callicott, J.B. (1994) 'The Conceptual Foundations of the Land Ethic' in Pierce and Van De Veer (1995).

Cherrett, J.M. (1989) 'Key Concepts: the Results of a Survey of Our Members' Opinions' in Cherrett, J.M. (ed.) *Ecological Concepts: the Contribution of Ecology to an Understanding of the Natural World* (Oxford: Blackwell Scientific Publications).

Clements, F.E. (1928) *Plant Succession and Indicators* (New York: H.W. Wilson Company).

Commoner, B. (1971) *The Closing Circle* (New York: Knopf).

Commission of the European Communities (1997) *Framework for Community Action in the Field of Water Policy*, COM (97) 49, incorporating COM (97) 614 and COM (98) 76, Brussels.
Conaghan, J. and Mansell, W. (1993) *The Wrongs of Tort* (London: Pluto).
Connell, J.H. (1978) 'Diversity in Tropical Rain Forests and Coral Reefs', *Science*, 199: 1302–1310.
Connell, J.H. and Slayter, R.O. (1977) 'Mechanisms of Succession in Natural Communities and their Role in Community Stability and Organization', *The American Naturalist*, 111: 1119–1144.
Craig, P.P. and Glasser, H. (1993) 'Ethics and Values in Environmental Policy: the Said and the UNCED', *Environmental Values*, 2: 137–157.
Day, J.M. and Tappan, M.B. (1996) 'The Narrative Approach to Moral Development: From the Epistemic Subject to Dialogical Selves', *Human Development*, 39: 67–82.
Devall, B. and Sessions, G. (1984) 'The Development of Natural Resources and the Integrity of Nature', *Environmental Ethics*, 6: 296–322.
Devlin, P. (1968) *The Enforcement of Morals* (London: Oxford University Press).
Dias, A. (1994) 'Judicial Activism in the Development and Enforcement of Environmental Law', *Journal of Environmental Law*, 6 (2): 243–262.
Drury, W.H. and Nisbet, I.C.T. (1973) 'Succession', *Journal of the Arnold Arboretum*, 54: 331–368.
Dryzeck, J.S. (1987) *Rational Ecology: Environment and Political Economy* (Oxford: Blackwell).
Dryzeck, J.S. (1992) 'Ecology and Discursive Democracy: Beyond Liberal Capitalism and the Administrative State', *Capitalism, Nature, Socialism*, 3: 18–42.
Dworkin, R.M. (1966) 'Lord Devlin and the Enforcement of Morals', *Yale Law Journal*, 75: 986–1005.
Dworkin, R. (1978) 'Liberalism' in Hampshire, S. (ed.) *Public and Private Morality* (Cambridge: Cambridge University Press).
Edmond, D.P. (1984) 'Co-operation in Nature: A New Foundation for Environmental Law', *Osgoode Hall Law Journal*, 22: 323–348.
Ehrlich, P. R. (1970) *The Population Bomb* (London: Ballantine).
Elton, C.S. (1927) *Animal Ecology* (New York: Macmillan).
Emmenegger, S. and Tschentscher, A. (1994) 'Taking Rights Seriously: The Long Way to Biocentricism in Environmental Law', *Georgetown International Environmental Law Review*, 6: 545–592.
ENDS (Environmental News Data Services) (1992) *Dangerous Substances in Water: a Practical Guide* (London: ENDS).
Evans, D. (1992) *A History of Nature Conservation in Britain* (London: Routledge).
Evans, F.C. (1956) 'Ecosystems as the Basic Unit in Ecology', *Science*, 123: 1127–1128.
Feldman. D. (1992) 'Public Interest Litigation and Constitutional Theory in Comparative Perspective', *Modern Law Review*, 55 (1): 44–72.
Finnis, J.M. (1980) *Natural Law and Natural Rights* (Oxford: Clarendon Press).
Foreman, D. (1991) *Confessions of an Eco-Warrior* (Boston: Harmony).

Freyfogle, E.T. (1990) 'The Land Ethic and Pilgrim Leopold', *University of Columbia Law Review*, 61: 217–256.
Freyfogle, E.T. (1994) 'The Ethical Strands of Environmental Law', *University of Illinois Law Review*, 1994: 819–846.
Glaweski, J. (1993) 'Environmental Provisions in a New South African Bill of Rights', *Journal of African Law*, 37: 177–184.
Goldsmith, E. (1988) 'Gaia: Some Implications for the Theoretical Ecologist', *The Ecologist*, 18: 64–74.
Goodin, R.E. (1992) *Green Political Theory* (Cambridge: Polity Press).
Goodpaster, K. (1978) 'On Being Morally Considerable', *Journal of Philosophy*, 75: 308–325.
Grant, V. (1981) *Plant Speciation*, 2nd edn (New York: Columbia University Press).
Grant, V. (1994) 'The Evolution of the Species Concept', *Biologisches Zentralblatt*, 113: 401–415.
Grierson, K.W. (1992) 'The Concept of Species and the Endangered Species Act', *Virginia Environmental Law Review*, 11: 463–498.
Guruswamy, L. and Tromans, S. (1986) 'Towards an Integrated Approach to Pollution Control', *Journal of Environmental and Planning Law*, 643–655.
Hale, M. (1677) *The Primitive Origination of Mankind* (London: W. Godbid).
Hanley, N. and Milne, J. (1996) 'Ethical Beliefs and Behaviour in Contingent Valuation Surveys', *Journal of Environmental Planning and Management*, 39: 255–272.
Hardaway, R.M. (1996) *Population, Law and the Environment* (Westport: Praeger Publishers).
Hardin, G. (1968) 'The Tragedy of the Commons', *Science*, 162: 1243–1248.
Hardin, G. (1977) *The Limits of Altruism* (Bloomington: Indiana University Press).
Hargrove, E.C. (1986) *Religion and Environmental Crisis* (Athens: University of Georgia Press).
Hargrove, E. (1989) *The Foundations of Environmental Ethics* (Englewood Cliffs: Prentice Hall).
Harrison, R. (1993) *Democracy* (London: Routledge).
Hart, H.L.A. (1963) *Law, Liberty and Morality* (London: Oxford University Press).
Hart, H.L.A. (1977) 'Immorality and Treason' in Dworkin, R.M. (ed.) *The Philosophy of Law* (Oxford: Oxford University Press).
Hayward, B.M. (1995) 'The Greening of Participatory Democracy: A Reconsideration of Theory', *Environmental Politics*, 4: 215–236.
Hill, T. Jr. (1983) 'Ideals of Human Excellence and Preserving Natural Environment', *Environmental Ethics*, 5: 211–224.
Hughes, G. (1962) 'Morals and the Criminal Law', *Yale Law Journal*, 71: 662–683.
IUCN (International Union for the Conservation of Nature and Natural Resources) (1980) *World Conservation Strategy: Living Resource Conservation for Sustainable Development*, IUCN, (Switzerland: Gland).
Kheel, M. (1985) 'The Liberation of Nature: a Circular Affair', *Environmental Ethics*, 7: 135–149.
Kohlberg, L. (1969) 'Stage and Sequence: the Cognitive Development Approach to

Socialization', in Goslin, D.A. (ed.) *Handbook of Socialization Theory and Research* (Chicago: Rand McNally).
Kohlberg, L. (1984) *The Psychology of Moral Development* (New York: Harper and Row).
Krämer, L. (1996) 'Public Interest Litigation in Environmental Matters before European Courts', *Journal of Environmental Law*, 8: 1-18.
Krutch, J.W. (1956) *The Great Chain of Life* (London: Country Book Club).
Kunich, J.C. (1994) 'The Fallacy of Deathbed Conservation under the Endangered Species Act', *Environmental Law*, 24: 501-571.
Leopold, A. (1966) *A Sand County Almanac* (New York: Oxford University Press).
List, P. (1993) *Radical Environmentalism: Philosophy and Tactics* (Belmont, Ca: Wadsworth Publishing Co.).
Lovelock, J. (1988) *The Ages of Gaia* (New York: Norton).
Lovelock, J. (1995) *Gaia: a New Look at Life on Earth* (Oxford: Oxford University Press).
McDonagh, S. (1986) *To Care for the Earth: a Call for a New Theology* (London: Geoffrey Chapman).
MacIntyre, A. (1985) *After Virtue: a Study in Moral Theory* (Notre Dame: University of Notre Dame Press).
McLaughlin, A. (1993) *Industrialism and Deep Ecology* (New York: New York University Press).
Marietta, D. (1988) 'Environmental Holism and Individuals', *Environmental Ethics*, 10: 251-258.
Marx, K. (1993) (originally 1939) *Grundrisse* (London: Penguin).
Masters, J.C. and Spencer, H.G. (1989) 'Why We Need a New Genetic Species Concept', *Systematic Zoology*, 38: 270-279.
Mayr, E. (1969) 'The Biological Meaning of Species', *Biological Journal of the Linnean Society*, 1: 311-320.
Mill, J.S. (1848) *Principles of Political Economy* (London: Longmans Green).
Mill, J.S. (1912) *Considerations on Representative Government* (Oxford: Oxford University Press).
Mill, J.S. (1972) 'On Liberty' in Acton, H.B. (ed.) *Utilitarianism, On Liberty, Considerations of Representative Government* (London: Dent and Sons).
Mitchell, B. (1967) *Law, Morality and Religion in a Secular State* (London: Oxford University Press).
Moncrief, L. (1974) 'The Cultural Basis for Our Environmental Crisis', *Science*, 170: 508-512.
Montefiore, H. (1970) *Can Man Survive?* (London: Fontana).
Muldoon, P. (1988) 'The Fight for An Environmental Bill of Rights', *Alternatives*, 15: 33-39.
Naess, A. (1973) 'The Shallow and the Deep, Long-Range Ecology Movement. A Summary', *Inquiry*, 16: 95-100.
Naess, A. (1984) 'A Defence of the Deep Ecology Movement', *Environmental Ethics*, 6: 265-270.
Naess, A. (1989) *Ecology, Community and Lifestyle* (Cambridge: Cambridge University Press).

Naess, A. (1995) 'Self Realization: An Ecological Approach to Being in the World' in Pierce, and Van De Veer (1995).
Odum, E.P. (1969) 'The Strategy of Ecosystem Development', *Science*, 164: 262–270.
O'Riordan, T. (1981) *Environmentalism* (London: Pion).
Ophuls, W. (1973) 'Leviathan or Oblivion' in Daly, H.E. (ed.) *Toward a Steady State Economy* (San Francisco: Freeman).
Ophuls, W. (1977) 'The Politics of the Sustainable Society' in Pirages, D. (ed.) *The Sustainable Society* (New York: Praeger).
Ophuls, W. and Boyan, A.S. (1992) *Ecology and the Politics of Scarcity Revisited* (New York: Freeman).
Orie, K.K. (1995) 'Constitutional Approach to Sustainable Environmental Management: Experience and Challenge', *Environmental Law and Policy*, 25: 43–51.
Passmore, J. (1974) *Man's Responsibility for Nature* (New York: Scribners).
Phillips, J. (1931) 'The Biotic Community', *Journal of Ecology*, 19: 1–24.
Phillips, J. (1934) 'Succession, Development, the Climax and the Complex Analysis of Concepts, I', *Journal of Ecology*, 22: 554–571.
Phillips, J. (1935) 'Succession, Development, the Climax and the Complex Analysis of Concepts II, III', *Journal of Ecology*, 23: 210–246, 288–508.
Pickett, S.T.A. and White, P.S. (1985) *The Ecology of Natural Disturbances and Patch Dynamics* (Orlando, FL: Academic Press).
Pierce, C. and Van De Veer, D. (eds) (1995) *People, Penguins and Plastic Trees: Basic Issues in Environmental Ethics*, 2nd edn (Belmont, CA: Wadsworth Publishing Company).
Plamenatz, J.P. (1973) *Democracy and Illusion* (London: Longman).
Plumwood, V. (1995) 'Has Democracy Failed Ecology; An Ecofeminist Perspective', *Environmental Politics*, 4 (4): 134–168.
Rabie, A. (1991) 'A Constitutional Right to Environmental Integrity – A German Perspective', *South African Journal on Human Rights*, 7: 208.
Rand, A. (1964) *Virtue of Selfishness: a New Concept of Egoism* (New York: Signet Books).
Rawls, J (1972) *A Theory of Justice* (Oxford: Clarendon).
Regan, T. (1983) *The Case for Animal Rights* (London: Routledge).
Regenmortel, M.H.V. (1992) 'Concept of Virus Species', *Biodiversity and Conservation*, 1: 263–266.
Robinson, D. (1993) 'Public Participation in Environmental Decision Making', *Environment and Planning Law Journal*, October: 321–329.
Robinson, D. and Dunkley, J. (eds) (1995) *Public Interest Perspectives in Environmental Law* (Chichester: Wiley Chancery).
Rodman, J. (1977) 'The Liberation of Nature?', *Inquiry*, 20: 83–131.
Rolston, H. (1988) *Environmental Ethics: Duties to and Values in the Natural World* (Philadelphia: Temple University Press).
Rolston, H. (1995) 'Duties to Endangered Species' in Elliot, R. (ed.) *Environmental Ethics* (Oxford: Oxford University Press).
Rousseau, J.J. (1984) *A Discourse on Inequality* (Middlesex: Penguin Books).

Royal Commission on Environmental Pollution (1988) *Best Practicable Environmental Option*, Twelfth Report, Cm 310, HMSO, London.
Sagoff, M. (1984) 'Animal Liberation and Environmental Ethics: Bad Marriage, Quick Divorce', *Osgoode Hall Law Journal*, 22 (2): 297–307.
Sagoff, M. (1988) *The Economy of the Earth: Philosophy, Law and Economics* (Cambridge: Cambridge University Press).
Sagoff, M. (1995) 'Can Environmentalists be Liberals?' in Elliot, R. (ed.) *Environmental Ethics* (Oxford: Oxford University Press).
Saward, M. (1993) 'Green Democracy', in Dobson, A. and Lucardie, P. (eds) *The Politics of Nature* (London: Routledge).
Schmelz, C. and Brandl, E.O. (1996) 'Environmental Protection and the Austrian Constitution', *European Public Law*, 2: 1–7.
Schindler, D.W. (1987) 'Is the Whole Really More Than the Sum of the Parts?' in Likens, G.E. et al. (eds) *Status and Future of Ecosystem Science* (New York: Institute of Ecosystem Studies).
Sikora, R.I. and Barry, B. (1978) *Obligations to Future Generations* (Philadelphia: Temple University Press).
Singer, P. (1976) *Animal Liberation: A New Ethic for our Treatment of Animals* (London: Jonathan Cape).
Sober, E. (1984) *The Nature of Selection: Evolutionary Theory in Philosophical Focus* (Cambridge, MA: MIT Press).
Stephen, J.F. (1967) (originally 1874) *Liberty, Equality, Fraternity* (London: Cambridge University Press).
Stone, C. (1972) 'Should Trees Have Standing? – Toward Legal Rights for Natural Objects', *Southern California Law Review*, 45: 450–501.
Tansley, A. (1935) 'The Use and Abuse of Vegetational Concepts and Terms', *Ecology*, 16: 284–307.
Tappan, M.B. (1997) 'Language, Culture and Moral Development', *Developmental Review*, 17: 78–100.
Taylor, P.W. (1986) *Respect for Nature: a Theory of Environmental Ethics* (Oxford: Princeton Press).
Thomas, K. (1984) *Man and the Natural World* (London: Penguin Books).
Thompson, A. (1985) 'Common Law, Statutes and Conservation Values: Do They Have Anything in Common?', *The Forestry Chronicle*, 61: 131–134.
Tribe, L. (1974) 'Ways Not To Think About Plastic Trees', *Yale Law Journal*, 83: 1315–1348.
UKELA (United Kingdom Environmental Law Association) (1987) *Best Practicable Environmental Option: a New Jerusalem?* (London: UKELA).
Van De Veer, D. (1979) 'Interspecific Justice', *Inquiry*, 22: 55–79.
Verschuuren, J. (1993) 'The Constitutional Right to Protection of the Environment in the Netherlands', *Osterreichische Zeitschrift fur Offentliches Recht und Volkerrechte*, 46: 67–77.
Waring, R.H. (1989) 'Ecosystems: Fluxes of Matter and Energy' in Cherrett, J.M. (1989).
Wenz, P. (1988) *Environmental Justice*, (New York: New York State University Press).

Westra, L (1993) 'The Ethics of Environmental Holism and the Democratic State: Are They in Conflict?', *Environmental Values*, 2: 125–136.

Wheeler, W.M. (1928) *The Social Insects: Their Origin and Evolution* (London: Paul, Trench and Trubner Ltd.).

White, L. Jr. (1967) 'The Historical Roots of Our Ecological Crisis', *Science*, 37: 1203–1207.

Wildlife and Conservation Special Committee (England and Wales) (1947) *Conservation of Nature in England and Wales* (London: HMSO).

Wilson, E.O. (1994) *The Diversity of Life* (London: Penguin).

Winpenny, J.T. (1991) *Values for the Environment: A Guide to Economic Assessment* (London: HMSO).

Young, I.M. (1990) *Justice and the Politics of Difference* (Princeton: Princeton University Press).

2 Challenging the Ethos of the European Union

A Green Perspective on European Union Policies and Programmes for Rural Development and the Environment[1]

David Wood

In order to accommodate the accession of new member states in Eastern Europe and meet the requirements of the World Trade Organization (WTO), the European Union (EU) has embarked upon major reforms of its basic constitution, the Common Agricultural Policy (CAP) and the Structural Funds. These reforms are embodied in the Treaty of Amsterdam and the 'Agenda 2000' reform process, which, amongst many other changes, formalise the EU's adoption of the goal of 'sustainable development'. This chapter, however, argues that despite promoting the rhetoric of 'sustainable development', the EU is premised on a fundamentally misguided driving force or ethos of economic growth and competitiveness. The EU is a key player in the global phase of capitalist industrialism, with a new form of state organisation and institutional development, a version of what McMichael (1998) has termed the 'global' state. Thus academic excitement about new forms of governance based on 'partnership' and 'subsidiarity' within the EU may well be misplaced, particularly if that excitement leads to a failure to remember or recognise the fundamental ethos of the Union.

The aim of this chapter is to confront such orthodoxies, being premised on a vision of society and governance based on the principles of ecological sustainability, social justice, real democracy, non-violence and liberation, in other words a radical Green agenda. This ideology has an understanding of the ideas of sustainable development, partnership and subsidiarity far removed from that of the Union, an understanding that is fundamentally localist and rooted in the revival of endogenous community economic, social and cultural structures. Within the framework of such a critique, the contradictions within the EU become apparent, and alternative possibilities can emerge.

Part One briefly outlines the radical view of globalisation and contrasts it with the localist Green philosophy. This approach, drawing on political ecology, stresses the importance both of local communities for environmental conservation, and of 'nature' in the constitution of community. Part Two considers the European Union's ethos and policy-making with particular emphasis on the Structural Funds and their relationship to environmental and agricultural policy, largely in the context of the rural. It examines not only the policies and programmes but also some of the arguments over their implementation and enforcement that have enjoyed a resurgence in recent academic literature. The conclusion discusses the potential roles of the EU, national, regional and local governments, NGOs, academics, and local people and communities, in a move to governance based on sustainability.

Part One: Globalisation and the Green Critique

The Process of Economic Globalisation

Globalisation has many forms. The most commonly understood interpretation refers to economic activity, and in particular the translation of the precepts of the capitalist market economy from a national through an international to a global scale (Yearley 1996). This process has been called 'the most fundamental redesign of the planet's economic arrangements since at least the industrial revolution' (Mander 1996a: 3). Concentration on the economic aspects of globalisation is justified because this is the key rationale for the promotion and extension of this phenomenon by its proponents, and as such it is part of the growing 'economisation' of the socio-political sphere (Shiva 1989), or the imposition of a new 'politicised market rule' (McMichael 1998). In this ideology the market economy, framed by the concepts of unlimited economic growth, consumerism and free trade (Daly and Cobb 1989; Douthwaite 1992; Ekins 1993; Wood 1997), is seen as the ideal vehicle for the provision of human wants (OECD 1993). The more radical interpretations, however, see globalisation not so much as a 'trend' or a 'force' but as a deliberate and controlled process of structural adjustment on a global scale carried out by transnational corporations, international financial organisations and supranational organisations, especially the United States, the Bretton Woods institutions (World Bank, International Monetary Fund and WTO), the Organisation for Economic Cooperation and Development (OECD) and the EU (Hildyard and Sexton 1996). Globalisation is thus the logical outcome of the process of 'development'. This has entailed absorbing 'backward' localities, mainly in Africa, Latin America and South Asia, into the market system, leading to the destruction of ecological systems, the increasing of inequality and the destruction of local cultural distinctiveness (Shiva 1989; Escobar 1995). Rural areas of the North were also considered to be underdeveloped and in need of modernisation: indeed this was one of the founding aims of the European Economic Community.[2] In addition, rural areas of these countries shared in the development experiments conducted in their colonies; the history of community development in the UK is particularly instructive here (Wright 1990).

But while the market system has concentrated the wealth produced using Southern resources and labour into the hands of Northern producers and consumers (Ekins 1993; Redclift 1996), this has not led to greater equity, even within the North. In the 1990s, income differentials between the richest and poorest regions in the EU have increased (CEC 1996; Mernagh and Commins 1997). And there is now evidence that welfare may not only be decreasing relatively but also absolutely. Jackson and Marks (1994) for example, calculated an 'Index of Sustainable Economic Welfare' (ISEW) for the UK from 1950–1990 which shows that although ISEW rose along with Gross National Product (GNP) until the 1970s, it has since fallen despite further rises in GNP. Analyses for the US, Germany and the Netherlands have shown the same pattern (Douthwaite 1996). Finally, globalisation has also been seen as the end of any possibility of full employment:

> ... to the global economy, people are not only increasingly unnecessary, but they and their demands for a living wage are a major source of economic inefficiency. Global corporations are acting to purge themselves of this unwanted burden. We are creating a system that has fewer places for people. (Korten 1995: 237)

Despite these criticisms, however, it is argued that globalisation processes are bound up with social, cultural and political forces at local and regional levels, as firms are 'territorially embedded' (Amin and Thrift 1994a). Furthermore it is also commonly argued that corporations, if they are not already, can be embedded within a locality and many development strategies that use inward investment depend on this. But others have countered that 'the prospects for greater local embeddedness of transnational corporations created by the new organizational forms appear to be limited to a minority of favoured places' (Dicken et al. 1994: 41), specifically economically and institutionally rich urban areas. The spatial distribution of such embeddedness is therefore a reflection of uneven development. But embeddedness is in any case frequently superficial, and some have seen it as yet further proof of the power of emerging global corporations to insinuate themselves into local markets without taking any part in the actual success or failure of the local economy. This sub-process of 'glocalisation' is 'rooted in the recognition that truly effective global reach can only be secured through capturing the local economy' (Hildyard et al. 1996: 130). The end result for those local economies, and especially those in rural areas, is that 'the local becomes just another field for the application of global rules, procedures, solutions and development models' (van Dijk and van der Ploeg 1995: ix).

For critics of globalisation such as Hirst and Thompson (1992, 1995), however, the nation state remains pivotal: the world 'remains an *international* system' (1995: 408) while 'the theorists of globalization deny both the need for strong international governance and the possibility of national level action' and are 'pessimists of the intellect and of the will' (1995: 429). In contrast, however, they appear over-optimistic about the possible regulatory role of 'common associations' (1995: 429), that is, consensual organisations with a global reach that can police globalised sectors, for example the World Trade Organization.[3]

Many of those who argue against theories of globalisation, however, seem to conflate several positions: support for globalisation, arguments that see globalisation as undesirable but inevitable, and those which recognise the process of globalisation but which argue that it must be opposed. Yet it is not pessimistic to argue that economic globalisation strategies are promoted by entities which possess enormous resources; it is simply a fact. But this does not prevent it being argued that globalisation must be opposed, nor from suggesting that global governance/government or nation states are not likely to provide that opposition. Other analysts argue that globalisation has a more dominant relationship with the state. Thus for McMichael, 'it is not that states are being eliminated, rather that they are being restructured from nation-states into ... "global" states, that is, institutions geared to securing global credit, and circuits of money and commodities, and legitimized by "consumer citizens"' (1998: 15).

'Forms of state' are certainly changing, and the EU is a clear example of this process (Caporaso 1996), but while nation states may not be as pivotal as Hirst and Thompson claim, they can (and do) actively encourage globalisation, and hence their own restructuring, by adopting neo-liberal objectives. Most importantly, it is unclear at what point the process of globalisation moves beyond the ability of states to limit it. Greens argue that this point is rapidly approaching but has not yet been reached (Hines 1998). Yet despite theoretical arguments, empirical evidence is lacking; there is no state, or group of states, that has taken the path of resistance. There is thus a critical distinction between *ability* to control or resist globalisation, and the *action* of doing so, an issue revisited in the conclusion.

Political Ecology: 'Denying the Global a Home'[4]

Evolving from a multitude of streams of influence including neo-Marxism, utopian and libertarian socialism (anarchism), and the new social movements of the 1960s (particularly the feminist, anti-development and peace movements), political ecology provides perhaps the most fruitful opposition to globalising ideologies.

In discussing the opportunities for such opposition, it is first necessary to distinguish political ecology, Green thinking, or 'ecologism' (Dobson 1995) from environmentalism. The latter, Dobson has convincingly argued, is merely an adjunct to other political theories and demands no rethinking; it is reformist and 'easily accommodated by other ideologies' (Dobson 1995: 7). Environmentalism also retains a reductionist scientific analysis of global environmental destruction, and therefore merely serves to find new ways to 'manage' discrete environmental problems (Redclift 1996). Green thinking, on the other hand, is a distinct ideology and represents:

> ... nothing less than a nonviolent revolution to overthrow our whole polluting, plundering and materialistic industrial society and, in its place, to create a new economic and social order which will allow human beings to live in harmony with the planet. (Porritt and Winner, in Dobson 1995: 9)[5]

The distinction between ecologism and environmentalism is fundamentally one between 'ecocentrism' or 'biocentrism' and 'anthropocentrism' (Dobson 1995; Naess 1989). Green thinking sees humanity as part of the natural world, and not as existing prior to it, or as being more important than it. This has its equivalent in the difference between 'sustainability' and 'sustainable development'. As Vandana Shiva (1992) points out, sustainability is essentially about the ability of natural systems to continue indefinitely to sustain and nurture life. Sustainable development is different. Redclift (1996: 48) claims that 'there is considerable confusion over *what* is to be sustained by sustainable development' (original emphasis); however, sustainable development by its own title places itself within the discourse of development, making it clear that what is to be sustained is development itself (Esteva 1992; for a general overview see Baker et al. 1997). It is a 'technocratic/ economistic discourse' (Barry 1996: 128), or the imposition of Northern environmentalism on development thinking (Adams 1995).

It is not surprising, therefore, that many commentators find the concept problematic: O'Riordan and Jäger, for example, note that sustainable development is 'struggling for recognition in a morass of ambiguity where the calls for real redistribution of power, and a much greater degree of economic independence at the local level are frankly unheeded because of their profoundly radical nature' (1995: 25). This is because sustainable development came about as a result of the Brundtland Commission's desire to sidetrack the profound and radical (anti-development) implications of sustainability, with a 'new era of economic growth' (WCED 1987: 1). This approach was confirmed by the Earth Summit in 1992, which saw 'growth as the principal means to stop the poor destroying the environment' (Chatterjee and Finger 1994: 168). It is, as Richardson notes, 'not only a political fudge; it is a sham. It attempts – unsuccessfully – to obscure the basic contradiction between the finiteness of the earth ... and the expansionary nature of industrial society' (1997: 57). Political ecology makes it quite clear that there can be no such conjunction. The earth is a finite space and its capacities are governed by the laws of thermodynamics. As such, infinite economic growth, in so much as it depends on increasing throughput, is a fallacy: 'an ever increasing flow of inputs of natural resources in the production processes to sustain the required growth inevitably results in liquidating of the natural capital stock that supplies this flow' (Haavelmo and Hansen 1992: 39; see also Daly and Cobb 1989; Daly 1996; Boothe 1998). Criticisms of this view, suggesting that economic growth is becoming less dependent on throughput (for example, Gerelli 1995), may be challenged both on the basis of its temporarily-bounded occurrence as a post-oil crisis phenomenon of the 1970s (Hinterberger et al. 1995), and because, even if it can still be observed, it is 'far from producing what is ecologically needed' (Weizsäcker 1995: 221). Essentially the market only responds after the event, and even then cannot be relied on to respond fast enough to ecological or social stimuli (Glasmeier 1994).

However, because of the politically attractive idea that present problems can be solved by 'business as usual', governments and supranational organisations have embraced sustainable development and environmental economics with immense fervour (Adams 1995; Yearley 1996). This has led, in turn, to sustainable development replacing the meaning of 'sustainability' in the minds of many such organisations (Shiva 1992); the OECD can now simply refer to sustainability as 'building the future into current decisions' (OECD 1993: 49) as if it were a component in a management strategy, and the European Commission can use 'sustainable development' and 'sustainable growth' as if they were compatible concepts (CEC 1997a).

Defining sustainability *per se*, however, is only part of the story. Wolfgang Sachs (1993) has noted that the location and scale of sustainability is vital to understanding the political arrangements resulting from the use of such a concept. Thus 'global' sustainability implies global institutions, surveillance and control (WCED 1987), whereas local strategies imply decentralisation, increased self-reliance and participatory governance. In this vein it has been proposed that 'sustainability presupposes community' (Achterberg 1996:

174) in political ecology. Kenny (1996: 16) states that 'community' is 'one of the most widely-used, but least analysed, terms in green political discourse', and indeed in wider development discourse. Kenny is so suspicious of the word that he rejects its primacy entirely. Some have observed that community has increasingly been used to denote the object of government, previously defined as national society, in new currents of thought about government and governance (Ward and McNicholas 1997). This is certainly an aspect of Green ideas about community. But political ecology proposes both a broadening and a deepening of the idea of community. It broadens it by extending community beyond the human to other species, to the earth itself, as well as to future generations – it can thus be characterised as a 'politics of advocacy' (Barry 1996: 128). But it also contains a deepening element in the sense that Greens embrace and encourage diversity and the liberation of those human 'others' oppressed by narrow conceptions of community: 'radical green politics is an emancipatory politics that seeks the maximization of the autonomy of human and non-human beings to "unfold in their own ways" ' (Eckersley, in Dobson 1995: 27).[6]

So, how can community be defined in a Green context? There are certainly utopian elements in the Green vision of the 'sustainable society' (GPEW 1997) but the Green interpretation of community is primarily practical. John Pearce captures some of this in advocating the notion of 'pragmatic community', 'one with which people feel comfortable and which will nonetheless "work" in the sense of serving its intended purpose' (Pearce 1994: 63). Both Pearce (1994) and Norgaard (1994) put forward the idea of 'nested communities', overlapping layers of community serving functions appropriate to their size and reach. This is the natural social outcome of the political principle of 'subsidiarity', which holds that 'nothing should be done centrally if it can be done equally well, or better, locally' (GPEW 1997: para. PG100). This principle cannot however be taken alone: Green theory states that the 'lower' body can and should 'judge for itself which functions carried out at a higher level it can do equally well, or better' (GPEW 1997: para. PG101).

There are two fundamental reasons for smaller communities taking bigger decisions. The first is that decisions can be taken as a result of direct knowledge of, and interaction with, the local environment (Norgaard 1994). This is not possible within the context of the global economic system. As a result of globalisation, links between people and local communities and their environments become weaker, and then redefined in terms of the new dominant global interpretation, for example, by stressing the role of the countryside as leisure space for tourism (CEC 1995a). The second reason is more complex, but is essentially that communities lead to the development of a 'relational self', rather than the purely individualistic self of capitalist society. Thus in a sustainable society, 'self-realisation would be achieved through reciprocity and interdependence rather than through autonomy' (Mathews 1995: 76). This in turn would predispose individuals to empathy and consequently to a more biocentric view (Naess 1989). This would lead to what Norgaard (1994) defines as a 'coevolutionary' approach, whereby a virtuous circle of interaction is created between people and nature leading to the blurring of the division between them.

Discussion of ecologically-based communities leads naturally on to consideration of bioregionalism (Sale 1985). Bioregionalism represents an attempt to reconnect communities with their natural environments primarily by the identification of localities with a bounded natural area, based on physical geography and biological characteristics. However this concept of bioregionalism may not necessarily accord with popular conceptions of place, especially in areas where industrialisation and globalisation have already overwhelmed many of the connections people once had with their environments.

Are other ways of thinking about geographical community therefore necessary? Douthwaite (1996), for example, considers the notion of 'spatial fields', which are socially or culturally-bounded areas based on various aspects of human interaction, for example, the distribution of local newspapers, or the prevalence of certain customs and dialects, or other factors that do not necessarily coincide with official ideas of place, or indeed with geographical space. Christopher Ray has put forward the concept of the 'culture economy', defined as an 'attempt by rural areas to localize economic control' and 'to (re)valorize place through its cultural identity' (1998a: 3). However such cultural and social factors are also involved in a complex relationship with capitalism and globalisation. Thus there are several 'modes' in which a culture economy approach can operate, varying from commoditisation to a rediscovery of culture leading to increased self-reliance. Green approaches in this typology can be located at the latter end of the scale. In some respects, bioregional thinking attempted to incorporate these cultural and social factors through the idea of the 'fuzzy boundary' which 'should be organic, changing with place and through time because it is dependent on its definition and interpretation by local people with their changing goals and understandings of their surroundings' (Stevenson and Ball 1998: 193). And, as has been noted above, diversity both within and between communities is a key Green value.

However Ray is not confident about the ability of localities (however defined) to follow the self-reliant trajectory. Instead he claims that realistically communities can only hope for a controlled engagement with the global economy. This argument has some factors in common with the 'new localist' agenda put forward by Clarke (1993) which argues that globalisation is creating new opportunities for local government to create 'new growth coalitions' at the local level. These rely on the potential for partnership between private and public organisations (see below in the context of the EU) to revitalise both political and economic development (Chandler 1993). However, the freedom offered local governments is largely illusory; the global economy is increasingly forcing local authorities to compete against each other for inward investment, effectively 'forcing localities to absorb private costs to increase private profits' (Korten 1995: 130). In addition, this sort of argument relies on too many of the aspects of globalising capitalism that are leading to the destruction of local cultures and the biosphere and the impoverishment of whole nations in the first place: consumerism, free trade, continuous economic growth and so on. It fails to examine the nature of corporate ideology and power that are key determinants of the new global economy (Mander 1996b) and does not question the right of European nations to enjoy high consumption lifestyles at the expense of the rest of the world. The strategy is therefore no more sustainable than present approaches.

This realisation has led to renewed consideration of self-reliance. Very importantly it must be noted that self-reliance does not mean no trade, or no other 'higher' bodies. As Arne Naess (1989) notes, the need for hospitals and so on is not precluded by the notion of community, nor is the crucial question of 'a mechanism to redistribute regional funds from the richer areas to the poorer areas' (Hines 1998: 12). For Douthwaite (1996), self-reliant strategies have three main aspects: first, that communities must use local resources to produce what they need for themselves; second, that world market prices must not determine what is produced; and finally, that as many inputs as possible must come from within the community. This means creating local currencies, exchange mechanisms and financial institutions to serve community rather than market needs; generating energy locally from renewable or continuous resources, and growing enough food ecologically and humanely to supply local people rather than growing chemically and intensively for surplus to sell on world markets. Some of these conditions have historical precedents, and growing present-day cases, for example, mutual Building Societies and Credit Unions (Douthwaite 1996), innovative local currency schemes like Local Exchange Trading Systems (LETS) (Lang 1994; Barnes et al. 1996; Meeker-Lowry 1996; Williams 1996; Mathewson and M'Gonigle 1997); cooperatively owned and managed 'Wind Guilds' in Denmark and Germany (Gipe 1995), and finally, the growing popularity of farmers' markets (Birkhölzer and Lorenz 1996) and Community-Supported Agriculture (CSA), or subscription farming (Douthwaite 1996).

Yet there is no single place where many such schemes operate together, and thus we cannot say exactly what kind of repercussions would occur in response to people-initiated self-reliance, should it become more widespread. Almost certainly, 'when communities get serious, the opposition will get serious too' (Douthwaite 1996: 117). In contrast, should a self-reliant trajectory be promoted at the state level, to what extent would that state be able to follow through its plans, given that people have come to expect the continued growth of the consumer society? With these hugely difficult questions in mind, it is to the policies and actions of one suprastate,[7] the European Union, that we now turn.

Part Two: Challenging the European Union

There are many ways in which the EU impacts upon local sustainability initiatives, which I will divide into three broad areas: first, its underlying ethos; second, the actual process of policy making, including agenda setting, institutional relationships and so on; and third, the implementation and enforcement of those policies. Of course, this is in some ways an arbitrary division and each area has a complex relationship with the others.

The Ethos of the European Union

The European Union is a capitalist organisation. This point is almost too obvious to state, yet it seems all too often ignored that as such it reflects the ideology, law and policy characteristic of capitalist industrialism. Its ethos is to make the European Union a strong and competitive economic power on world markets (CEC 1997a). With respect to rural areas, European Union Commissioner Padraig Flynn has stated that the aim of policy is 'integration of European Union rural areas into the rapidly globalizing world economy' (Flynn, in Mernagh and Commins 1997: i).

At the same time, the EU tries to mitigate the worst effects of those markets on its population. This mitigation is carried out both by direct aid (such as the Structural Funds, as discussed below) and protectionist policies (such as import tariffs in the CAP), but also by continually aiming to increase production and consumption (the throughput of energy) overall with the aim of raising the poorest along with the rich. Because this requires ever increasing resources and ever more capacious sinks for waste, it is unsustainable. It is also unjust, effectively involving the export of its injustice and unsustainability to areas less able to do the same for their people. In the Netherlands, generally considered to be one of the exemplars of sustainable development within Europe, for example, 1,900 per cent of available ecologically productive land is used. It appropriates 100,000–140,000 square kilometres of arable land, five to seven times its actual agricultural area, from other countries, mainly in the South (Wackernagel and Rees 1996). As the 'ecological footprint' of the Union increases through the continuous rise in its standard of living, its negative effects both on the global environment and on places and people in the South multiply.

But the EU refuses to take any direct responsibility for the way in which it operates, referring to the rationale behind policy with phrases like 'the Union will have to adjust to the continued process of globalization' (CEC 1997a: 8). This implies that the market is beyond control and that Europe is merely following an inevitable economic tide. In fact the European Community is a key player in the growth of the global free market, and the EU remains one of the three regions (the 'triads') vital to its dominance (Hildyard et al. 1996). This attitude is part of the political ideology of globalisation and results in particular policy choices with very specific kinds of results in terms of environmental destruction and income and quality-of-life disparity at global and local levels. It also involves the deliberate and anti-democratic ceding of the already limited popular mandate of the EU to unelected, unaccountable yet extraordinarily biased global bodies like the WTO which operate largely in the interests of the transnational corporations (Scott 1995; Nader and Wallach 1996; Retallack 1997).

The clearest example of the massive internal contradictions in EU thinking is the revised Article 2 of the Treaty Establishing the Community[8] which states that the aims of the Community are:

> ... to promote throughout the Community a harmonious, balanced and sustainable development of economic activities, a high level of employment and of social protection, equality between men and women, sustainable and non-inflationary growth, a high degree of competitiveness and convergence of economic performance, a high level of protection and improvement of the quality of the environment, the raising of the standard of living and quality of life, and economic and social cohesion and solidarity among Member States. (Article 2 EC)

Excitement amongst environmentalists at the inclusion of 'sustainable development' should clearly be tempered by the other aims, including 'sustainable ... growth', as well as stress on 'competitiveness' and 'raising the standard of living'. That these are all considered compatible with 'equality', 'social cohesion' and 'raising of the ... quality of life' shows the bankruptcy of the aims of the EU in Green eyes. The basis of the Union is clearly anthropocentric. Environmental considerations are important only in so far as they enhance competitiveness: 'the environment is no longer seen in a vacuum, but as an essential factor in development with specific scope for economic initiative, innovation and job creation, not to mention competitive advantage' (CEC 1995b: 6). Competition inevitably means that there will be winners and losers in the globalised economy (Hines 1998), but the EU is determined that it should be 'well placed to draw advantage from this process' (CEC 1997a: 8), in other words to *cause* poorer nations, communities and people, other species and the planet as a whole to lose.

Policy Making in the European Union

The EU's ethos and the policies which flow from it, however, are not static. Numerous additions and clarifications have been made to the Treaty of Rome over the years of which the Amsterdam amendments are only the latest. Institutions have been set up and evolved, new nations have joined, bureaucracies have been created, and thousands of Regulations, Directives, Recommendations and Opinions have been issued. Broadly speaking there are three mainstream theoretical currents in the way in which policy making and institutional development in the EU are discussed. The first is the 'supranational' or 'neofunctional' approach (for example, Newman 1996), which sees elites in EU institutions, transnational and supranational forces as critical and which is adopted both by those who see a federal Europe as the ultimate goal of the Union (integrationists) and by opponents of this project. The second current is the 'intergovernmental' approach (for example, Moravcsik 1993), which stresses the role of national governments negotiating and competing to promote their own interests, or those of national interest groups. Finally, emerging ideas of 'multilevel' or 'post-parliamentary' governance (for example, Andersen and Burns 1996; Marks et al. 1996) attempts to fuse the two former currents. All these approaches have merit, and each is probably particularly apt for explaining particular developments.

An area where the more neofunctionalist approach seems useful is that of agenda setting. Agenda setting is crucial to the process of policy making. Peters has argued that 'in general ... the EU will adopt the instruments that will evoke the least opposition from national or industrial sources' (1996: 3). But this is too weak. The EU's agenda is often set by industrial sources, whether directly through the lobbying of groups like the European Round Table of industrialists (ERT), or indirectly through national governments, whose policies increasingly reflect corporate interests. The ERT, comprised of bosses from the largest European TNCs, is particularly crucial and underestimated by most. They have been called 'Europe's corporate rulers' (Hines 1998), and Cowles (1995) has shown how the ERT effectively set the agenda for the Single European Act, which determined the shape for European integration, and in addition has changed the nature of cohesion policy through its successful advocacy of 'Trans-European Networks' (TENs) in transport, telecommunications and energy, included as Title XV (ex-Title XII) of the revised Treaty Establishing the Community. The European Commission claim that the TENs will 'serve to enhance ... sustainable development' (CEC 1997a: 12), but in fact they have highlighted the unsustainable reality behind the sustainable development rhetoric of the EU, leading to huge protests across Europe (particularly the anti-roads movement in the UK, the Valle d'Aspe conflict on the Spanish/French border and the movement against the Scanlink project to link Denmark and Sweden) and the forced resignation of ecologically-minded opponents from EU posts, for example, former Environment Commissioner Carlo Ripa di Meana.[9] The influence of the ERT and other corporate lobby groups such as the Union of Industrial and Employers' Confederations of Europe over the Intergovernmental Conference process leading to the Treaty of Amsterdam was also crucial (CEO 1997).

The European Court of Justice has also been considered by some to be important in setting the agenda, and in making policy, although the nature of its contribution is contested. Newman (1996) claims that its role in speeding integration and in sharpening the pro-market orientation of the Community has been crucial, particularly when political problems were leading to stalemate in the other institutions in the 1970s. Essentially the ECJ made policy through the extended interpretation of Treaty Articles, Regulations and Directives, and Scott (1998a) provides ample evidence of the Court's role in the environmental field. However others, for example Wincott (1996), argue that its role is far more reflective of a wider legislative and policy process, and is enabled by other developments in the Union, but it has been well argued that the focus of the ECJ has been more on market integration than regulation (Weatherill 1997). What is certain is that the ECJ has strengthened the corporate bias of the Union (for example, the Philip Morris case, which limited the ability of individual governments to control mergers[10]). The Court has also circumscribed the efforts of communities and individuals to fight for their social, economic and environmental rights against the Commission, the crucial question of *locus standi* remaining very much unresolved (Scott 1998a). However it has strengthened the rights of legal individuals where individual states are involved in enforcing Community law, thus privileging enforcement over good governance (Weatherill 1997; Scott 1998a).

Implementation and Enforcement: the Example of the Structural Funds

Policies are experienced practically through their implementation and enforcement. A major example is the linked collection of targeted budgets known collectively as the Structural Funds, encompassing the European Regional Development Fund (ERDF); the European Social Fund (ESF); the Guidance Section of the European Agriculture Guidance and Guarantee Funds (EAGGF); and the Financial Instrument for Fisheries Guidance (FIFG). The money provided by these funds at present comes under six headings, or

'Objectives'. However these will soon be abolished and replaced by three revised Objectives, following the Agenda 2000 reform proposals (CEC 1997a, b, c).

The reform of the Structural Funds (CEC 1998b) proposes two territorial measures, Objectives 1 and 2; and one horizontal measure, Objective 3, aimed at improving levels of training and education. In addition, there are at present 13 'Community Initiatives', defined as inter-regional, 'bottom-up' and high local-profile development programmes (CEC 1998d). Again these programmes will be reformed into three: one for cross-border, interregional and transnational cooperation; another for rural development, and a third for human resources and equal opportunities. This section examines the reformed Funds and their implementation in rural areas by looking at three of the defining phrases used, and finally at the relationship between agricultural policy and these rural development initiatives.

Sustainable development The concept of development embodied by the Structual Funds is the classic modernist discourse identified earlier. The document outlining the reforms to the Funds defines the components of sustainable economic development as 'growth, competitiveness and employment' (CEC 1998b). Both the old and new Objective 1 thus identify areas which are 'lagging behind' the rest in some way (CEC 1998b: 14). These areas are identified not through some carefully thought-out quality-of-life indicators, nor indeed by simply asking people how happy they are or how they think their lives could be improved, but by the levels of Gross Domestic Product (GDP) per head at the regional (NUTS II) level. 'Success' in development programmes is thus judged on the rate of growth of this indicator: 'Community policymakers ... remain fully and apparently unrepentantly rooted to a conception of development which is narrowly economic in its conception ... it is capital and commercial activity which is perceived by the Community as implying development' (Scott 1995: 42).

The underlying and unchallenged fact is that even the Structural Funds' 'threshold' of 75 per cent of the average European Union GDP per head is a staggering standard of living as far as the vast majority of the world's population are concerned, and is a higher level of throughput in the economy than recent work on 'ecological footprinting' (Wackernagel and Rees 1996) suggests that the world can afford for Europe to have. No EU measures are targeted at bringing down the GDP of those countries over the Union average. Convergence between the member states' GDPs is only upward, and this is not questioned.

This insistence on economic above all other criteria can be immensely destructive to local initiatives within the Union. Steven Syrett's research on Local Economic Initiatives (LEIs) in Portugal has shown that:

Integration into a free-trade Europe provides a dominant economic agenda which sets the context for endogenous development strategies. Within this context, the need for LEIs to operate profitably within a capitalist market place has resulted in the rapid abandonment of policies which attempted to prioritize social as well as economic criteria. (Syrett 1995: 234)

This also leads to the abandonment of any real environmental criteria. Environmental objectives were incorporated into the Structural Funds in the 1993 reforms, as a result of the EU's Fifth Environmental Action Programme, 'Towards Sustainability' (CEC 1993), a dominant theme of which was the integration of environmental protection measures into policy making in other sectors. The environmental action programmes, however, have no direct legal force; in the words of the Commission it was only 'a policy instrument used by the European Commission to encourage its own departments, the authorities in the member states, and the social and economic partners to give more consideration to environmental issues' (CEC 1995b: 6–7). One would therefore have expected the reforms of the Structural Funds to have included more concrete integration of environmental provisions. However, apart from the requirement that all programmes should comply with the existing Environmental Impact Assessment Directive,[11] the only new introduction was 'a requirement for environmental information' (CEC 1995c: 8). And the responsibility for researching and publishing this information, together with any action that might flow from it, was left entirely in the hands of member states (CEC 1995c). It is notable that subsequent challenges to the implementation of the Structural Funds on environmental grounds brought to the European Court of Justice have been rejected due to the Court's decision not to recognise the *locus standi* of individuals, communities or groups complaining about environmental damage and because of the difficulties of reviewing Community decisions against the Community's own environmental policy (Krämer 1996; Scott 1998a). It has also been noted that Agenda 2000 'appears to give environmental protection a low priority in new member states' (Jordan 1998: 235). The proposed reforms of the Structural Funds do little to remedy this situation: the new Objective 2 includes a new category for *urban* areas with 'a particularly degraded environmental situation' (CEC 1998c), but the detail makes clear that the solutions are likely to be much the same as before, on the grounds that economic and social measures are preventative, and therefore more suited to sustainability (CEC 1998b). Unfortunately, the Commission again fails to recognise that it is its economic and social policies that have contributed to the degradation of the environment (urban or rural) in the first place.

Coupled with this is a belief that far higher levels of formal employment are possible within a competitive global marketplace, and that integrating individuals further into international circuits of capital and labour ('social inclusion'[12]) is the solution to damage that is largely the result of capitalism in the first place. For example, in the EC's First Report on Economic and Social Cohesion (CEC 1996) it is noted that many countries, including two of the poorest 'cohesion countries' (Greece and Spain), have seen an increase in unemployment despite previous EU efforts.

Partnership and subsidiarity A key word in the Structural Funds since the 1988 reforms has been 'partnership'. According to the Commission, this principle should 'enable all concerned to be involved in the preparation, implementing, monitoring and evaluation of community funding' (CEC 1998b: 9). 'All concerned' are currently defined as the Commission, the government of the Member State, and 'the economic and social partners, designated by the Member State at national, regional, local, or other level'.[13] However, the reformed Funds should 'broaden' and 'deepen' the partnership principle, by making sure of the continuous involvement of partners, and by including local authorities and environmental interests (CEC 1998c). Joanne Scott has argued that, in the context of civic republican ideals, 'it is apparent that the concept of partnership holds considerable promise. It creates a space for the reception of voices previously excluded from the policy process ... [and] constructs a public role for private actors' (Scott 1998b: 181). Scott, however, recognises that there are many problems with partnership, and her case-study of the Highlands and Islands of Scotland Objective 1 region shows how 'far removed from experience in the implementation of Community structural funding' (1998b: 187) such ideals are. This is confirmed by broader surveys of partnerships in the UK, for example Bache et al. (1996) and Geddes and Bennington, the latter commenting that most partnership mechanisms 'appear to have limited results, especially in involving and empowering the most excluded groups and communities' (1995: 104). This is largely because 'partnership' has often been treated merely as a tool for development, but 'partnership is not a technique ... shared agendas give partnership a *political* dimension' (Carton et al. nd: 97).[14]

In the literature on development, partnership is seen in the wider context of participation in decision making. Many European studies, both theoretical and empirical, have been carried out in this area (for example Hawker and Mackinnon 1989; Stohr 1990; Bryden and Watson 1991; Baxter 1994; Bryden et al. 1995; Lowe et al. 1998). Most place partnership some way below 'ideal' levels of community involvement. In any case, the EU is not advocating partnership primarily because of concerns for democracy and accountability, but rather it is included as 'a means of ensuring the efficiency of the funds' (CEC 1998c: 9), thus attempting to ignore the social and political dimensions. Irish studies have noted the 'absence of any legal basis for negotiation between government and social partners' (Walsh et al. nd: 19), and the actual definition of who is to be a partner is ultimately left at the national level even within the revised Funds. Debates about partnership and participation thus involve much discussion of the appropriate level of action. In this context, then, the European Community endorses the principle of subsidiarity:

> In areas which do not fall within its exclusive competence, the Community shall take action, in accordance with the principle of subsidiarity, only if and insofar as the objectives of the proposed action cannot be sufficiently achieved by the Member States and can therefore, by reason of the scale or effects of the proposed action, be better achieved by the Community. (Article 5 EC, ex-article 3b)

However, it is clear from this article that, unlike in political ecology, the choice of decisions to be taken at a lower level will be predetermined at a higher level, in this case the nation state. This is because the principle of subsidiarity within the EU came about largely as a result of intergovernmental wrangling over the allocation of Structural Funding. It is thus a sop to national governments and does not represent any move towards strong local democracy, or local control over development.

Thus where ideas of local involvement in development are weak, as in Greece, paternalistic governments can have 'a negative effect on the development of partnerships' (Robolis et al. 1996: 3). In contrast, others have argued that the EU requirement for development partnership should be abandoned and should not be used to justify the retreat of the state from social policy (le Gales and Londe 1996). Moreover, the notion of 'partnership' is further complicated by differing cultural and linguistic interpretations of the word, as a recent report from Spain noted:

> Partnership is a neologism that has come from foreign parts, and has been imposed by European structures and, unless it is sifted through each country's socio-cultural realities, there is a clear danger of it being seen as imported, passing fashion, or a piece of cultural imperialism. (Loza et al. 1996: 6)

A more hopeful sign is the emphasis in the LEADER (I and II) Community Initiatives on 'capacity-building' (Asby and Midmore 1996). This involves building the confidence and capabilities of local people to create their own solutions to problems in their areas. As such it has the potential to generate any kind of political and social response from people, not just the answers expected by the EU. The process initiated by LEADER has been seen as one of 'identity construction', and an extension of personal growth concepts to a community level (Ray 1997). LEADER is perhaps subject to the same kind of criticism on grounds of paternalism as were earlier *animation rurale* efforts (Midgely 1986). This however is not the main criticism of LEADER. The main problem is that, even in its second incarnation, it still has too much in common with other EU development programmes in terms of its time limitations and overall objectives. As Baxter notes:

> The relatively short, tight timescale for the developments within the LEADER programme require hierarchical organizations and control but are not conducive to the evolution of naturally forming grassroots movements with long-term horizons – an essential feature of any sustainable future. (Baxter 1994: 22)

Thus genuinely sustainable movements are only likely to evolve from LEADER either indirectly, through individuals and groups challenging received wisdom as a result of newly developed capacities and strong cultural awareness, or by new and existing initiatives 'piggy-backing' themselves onto LEADER (or indeed other EU Initiatives or Objectives) to receive funds and information for goals contrary to Union policies. This in itself is dangerous for those groups as studies have noted 'a tendency for funding agencies to impose their own ideas on local initiatives ... Many [community initiatives] narrowed their aims in response to the functional specializations of funding agencies to which the initiatives all must go for support' (Bryden and Watson 1991: 28). This 'asymmetrical interdependence' (Bache et al. 1996: 317) exists across the range of EU programmes for development.

The reform of the Community Initiatives has left one Initiative for rural development (CEC 1998c) but it remains to be seen how much of the LEADER programmes' philosophy or structure it will adopt (Ray 1998b). As with any participatory local policy, it would need a wider socio-political framework in which to operate if it was to be truly effective, one which delegated real power to the local level. Such a framework would certainly have to take greater account of the role of the Common Agricultural Policy.

Agriculture and rural development The Structural Funds and Community Initiatives constitute less than a third of the EU's budget, and rural areas receive only a proportion of this. Thus, for most rural areas, the CAP is still the dominant influence, absorbing about 50 per cent of the Union's budget (CEC 1998a). Agriculture policy in the EU is almost unique in its supranational status (Hoggart et al. 1995). Yet many have seen the course of the CAP as a series of blows for small traditional farmers. As far as peasant farmers are concerned, it has been argued that 'the result of decisions taken so far is total failure' (Rosener 1994: 208). The European Commission, although it recognises the need for reform, attributes many of the negative reactions to a public relations problem, referring to the 'bad image of the

CAP in the minds of the public' (CEC 1998c: 3). The CAP also contradicts the efforts of Regional Development policy by favouring big farmers and highly integrated regions able to take full advantage of the subsidies offered while also being competitive on the world market, thus leading to further imbalances between regions. As Scott has commented 'seventy percent of guaranteed funds, or fully forty percent of the entire Community budget, is in effect working against the Community's regional policy objectives' (1995: 105).

But there is no reason why we should be surprised by this. The ethos of the EU is primarily economic, and regional policy is simply a small attempt to compensate for some of the effects of uneven development. It cannot *fully* compensate for these effects because that would make the Union as a whole uncompetitive. The overall effect therefore is not, for example, to stop the massive movement of agricultural workers from poorer peripheral regions to the industrial core,[15] but to increase it.

The EU, however, is not the only hand driving Europe's agricultural policy. The GATT negotiations have had the biggest effect on attempts to reform the CAP (McMichael 1994), despite the denials of some commentators (for example, Hoggart et al. 1995). For in spite of the Blair House accord that temporarily 'green boxes' aspects of the reformed CAP outside GATT-negotiated agreements (Winter 1996), the new WTO rules make it plain that the CAP cannot continue forever. The only difference that this will have on rural areas is to increase the trends towards core and peripheral development that are already evident, and make rural communities more dependent on transnational corporations:

> It is hard to imagine that agricultural development will take an extremely endogenous character. As a matter of fact, the introduction of greater market responsibility into agriculture policies will force agriculture to integrate with agribusiness both in terms of processing and intermediate products supply. (van Dijk 1995: 85)

The Agenda 2000 process has proposed exactly this route: to make the CAP more market-oriented, while at the same time trying to reintegrate rural development considerations as a 'second pillar' in the CAP (CEC 1998c). Thus money for rural development will now come more from the Guarantee fund within EAGGF, rather than the Guidance section. This can only further lessen already weak democratic control over rural development, as the European Parliament is not required to approve funding in this area (Lowe and Ward 1998).

Conclusion

The Structural Funds are a key component of 'the European model of society' (CEC 1996: 115). However, as we have seen, this model is contradictory and dangerous. It advocates facing the challenges of globalisation by speeding up that process, tackling environmental destruction by promoting the very forces that destroy the environment, and protecting the jobs and communities of its people by integrating them into a world market system dominated by transnational corporations that have no interest in their welfare. This is not just dangerous for the Union, but globally. As Susan Baker comments, the EU's position as a 'world leader' in environmental issues may lead to other nations copying the Union's stance in adopting a weak form of sustainable development (Baker 1997).

The most important questions for the environment and for local communities and people are: can the EU change direction? Can it take the necessary steps to resist globalisation? If so, will it? Some place their faith in institutional reform, more specifically the creation of strong cross-sectoral agencies to deal with the perceived implementation gap (Weatherill 1997). However, how such agencies would be able to function within the overall context of fundamental EU ambitions is unclear. Greens propose a far more radical reorientation of the Union. It could, for example: facilitate the relocalisation of agriculture and promote low-input, organic and permacultural methods of farming; provide funds and support for locally-controlled renewable energy generation (something it did to a very limited extent through the old VALOREN Community Initiative), and legislate to allow local currencies and banks. For these policies to work, the EU would have to control and break up transnational corporations, requiring that companies site where they wished to sell and kept profits within the community, and put new controls on the movement of goods and capital (Hines 1998). The Union would essentially take responsibility for setting the 'framing conditions' (Daly 1996) for economic activities and recognise the importance of subordinating the market to ecological, social and cultural needs.

But these initiatives go against the current ethos of the Union. Van Dijk's conclusion that 'in Europe, there is no policy at hand to guide processes of endogenous development' (van Dijk 1995: 89) will still be true after the institution of the Agenda 2000 reforms. The EU is continuing in its efforts to create a single currency whilst limiting the ability of smaller areas to support their own financial institutions,[16] create Trans-European Networks in energy and transport, and move towards a more market-centred CAP. The EU has also fully signed up to the WTO and is thus fearful of economic reprisals from trading partners and competitors. But, most importantly, the Union's policies are not amenable to change through democratic means: the

European Parliament has no effective power (Viola 1997), and the political agenda is set by industrial interest groups. In any case all the major European political parties, except the Greens, Communists and some extreme right parties, are more firmly committed than ever to the corporate economic worldview. Qualified Majority Voting in the Council of Ministers could provide the opportunity for member states to change the direction of the Union, but the same neo-liberal characteristics apply to political parties within nations as to the European Parliament. Their governments seem likely to continue their commitment to the free market system.

This severely hampers the likelihood of national governments themselves being any better potential regulators of globalisation. In the UK, Labour has talked of 'greening' the WTO, but unless it is prepared to seriously challenge transnational corporations this reformism will have little impact. The Government's attitude to the Multilateral Agreement on Investment (MAI) (see CEO 1998) has highlighted the shortcomings of its approach to globalisation, with a secretive approach dismissive of the public's right to know about the issues, let alone to debate them. Local governments in the UK are largely powerless, though in some parts of Europe strong regional governments motivated by cultural and ecological concerns could have an influence (Marshal 1998).

It seems that it is down to local communities. The only sustainable alternative is not to take part in this process, to fight against it. In the short term, this is the more difficult alternative. It goes against everything that our current dominant political, economic, social and cultural models promote. Is it therefore unrealistic? In reply I can only ask (paraphrasing Mander 1996a): Why is a change of direction considered unrealistic when the present path is impossible? Ordinary people must continue in their efforts to create viable alternatives: start and maintain LETS schemes, Credit Unions, etc.; work with farmers to create CSA and open local shops selling local produce; create local energy cooperatives; protest every aspect of globalisation, campaign for land redistribution and so on. As Douthwaite suggests, 'only when a community has demonstrated that it can build an independent parallel economy that works well, will politicians support the new approach and other communities have the faith to begin to build one themselves' (1996: 361). But we should not be afraid to use the funds and networks provided by the Structural Funds and Community Initiatives as well as other schemes like Local Agenda 21 to promote sustainability. Even conventional projects can be 'successful' not because they succeed in further integrating people and communities into patterns of capitalist production and consumption, but because they 'can represent significant points of concrete and symbolic resistance for established communities and create alternative political possibilities' (Syrett 1995: 322–323).

These efforts must be networked across Europe and across the world; sympathetic individuals within governments at all levels must be nurtured. The end result would be a kind of slow secession from the conventional economy combined with a constructive engagement at the personal level with those remaining inside. Academics are part of this process and can aid it by revealing the failings of current approaches, by uncovering and disseminating new information, insights and approaches. Alternatively, in failing to address the critical relationship of globalisation and sustainability and concentrating on reformist measures, we can hide the need for change.

Notes

1. This chapter is dedicated to the memory of Dick Richardson, scholar of political ecology and Green Party activist. It draws substantially on a previous working paper (Wood 1997). I would like to thank those who commented on earlier drafts.
2. Preamble, Treaty of Rome 1957.
3. The list of provisos that they give undermines their initial thesis: 'provided it develops a broader agenda and some concern for the consequences of its policies for employment and output in advanced and developing countries alike' (Hirst and Thompson 1995: 429). These concerns are precisely those for which the WTO is seeking to avoid taking responsibility; the WTO's tribunal system, for example, exists to undermine regulatory regimes operating in favour of the environment or social justice (Retallack 1997).
4. The title of an editorial in the *Ecologist* (Hildyard and Sexton 1996) – a particularly apt description of what it means to be opposed to globalisation.
5. I would qualify this by stating that political ecology does not envisage one monolithic new order, but a multitude of varying interpretations of 'the sustainable society' (GPEW 1997).
6. There is unfortunately little space here to delve into Green conceptions of rights. Some have argued that there is a very strong conception of 'the good life' in some currents of Green thought, particularly Deep Ecology, which would limit individual rights in a sustainable society. However, this argument is specious, ignoring the fact that all rights are framed and limited by societies and by the natural environment. In contrast to present frameworks, however, the Green conception asserts the Hegelian notion that the recognition of natural limits to human activity can actually empower individuals, as it prevents others from being able to destroy or enclose for personal gain the common environment which allows people (and other species) to flourish. Individual rights therefore have the concomitant responsibility not to compromise the rights of others (Eckersley 1992). See also the discussion of 'relational self' and community later in this chapter.
7. As I have already indicated, I believe that the EU can be considered as a state in a new and evolving form. However I also believe the argument about what one calls the EU to be less important than an analysis of what it does.
8. All references to the Treaty Establishing the Community refer to the Treaty of Rome 1957, as amended by subsequent Treaties up to and including the Treaty of Amsterdam (1997). At the time of writing the Treaty of Amsterdam had yet to enter into force, thus

any change in Article or Title numbering is noted, the previous version being referred to as 'ex-article ... ' and 'ex-title ... '.
9 Intergovernmentalists might argue that this had more to do with appeasing the UK government. Ripa di Meana had objected in particular to the manner in which the M3 motorway extension through Twyford Down in Hampshire in the south of England had been planned and built (see Bryant 1996).
10 Linked Cases 142/84 and 156/84 [1987] ECR 4487.
11 Council Directive 85/337/EEC, OJ L175/40, 5.7.85.
12 See Mernagh and Commins (1997) for the official line on the use of 'inclusion'/ 'exclusion' and why 'social exclusion' has come to replace 'poverty' in EU policy discourse.
13 European Council Regulation 2081/93/EEC, OJ L193/5, 31.7.93, Article 4.1.
14 Author's translation. The original reads: 'le partenariat n'est pas une technique ... l'agenda commun donne au partenariat une dimension *politique*.'
15 Overall migration figures for the European Union show that the biggest movements are still from the more rural European nations (Spain, Portugal, Greece, Ireland) to the industrial 'core' (the Netherlands, Belgium, Germany, UK) (Hoggart et al. 1995). While these figures do not prove that rural people are moving to urban areas, they do suggest it. They also suggest that inequality within the EU, and in particular between the poorest regions of poorer nations and the richest areas of the richer nations, is still wrong, whatever the GDP figures may show.
16 The EU has made it virtually impossible for communities to set up new Building Societies, by requiring initial capitalisation of ECU 1 million, arbitrarily rounded up to £1 million by the UK government, way beyond the means of almost all communities (Douthwaite 1996). See Directive 93/30/EEC, OJ L110, 28.4.92, p. 52 transposed into UK law in the Building Societies (Designated Capital Resources) Order 1992, SI 1992/1611 and the Building Societies (Supplemental Capital) (Amendment) Order 1992, SI 1992/1612.

References

Achterberg, W. (1996) 'Sustainability, Community and Democracy', in Doherty and de Geus (eds) (1996: 170–187).

Adams, W.M. (1995) 'Green Development Theory? Environmentalism and Sustainable Development', in Crush (ed.) (1995: 87–99).

Amin, A. and Thrift, N. (eds) (1994a) *Globalization, Institutions and Regional Development in Europe* (Oxford: Oxford University Press).

Amin, A. and Thrift, N. (1994a) 'Living in the Global', in Amin and Thrift (eds) (1994: 1–22).

Andersen, S.S. and Burns, T. (1996) 'The European Union and the Erosion of Parliamentary Democracy: a Study of Post-Parliamentary Governance', in Andersen, S.S. and Eliassen, K.A. (eds) *The European Union: How Democratic is it?* (London: Sage, 227–251).

Asby, J. and Midmore, P. (1996) 'Human Capacity Building in Rural Areas: The Importance of Community Development', in Midmore, P. and Hughes, G. (eds) *Rural Wales: An Economic and Social Perspective* (Aberystwyth: Welsh Institute of Rural Studies).

Bache, I., George, S. and Rhodes, R.A.W. (1996) 'The European Union, Cohesion Policy and Subnational Authorities in the United Kingdom', in Hooghe, L. (ed.) *Cohesion Policy and European Integration: Building Multi-Level Governance* (Buckingham: Open University Press, 294–318).

Baker, S. (1997) 'The evolution of European Union environmental policy: from growth to sustainable development', in Baker et al. (eds) (1997: 91–106).

Baker, S., Kousis, M., Richardson, D., and Young, S. (eds) (1997) *The Politics of Sustainable Development: Theory, Policy and Practice within the European Union* (London: Routledge).

Baker, S., Kousis, M., Richardson, D., and Young, S. (1997a) 'Introduction: the theory and practice of sustainable development in EU perspective', in Baker et al. (eds) (1997: 91–106).

Barnes, H., North, P., and Walker, P. (1996) *LETS on Low Income* (London: New Economics Foundation).

Barry, J. (1996) 'Sustainability, Political Judgement and Citizenship: Connecting Green Politics and Democracy', in Doherty and de Geus (eds) (1996: 113–131).

Baxter, S.H. (1994) *Experiences in Participation: A Review of Current Practice in Rural Development Programmes* (Inverness: Scottish Natural Heritage North-West Region).

Birkhölzer, K. and Lorenz, G. (1996) *The Role of Partnerships in Promoting Social Cohesion: Local Partnerships to Combat Social Exclusion and Promote Social Cohesion in the Federal Republic of Germany*, commissioned by the European Foundation for the Improvement of Living and Working Conditions (Berlin: Technologie-Netzwerk Berlin eV).

Boothe, D.E. (1998) *The Environmental Consequences of Growth: Steady-State Economics as an Alternative to Ecological Decline* (London: Routledge).

Bryant, B. (1996) *Twyford Down: Roads, Campaigning and Environmental Law* (London: E & FN Spon).

Bryden, J. and Watson, D. (1991) *Local Initiatives and Sustainable Development in Rural Scotland* (Aberdeen: Arkleton Trust & Scottish Development Department).

Bryden, J., Watson, D., Storey, C. and Alpha, J. van (1995) *Community Involvement and Rural Policy: Research Report to the Scottish Office* (Aberdeen: Arkleton Trust).

Caporaso, J.A. (1996) 'The European Union and Forms of State: Westphalian, Regulatory or Post-Modern?', *Journal of Common Market Studies*, 34 (1): 29–52.

Carton, B., Delogne, R., Nicase, I. and Stengele, A. (nd) *Le role des partenariats locaux dans la lutte contre l'exclusion sociale*, commissioned by the European Foundation for the Improvement of Living and Working Conditions (Hoger Instituut voor Arbeid, Katholieke Universiteit Leuven).

CEC (Commission of the European Communities) (1993) *Towards Sustainability: A European Community Programme of Policy and Action in Relation to the Environment and Sustainable Development*. (5th Environmental Action Programme) (Brussels: CEC DG XI).

CEC (Commission of the European Communities) (1995a) *The Role of the Union in the Field of Tourism (Commission Green Paper)* (Brussels: CEC DG XXIII).

CEC (Commission of the European Communities) (1995b) *The Environment and the Regions: Towards Sustainability* (Luxembourg: Office for Official Publications of the European Communities).
CEC (Commission of the European Communities) (1995c) *The Implementation of the Reform of the Structural Funds in 1993. Fifth Annual Report* (Luxembourg: Office for Official Publications of the European Communities).
CEC (Commission of the European Communities) (1996) *First Report on Economic and Social Cohesion* (Luxembourg: Office for Official Publications of the European Communities).
CEC (Commission of the European Communities) (1997a) *Agenda 2000 – Volume I. For a Stronger and Wider Union*, DOC/97/6 (Strasbourg: CEC).
CEC (Commission of the European Communities) (1997b) *Agenda 2000 – Volume 2. Reinforcing the Pre-Accession Strategy*, DOC 97/7 (Brussels: CEC).
CEC (Commission of the European Communities) (1997c) *Agenda 2000 – Volume 3. Summary and Conclusions of the opinion of the Commission concerning the Applications for Membership to the European Union presented by the candidate countries*, DOC 97/8 (Strasbourg/Brussels: CEC).
CEC (Commission of the European Communities) (1998a) *Proposal for Council Regulations (EC) laying down general provisions on the Structural Funds*, COM (1998) 131 Final (Brussels: CEC).
CEC (Commission of the European Communities) (1998b) *Proposal for Council Regulations (EC) concerning the reforms of the Common Agricultural Policy*, COM (1998) 158 Final (Brussels: CEC).
CEC (Commission of the European Communities) (1998c) *Proposed Regulations Governing the Reform of the Structural Funds 2000–2006: Comparative Analysis*, Preliminary Version (Luxembourg: Office for Official Publications of the European Communities).
CEC (Commission of the European Communities) (1998d) *Guide to the Community Initiatives 1994–99, Volume 2* (Luxembourg: Office for Official Publications of the European Communities).
CEO (Corporate Europe Observatory) (1997) *Europe Inc. – Dangerous Liaisons Between EU Institutions and Industry* (Amsterdam: CEO).
CEO (Corporate Europe Observatory) (1998) MAIGALOMANIA! Citizens and the Environment Sacrificed to Corporate Investment Agenda. http://www.xs4all.nl/~ceo/mai/
Chandler, J.A. (1993) 'Local Authorities and Economic Development in Britain', in Goetz and Clarke (eds) (1993).
Chatterjee, P. and Finger, M. (1994) *The Earth Brokers: Power, Politics and World Development* (London: Routledge).
Clarke, S.E. (1993) 'The New Localism: Local Politics in a Global Era', in Goetz and Clarke (eds) (1993).
Cowles, M.G. (1995) 'Setting the Agenda for a New Europe: the ERT and EC 1992', *Journal of Common Market Studies*, 33 (4): 501–526.
Crush, J. (ed.) *Power of Development* (London: Routledge).
Daly, H.E. (1996) *Beyond Growth: The Economics of Sustainable Development* (Boston, MA: Beacon Press).

Daly, H.E. and Cobb, J.B. (1989) *For the Common Good: Redirecting the Economy towards Community, the Environment and a Sustainable Future* (London: Green Print).

Dicken, P., Forsgren, M. and Malmberg, M. (1994) 'The Local Embeddedness of Transnational Corporations', in Amin and Thrift (eds) (1994: 23–45).

van Dijk, G. (1995) 'Policy Failure and Endogenous Development in European Agriculture', in van Dijk, G. and van der Ploeg, J.D. (eds) *Beyond Modernisation: The Impact of Endogenous Rural Development* (Assen – Netherlands: Van Gorcum: 70–86).

van Dijk, G. and van der Ploeg, J.D. (1995) 'Is There Anything Beyond Modernisation?', in van Dijk, G. and van der Ploeg, J.D. (eds) *Beyond Modernisation: The Impact of Endogenous Rural Development* (Assen – Netherlands: Van Gorcum: vii–xiii).

Dobson, A. (1995) *Green Political Thought* (2nd edn) (London: Routledge).

Doherty, B. and de Geus, M. (eds) (1996) *Democracy & Green Political Thought: Sustainability, Rights & Citizenship* (London: Routledge).

Douthwaite, R. (1992) *The Growth Illusion: How Economic Growth has Enriched the Few, Impoverished the Many and Endangered the Planet* (Dartington: Green Books).

Douthwaite, R. (1996) *Short Circuit: Strengthening Local Economies for Security in an Unstable World* (Dartington: Green Books).

Duff, A. (1993) 'Towards a Definition of Subsidiarity', in Duff, A. (ed.) *Subsidiarity within the European Community: A Federal Trust Report* (London: Federal Trust for Education and Research: 7–32).

Durning, A.T. (1992) *How Much is Enough? The Consumer Society and the Future of the Earth* (London: Earthscan).

Eckersley, R. (1992) *Environmentalism and Political Theory* (Cambridge: Cambridge University Press).

Ecologist (1993) *Whose Common Future? Reclaiming the Commons* (London: Earthscan).

Ekins, P. (1993) *Trading Off the Future: Making World Trade Environmentally Sustainable* (London: New Economics Foundation).

Escobar, A. (1995) 'Imagining a Post-Development Era', in Crush (ed.) (1995: 221–227).

Esteva, G. (1992) 'Development', in Sachs, W. (ed.) *The Development Dictionary: A Guide to Knowledge as Power* (London: Zed Books: 6–25).

Friedmann, J. (1992) *Empowerment* (Cambridge, MA: Blackwell).

le Gales, P. and Londe, P. (1996) *The Role of Partnerships in Combating Social Exclusion: Final Report – France*, Commissioned by the European Foundation for the Improvement of Living and Working Conditions (Rennes: Centre de Recherches Administratives et Politiques, IEP).

Geddes, M. and Bennington, J. (1995) *The Role of Partnerships in Promoting Social Cohesion: Research Report for the United Kingdom*, Commissioned by the European Foundation for the Improvement of Living and Working Conditions (Local Government Centre, Warwick Business School, University of Warwick).

Gerelli, E. (1995) 'Facing the Uncertainties of Global Environmental Change: Strategies for Sustainability', in Jäger et al. (eds) (1995) *Global Environmental Change and Sustainable Development in Europe* (Luxembourg: CEC, DGXI).

Gipe, P. (1995) *Wind Energy Comes of Age* (New York: John Wiley & Sons).

Glasmeier, A. (1994) 'Flexible Districts: Flexible Regions? The Institutional and Cultural Limits to Districts in an Era of Globalization and Technological Paradigm Shifts', in Amin and Thrift (eds) (1994a).

Goetz, E.G. and Clarke, S.E. (eds) (1993) *The New Localism: comparative urban politics in a global era* (Newbury Park CA: Sage).

GPEW (Green Party of England and Wales) (1997) *Manifesto for a Sustainable Society*, updated after Spring Conference 1997 (London: GPEW).

Haavelmo, T. and Hansen, S. (1992) 'On the Strategy of Trying to Reduce Economic Inequality by Expanding the Scale of Economic Activity', in Goodland, R. et al. (eds), *Population, Technology and Lifestyle: The Transition to Sustainability* (Washington: Island Press).

Hawker, C. and Mackinnon, N. (1989) *Factors in the Design of Community-Based Rural Development in Europe* (Aberdeen: Arkleton Trust and Scottish Development Association).

Hildyard, N., Hines, C. and Lang, T. (1996) 'Who Competes? Changing Landscapes of Corporate Control', *Ecologist*, 26 (4): 125–144.

Hildyard, N. and Sexton, S. (1996) 'Denying the Global a Home', *Ecologist*, 26 (4): 123–124.

Hines, C. (edited by Merry, P. and Lucas, C.) (1998) *Act Local, Act Global, Greening the European Union – A Challenge to Globalisation*, Green Briefings, European Series 2 (London: Green Party of England and Wales).

Hinterberger, F., Luks, F. and Welfeis, M.J. (1995) 'Commentary on "Facing the Uncertainties of Global Environmental Change: Strategies for Sustainability"', in Jäger et al. (eds) (1995).

Hirst, P. and Thompson, G. (1992) 'The Problem of "Globalisation": International Economic Relations, National Economic Management and the Form of Trading Blocs', *Economy and Society*, 21 (4): 357–396.

Hirst, P. and Thompson, G. (1995) 'Globalization and the Future of the Nation-State', *Economy and Society*, 24 (3): 408–442.

Hoggart, K., Buller, H., and Black, R. (1995) *Rural Europe: Identity and Change* (London: Arnold).

Jackson, T. and Marks, N. (1994) *Measuring Sustainable Economic Welfare: A Pilot Index 1950–1990* (Stockholm: Stockholm Environmental Institute).

Jäger, J., Liberatore, A. and Grunflach, K. (eds) (1995) *Global Environmental Change and Sustainable Development in Europe* (Luxembourg: CEC, DGXI).

Jordan, A. (1998) 'Step Change or Stasis? EC Environmental Policy after the Amsterdam Treaty', *Environmental Politics*, 7 (1): 227–236.

Kenny, M. (1996) 'Paradoxes of Community', in Doherty and de Geus (eds) (1996: 19–35).

Korten, D.C. (1995) *When Corporations Rule the World* (West Hartford, CT: Kumarian Press).

Krämer, L. (1996), 'Public Interest Litigation in Environmental Matters Before European Courts', *Journal of Environmental Law*, 8 (1): 1–18.

Lang, P. (1994) *LETS Work: Rebuilding the Local Economy* (Bristol: Grover).

Lowe, P., Ray, C., Ward, N., Wood, D. and Woodward, R. (1998) *Participation in Rural Development: A Review of European Experience*, Commissioned by the European Foundation for the Improvement of Living and Working Conditions (Centre for Rural Economy Research Report, University of Newcastle upon Tyne).

Lowe, P. and Ward, N. (1998) *A Second Pillar for the CAP? The European Rural Development Regulation and its Implications for the UK*, Centre for Rural Economy Working Paper 36 (University of Newcastle upon Tyne).

Loza, J., Aguilar, M. and Just, A.M. (1996) *The Role of Partnerships in Promoting Social Cohesion: National Report for Spain (draft)*, Commissioned by the European Foundation for the Improvement of Living and Working Conditions (Gabinet d'Estudis Socials).

Mander, J. and Goldsmith, E. (eds) (1996) *The Case Against the Global Economy – and for a turn towards the Local* (San Francisco, CA: Sierra Club Books).

Mander, J. (1996a) 'Facing the Rising Tide', in Mander and Goldsmith (eds) (1996: 3–19).

Mander, J. (1996b) 'The Rules of Corporate Behaviour', in Mander and Goldsmith (eds) (1996: 309–322).

Marks, G., Hooghe, L. and Blank, K. (1996) 'European Integration from the 1980s: state-centric vs. multi-level governance', *Journal of Common Market Studies*, 34(3): 341–378.

Marshal, J. (1998) 'The Conditions for Environmentally Intelligent Regional Governance: Reflections from Lower Saxony', *Journal of Environmental Planning and Management*, 41(4): 421–444.

Mathews, F. (1995) 'Community and the Ecological Self', *Environmental Politics*, 4(4): 66–100.

Mathewson, A. and M'Gonigle, M. (1997) 'Eco-Investing: Financial Sustainable Economic Development', *Local Environment*, 2(2): 155–170.

McMichael, P. (1994) 'GATT, Global Regulation and the Construction of a New Hegemonic Order', in Lowe, P. et al. (eds) (1994) *Regulating Agriculture* (London: David Fulton: 163–190).

McMichael, P. (1998) 'Globalisation as Politicised Market Rule', paper presented to the *Review of International Political Economy* conference on 'Globalization, State and Violence', University of Sussex, 15–17 April 1998.

Meeker-Lowry, S. (1996) 'Community Money: The Potential of Local Currency', in Mander and Goldsmith (eds) (1996: 446–459).

Mernagh, M. and Commins, P. (1997) *In From the Margins – Social Inclusion and Rural Development in the Europe of the New Millennium: Some Lessons from Poverty 3* (Dublin: SICCDA).

Midgely, J. (1986) 'Community Participation: History, Concepts and Controversies', in Midgely, J. et al. (eds) *Community Participation, Social Development and the State* (London: Methuen).

Moravcsik, A. (1993) 'Preferences and Power in the European Community: A

Liberal Intergovernmental Approach', *Journal of Common Market Studies*, 31(4): 473–524.

Nader, R. and Wallach, L. (1996) 'GATT, NAFTA, and the Subversion of Democracy', in Mander and Goldsmith (eds) (1996: 92–107).

Naess, A. (1989) *Ecology, Community and Lifestyle: Outline of an Ecosophy*, trans. and ed. Rothenberg, D. (Cambridge: Cambridge University Press).

Newman, M. (1996) *Democracy, Sovereignty and the European Union* (London: C. Hurst and Co.).

Norgaard, R.B. (1994) *Development Betrayed: The End of Progress and a Coevolutionary Revisioning of the Future* (London: Routledge).

OECD (Organisation for Economic Co-operation and Development) (1993) *What Future for Our Countryside? A Rural Development Policy* (Paris: OECD).

O'Riordan, T. and Jäger, J. (1995) 'Global Environmental Change and Sustainable Development', in Jäger et al. (eds) (1995: 17–34).

Pearce, J. (1994) *At the Heart of the Community Economy* (London: Calouste Gulbenkian Foundation).

Peters, G. (1996) 'Agenda-Setting in the European Union', in Richard, J.J. (ed.) *European Union: Power and Policy-Making* (London: Routledge: 61–74).

Ray, C. (1997) *The Dialectic of Local Development: The Case of the EU LEADER I Rural Development Programme*, Centre for Rural Economy Working Paper 23 (University of Newcastle upon Tyne).

Ray, C. (1998a) 'Culture, Intellectual Property and Territorial Rural Development', *Socologia Ruralis*, 38(1): 3–20.

Ray, C. (1998b) *New Places and Space for Rural Development in the European Union: An Analysis of the UK LEADER II Programme*, Centre for Rural Economy Working Paper 34 (University of Newcastle upon Tyne).

Redclift, M. (1996) *Wasted: Counting the Costs of Global Consumption* (London: Earthscan).

Retallack, S. (1997) 'The WTO's Record So Far – Corporations: 3; Humanity and the Environment: 0', *Ecologist*, 27(4): 136–137.

Richardson, D. (1997) 'The politics of sustainable development', in Baker et al. (eds) (1997: 43–60).

Robolis, S., Papdogamvros, V., Dimoulas, K. and Sidira, V. (1996) *The Role of Partnerships in Promoting Social Cohesion: Research Report for Greece*, WP 96/30/EN (Dublin: European Foundation for the Improvement of Living and Working Conditions).

Rosener, W. (1994) *The Peasantry of Europe*, trans. Barker, T.M. (Oxford: Blackwell).

Sachs, W. (1993) *Global Ecology: a New Arena of Global Conflict* (London: Zed Books).

Sale, K. (1985) *Dwellers in the Land: the Bioregional Vision* (San Francisco, CA: Sierra Club Books).

Scott, J. (1995) *Development Dilemmas in the European Community: Rethinking Regional Policy* (Buckingham: Open University Press).

Scott, J. (1998a) *EC Environmental Law* (New York: Longman).

Scott, J. (1998b) 'Law, Legitimacy and EC Governance: Prospects for "Partnerships"', *Journal of Common Market Studies*, 36(2): 175–194.
Shiva, V. (1989) *Staying Alive: Women, Ecology & Development* (London: Zed Books).
Shiva, V. (1992) 'Recovering the Real Meaning of Sustainability', in Cooper D.E. and Palmer J.A. (eds) *The Environment in Question* (London: Routledge: 187–193).
Stevenson, F. and Ball, J. (1998) 'Sustainability and Materiality: the Bioregional and Cultural Challenge to Evaluation', *Local Environment*, 3(2): 191–209.
Stohr, W.B. (ed.) (1990) *Global Challenge and Local Response: Initiatives for Economic Regeneration in Contemporary Europe* (London: Mansell).
Syrett, S. (1995) *Local Development: Locality and Economic Initiatives in Portugal* (Aldershot: Avebury).
Viola, D.M. (1997) 'Forging European Union: What Role for the European Parliament', in Landau, A. and Whitman, R. (eds) *Rethinking the European Union: Institutions, Interests and Identities* (Basingstoke: Macmillan: 111–128).
Wackernagel, M. and Rees, W. (1996) *Our Ecological Footprint: Reducing Human Impact on the Earth* (Vancouver, BC: New Society Publishers).
Walsh, J., Craig, S. and McCafferty, D. (nd) *The Role of Partnerships in Promoting Social Cohesion: National Report for Ireland (draft)*, Commissioned by the European Foundation for the Improvement of Living and Working Conditions (Dublin: Combat Poverty Agency).
Ward, N. and McNicholas, K. (1997) *Reconfiguring Rural Development in the UK: Objective 5b and the New Rural Governance*, Centre for Rural Economy Working Paper 24 (University of Newcastle upon Tyne).
WCED (World Commission on Environment and Development) (1987) *Our Common Future* (Oxford: Oxford University Press).
Weatherill, S. (1997) 'Constitutional Issues in the Implementation of EC Law: Addressing the Imbalance in favour of Market Deregulation', paper for the fifth international conference of the European Community Studies Association, Seattle, May 29th–June 1st, 1997.
Weizsäcker, E.U. von (1995), 'Commentary on "Facing the Uncertainties of Global Environmental Change: Strategies for Sustainability"', in Jäger et al. (eds) (1995).
Williams, C. (1996) 'Local Purchasing Schemes and Rural Development: an Evaluation of Local Exchange and Trading Schemes', *Journal of Rural Studies*, 12(3): 231–244.
Wincott, D. (1996) 'The Court of Justice and the European Policy Process', in Richards, J.J. (ed.) *European Union: Power and Policy-Making* (London: Routledge: 170–186).
Winter, M. (1996) *Rural Politics* (London: Routledge).
Wood, D. (1997) *Globalisation, Community Participation and Sustainable Rural Development: a Green Critique of European Union Rural Development Policy*, Centre for Rural Economy Working Paper 29 (University of Newcastle upon Tyne).
Wright, S. (1990) 'Development Theory and Community Development Practice',

in Buller, H. and Wright, S. (eds) (1990) *Rural Development; Problems And Practices* (Aldershot: Avebury: 41–64).

Yearley, S. (1996) *Sociology, Environmentalism, Globalisation* (London: Sage).

PART II
NATURE AND IDENTITY

3 Capturing Values for Nature: Ecological, Economic and Cultural Perspectives

Carolyn Harrison, Jacquelin Burgess and Judy Clark

Introduction

Geographers and environmentalists concerned to see society moving in the direction of sustainable development face an enduring challenge: how to value nature and protect it. In this chapter we highlight the concepts of 'natural/environmental capital' because this approach has gained considerable support amongst environmental agencies, and central and local government in the last five years (Gillespie and Shepherd 1995, 1996; Environmental Resources Management 1995; CAG/LUC 1997). In essence, the concept draws on an economic metaphor to depict natural stock and flows as capital and interest. When extended to include natural areas as sinks as well as source areas, the concept accommodates the ability of wetlands and river systems, for example, to assimilate pollution and waste.

Expressed in this way, the concept of natural capital has appeal because it meshes well with utilitarian objectives of sustainable development if not utopian ones (see Chapter 1). Through its depiction of nature as environmental assets which provide a continuous stream of services and benefits to society, as long as the stock of natural capital is not eroded, the concept focuses attention on those natural processes often taken for granted or ignored in more conventional ways of environmental appraisal and auditing. Hence, natural capital appears to place nature on an equal footing with economic interests in debates about development. In addition, the concept proves attractive because it gains authority and legitimacy through association with the discipline of economics. But, as we aim to show, natural capital is just one among several approaches to valuing nature (Foster 1997a) and there is no reason to believe that it is necessarily correct or an approach which finds support amongst the wider public.

We begin by discussing briefly the distinctions between 'meanings' and 'values' for nature, arguing that the former reside in the domain of representation whereas the latter are irrevocably social and entail moral arguments which generate conflict between different interests. Further, values find expression in actions of different kinds. Recent changes in the institutional context of nature conservation in Britain have played an influential role in how nature is valued in planning policies and so we briefly review the changing context of nature conservation in the UK which has facilitated the coining of a new metaphor for nature – that of 'natural capital.' Not feeling at all comfortable with 'natural capital', and noting its singular lack of resonance in the discourses of lay publics, set us thinking about the different and incommensurable ways there are of valuing nature. Thus, we then explore a typology of four commonly used approaches which help to clarify different assumptions and world views. The typology reveals the importance of dialogue between disciplines which have fundamentally different epistemologies but equally valid claims to the study of values for nature. Finally, we address the argument that there is no alternative to expert-driven systems of valuation for environmental policy making. Drawing on recent research for the Environment Agency, we will demonstrate that it is possible to combine the strengths of an analytical process which is rigorous and defensible, with a more inclusive and deliberative approach to agreeing values for nature and courses of action.

Nature Conservation Values

For analytical purposes, it is useful to distinguish between meanings and values whilst acknowledging that both are embodied in different kinds of knowledges, and inseparable from, actions and practices. *Meanings* are fundamentally bound up in representations in discourses of many different kinds. Meanings are profoundly personal, intimately connected with our own life experiences. Think of the wrenching pain felt when returning to a much-loved landscape of childhood to find that the sense of wildness and wide skies, the smell of clean air and boggy ground, the screeching of swifts have vanished. Interwoven with these personal experiences, meanings for nature are also profoundly social in character: finding expression in local dialects and cultural practices, in metaphor, in literature, the visual arts, mass media and the texts of popular culture (Williams 1973). Meanings for nature are both contextual and contingent, varying across space and changing through time. How are meanings conceptually different from values? Whilst we might agree to differ about personal meanings of nature – one person may be deeply moved by the haunting beauty of salt marshes whilst another might find then drab, boring and uninspiring – environmental values engender conflicts over choices and demand the rationalisation of courses of action. *Values* are the reasons given for actions. They are invoked to account for, and to make judgements about, the actions of individuals and institutions whilst, at the same time, finding embodiment in social organisation. O'Brien and Guerrier put this well:

> Values are important in the debate about the environment not because some value or other in itself can or should be described as 'right' or 'wrong', but because value systems refer to the underlying principles about the 'proper conduct' of life in general and about ways of interpreting specific events in terms of more extensive commitments to particular social arrangements and political orders. They indicate the cultural plurality – and often ambiguity – within which notions of 'rightness' and 'wrongness' are formulated, maintained, contested and changed. (O'Brien and Guerrier 1995: xiv)

Thus, conservation values are fundamentally concerned with the rationalisations of right or proper conduct in relation to the living world. But the situation is more complex, for nature conservation is also an activity enmeshed in biological systems which have their own trajectories of change, and new understandings of the way the natural world functions cause us to reassess tenets we thought were universal. Witness, for example, the debates within ecology about the relationship between diversity, stability and disturbance (Pickett and White 1985). Moreover, conservation values are embedded in social systems which generate their own value shifts over time – changing attitudes to wilderness and wildness for example, and to weeds and alien species (Adams 1997). For all these reasons elucidating conservation values is a complex process.

But more than this, as philosophers remind us (Holland and Rawles 1993), values are not things we always argue from, but what we reason towards. Often it is only through open and sustained debate that 'values', whose relative stability distinguishes them from more subjective and labile personal preferences, are revealed. Having recourse, therefore, to what Foster (1997a) calls a 'purity of process', through which attention is focused on the way value judgements about nature are made, seems essential if 'objectivity' and a 'disinterestedness' are to be secured. The requirement for such deliberation is all the more pressing in the case of sustainable development because sustainable development seeks to ensure that all who have a stake in the future of society are involved in decisions about its trajectory. Recent efforts devoted to developing more deliberative and inclusive approaches to valuing nature as part of the Local Agenda 21 (LA21) process, for example, reflect these twin concerns (LGMB 1993; Wilcox 1994). When valuing nature is approached through an inclusive and deliberative process, we can be more certain that methods of environmental appraisal which appeal to universal values do just that. Equally, because stakeholders are involved in this process, policies based on these agreed values will gain wider support than those 'values' elicited through a process confined to expert groups alone – whether these are groups of conservation scientists, economists or planners.

The Changing Institutional Context of Nature Conservation in Britain

Revealing conservation values is difficult enough at any time, but problems are compounded when institutions charged with the task of conserving nature also change. In Britain, institutional change which accompanied both the dismemberment of the Nature Conservancy Council (NCC) in 1991 and the establishment of an Environment Agency (the Agency) in 1995, has a material bearing on how nature is valued in national and local policies.

Prior to 1991, the NCC was responsible for nature conservation policies on a national scale and advised central government on the importance and significance of nature conservation. However, throughout the 1980s, the NCC's authority and ability to 'stand up for nature' was repeatedly challenged by a central government convinced of the correctness of the free market as the means of achieving a balance between development and conservation. Threatened with privatisation by the Secretary of State in 1986 and by the politicisation of the SSSI system which was increasingly seen by government and the private sector as an unreasonable obstacle to development (Marren 1993), the NCC found its scientific approach to valuing nature repeatedly contested. On their establishment, therefore, it was not surprising to find each of the four country-based organisations which succeeded the NCC needing to forge new identities, including new ways of valuing nature.

In the case of English Nature (EN) and the new Countryside Commission now restricted to England, the concept of 'Natural Capital' appeared to recommend itself as a novel way of valuing nature and the environment. Constructing the environment through an economic metaphor meant that an argument could be advanced that all forms of natural capital, like human capital, are interchangeable through the medium of money. Thus, natural capital could be regarded as offering an acceptable way forward in the political climate of the early 1990s. In addition, the concept of natural capital meshed well with a new institutional culture which, at least in the case of EN, appeared to embrace the values of a free-market through talk of 'good customer relations' and 'reconciling nature conservation with other land uses ...' (Marren 1993). The fact that by 1996, this approach to valuing nature seemed to have outgrown 'the strength of its foundations' and to require review (CAG/LUC 1997) is perhaps a measure of the growing maturity EN now seeks to express in a changed political climate.

The establishment of the Environment Agency in 1995 brought together Her Majesty's Inspectorate of Pollution, local waste regulation authorities and the National Rivers Authority. With the objective of providing an integrated and holistic approach to the environment, the Agency also inherited conservation duties, including the duty to promote conservation in riverine and estuarine habitats. Of particular relevance to our concern with valuing nature is s.39 of the Environment Act 1995. This states that in respect of its policies, programmes and projects, the Agency has a duty to consider the costs and benefits of its actions; that is, not only its internal costs and benefits but also costs and benefits incurred by other organisations, individuals, society as a whole and the environment. Environmentalists were quick to point out that the prospects for nature conservation would depend on how the Agency came to interpret these duties (Burton 1995).

The Agency is not committed to any particular methods of appraising costs and benefits although historically cost-benefit analysis had been regularly employed by its parent organisations for appraising larger-scale programmes and projects. As the national organisation with the most wide-ranging environmental remit and arguably the most influential one in terms of how the value of nature is determined, the Agency has a particularly important role to play in advancing sustainable development. How the Agency might interpret these duties in the specific context of producing Local Environment Agency Plans (LEAPs) for all the river catchments in England and Wales is the subject of our case study reported below.

Approaches to Valuing Nature

With these considerations in mind, we turn now to a typology of common approaches to valuing nature (see Table 3.1 below).

Free Market Approaches

Where values are determined by the free market and are expressed through private ownership, nature is afforded protection through the good offices of the landowner. On nature reserves owned, leased or managed by nature conservation agencies and wildlife trusts, the intention of the landowner

Table 3.1 A Typology of Approaches to Valuing Nature

Value of nature determined by ...	Value of nature expressed through ...	Nature best protected by ...
Free market	**Private ownership**	**Property rights**
Science	**Scientific criteria**	**Standards and regulations** (legislation)
Individual use (preferences)	**Willingness to pay/accept** (contingent valuation)	**Economic efficiency** (cost-benefit analysis)
Common good, ethical, moral concerns	**Social consensus**	**Political process**

towards nature is clear. This is not necessarily the case for the wider countryside where management agreements favouring nature have to be negotiated individually with each landlord. In practice, the numerous agri-environmental schemes now operating in the UK are based on this approach, albeit within a market framework that is protected from the full rigours of free competition (Bishop and Phillips 1993). By the end of 1994 some 4 per cent of the total agricultural land area of England was covered by management agreements under the two major farmland conservation schemes: Environmentally Sensitive Areas (ESAs) and Countryside Stewardship (CS).

The basis of these voluntary schemes is compensation for profits forgone when the farmer agrees to farm in environmentally conscious ways. Although payment is not a true market price, levels have been set to reflect what farmers would find acceptable (Billsborough 1997). Given the underlying values of private ownership upon which the approach is based, therefore, the high level of uptake of these schemes by farmers in the target areas (Land Use Consultants 1995) is not surprising. However, as Whitby et al. (1996) note, once farmers are exposed to the full force of international competition, continued government support for these schemes will be severely tested. Likewise, as the public become better informed about how these schemes are funded and administered, and acknowledge the consequences of this continued support for food prices paid at supermarket checkouts, existing tacit public support for this approach – including its approach to valuing nature – cannot be guaranteed either.

Scientific Approach

The dominant means of protecting nature in Britain is through a process of key site selection and the use of legislation to protect these sites. Science has informed the evaluative process on which the legislative framework associated with designations such as Sites of Special Scientific Interest (SSSIs) (Ratcliffe 1977), National Nature Reserves (NNRs), Local Nature Reserves (LNRs) and a whole host of other national and international designations is based. Over 2 million hectares of land are protected through these designations in the UK, although as annual reports of English Nature, for example, reveal, the degree of protection afforded to sites is far from absolute. Throughout the 1980s and early 1990s agricultural activities, pollution and a series of miscellaneous activities continued to inflict both long-term and short-term damage to SSSIs (Comptroller and Auditor General 1994; House of Commons Committee of Public Accounts 1995; DOE 1996). SSSIs, regarded as the 'jewels in the crown' of our natural heritage, were thought to require the highest possible – if not 'absolute' – protection because they supported populations of organisms thought by conservation scientists to be most at risk from extinction. The determination of some landowners to damage valued habitats through the pursuit of their own profit-motivated approach points to both loopholes in existing legislation and to the fact that legislation can never confer absolute protection in an imperfect world.

Friends of the Earth and other voluntary sector organisations continue to press for improvement to existing SSSI legislation but, in practice, resort to legislation as a means of protecting nature, without also securing the political will to uphold it, will always prove inadequate. The weakness of a legislative approach to site protection based on science alone has been exposed in particular through evidence heard at several high-profile planning enquiries involving the impact of proposed development on SSSIs.

Conflicting expert evidence presented in public enquiries about the correctness and robustness of the criteria used to evaluate and designate sites undermine the objectivity and disinterestedness of a scientific approach to nature conservation. For example, the debate surrounding Rainham Marshes SSSI on the eastern edge of London (Harrison and Burgess 1994) and the several cases discussed by Cowell (1997) exposed the double-edged sword which science offers when it moves out of the laboratory and into the social and political arena (Yearly 1991; Harrison 1993). In effect these public inquiries reveal how difficult it is to defend values for nature based on a scientific process which purports to be 'objective' and value-free, but which at the same time makes appeals to universal values. These bruising litigious experiences confirm that an approach to valuing nature based on science, unless accompanied by the political will to support it, is open to challenge. The reluctance of national agencies to use their compulsory powers to support their own judgements – admittedly more through lack of financial resources than lack of commitment – merely serves to emphasise this point.

Individual Use-value Approach

This approach is closely aligned with the practices of the former Department of Transport and its heavy reliance on cost-benefit analysis (CBA) for assessing the impact of road schemes. Judgements guided by CBA, including those about how to value and protect nature, are based on economic efficiency. Given its (apparent) ability to express all costs and benefits in the common unit of money, CBA proves to be an attractive approach. Moreover, through the use of contingent valuation methods (CVM) to reveal public preferences for different environmental scenarios, CBA also claims to be a democratic process.

In a CVM survey, respondents engage in a bidding process set up to represent an artificial market for environmental goods and services (Bateman and Turner 1993). For example, respondents might be asked to indicate what they would be willing to pay to conserve a natural area threatened by development, or less often, because the sums of money are usually much larger, what they would be willing to accept by way of compensation were the area to be damaged or lost. Summing the amounts individuals are prepared to pay or accept provides the means of gauging how society values nature. This aggregate sum is then used to assess the economic efficiency of projects and policies such as agri-environmental schemes and forestry programmes.

CBA has been criticised on a number of grounds; most especially for its assumption that the plural values which reside in nature and the countryside are commensurable, but also because CVM elicits individual preferences and not the disinterested and attentive responses solicited through Foster's deliberative approach mentioned earlier (see O'Neill 1993; Foster 1997). Support for these approaches amongst the public has also been challenged. For example, in a recent study conducted with members of the public who had responded to a CVM survey undertaken about a wildlife enhancement scheme (Burgess et al. 1998a), local residents and visitors alike felt very strongly that the CVM conceals the purposes to which it is put. Had they known how the findings were to be used, several respondents said that they would not have participated in the CVM survey. Although widely criticised by institutional economists such as Jacobs (1994) and Hodgson (1997), CBA and CVM continue to be widely used, especially for environmental appraisal of large projects (see Chapter 1).

Common Good Approaches

Basing a value system on a concept of 'common good' implies embracing ethical and moral concerns as well as popular values for particular places, natural features and their attributes. One outcome of the engagement of Local Authorities with policies for sustainable development and the Local Agenda 21 (LA21) process has been a concern to promote more participative forms of democracy in their decision-making processes. Several authorities have been keen to discover what nature needs protecting through a process of consensus building. Using a variety of methods such as visioning conferences, community panels, village appraisals, focus groups and planning for real, members of the public have been encouraged to determine their own sustainability indicators (LGMB 1993; Burgess et al. 1998b).

What emerges from this deliberative process supports the arguments made by cultural geographers and activists concerned with the cultural significance of nature, places and landscapes (Lowenthal 1978; Gold and Burgess 1982; Mabey et al. 1984; Mabey 1996). People from all walks of life value the natural world not just for its features and objects but for a wide range of other less tangible benefits which accrue to society. For example, people value the sense of place and local distinctiveness which reside in the particular juxtaposition of features such as pond and hedgerow, well-loved buildings and unpaved road. Places are also valued for their attributes and qualities. For example, the sense of vitality and security which comes from knowing that public spaces are well cared for means that natural spaces are perceived to be accessible to anyone wishing to use them. 'Accessible nature' is hence more than the sum of its existing features (English Nature 1995). Existing methods of scientific valuation which value species and habitats as objects but ignore the cultural and social significance of nature's attributes, fail to capture these less tangible values or the benefits they provide. By contrast, with their emphasis on equity and distributive justice for both existing and future generations, deliberative and inclusionary methods of valuing nature consistently confirm the universal significance of the moral and ethical dimensions of valuation.

From Natural to Environmental Capital

Evident from this brief review of four approaches to valuing nature is the fact that each tries to capture what is an extremely complex, subtle, and elusive process. The simplification involved, the masking of some assumptions and privileging of others, and the presence or absence of an inclusionary approach, mean that all approaches are likely to be contested. It is also clear that institutions can mediate in this process of valuation. The genesis of the concept of natural capital (and its new reformulation as the concept of 'environmental capital') illustrates how an economic approach to valuing nature has attempted to capture scientific and common good values.

Based on the simple economic metaphor that natural stocks and flows are like capital and interest, natural capital was classified into three categories: critical, constant and tradable (see Table 3.2).

Table 3.2 Natural Capital

Critical natural capital – assets which are important, irreplaceable and cannot be substituted by anything else. They should be given the highest possible – some would say 'absolute' – protection like SSSIs, RAMSAR sites and SPAs.

Constant natural capital – assets which are not individually unique or irreplaceable but the total stock of these assets needs to be maintained at or above a given 'threshold'.

Tradable natural capital – assets for which there is no minimum threshold level of required maintenance. These assets can be traded for non-environmental gains.

In a series of research reports published in the mid-1990s, English Nature provided worked examples of how this approach might be applied to ecosystems, habitats and species in different geographical contexts (Gillespie and Shepherd 1995, 1996). In practice the approach makes a number of assumptions about reversibility, substitutability, importance and scarcity or threshold in relation to some desired level, all of which need to be reviewed at particular spatial scales (Holland 1994, 1996). For example, nationally common habitats may be regarded as important by local residents especially if they are declining locally. On the other hand, species that are rare on a national scale may be common locally and hence overlooked in terms of their local importance. The concept of substitutability proved problematic too for an environmental movement wedded to a concept of natural equilibrium. However, the economic metaphor is such a dominant one that the risk of treating all natural capital as potentially 'tradable', seemed ever present, and it was this attendant risk which environmentalists found most unacceptable (Buckley 1995). Adopting a natural capital approach appeared to mean that protecting nature would become an increasingly risky business!

Although never formally linked to the site designation system of SSSIs and the like, the concept of natural capital proved influential within country agencies, county and local planning authorities and in voluntary sector organisations. Moreover, as each organisation tried to extend nature conservation policies into the wider countryside where developers still pressed their claims, the risk that all natural capital could be regarded as potentially tradable seemed to be reinforced by other environmental policies. For example, the extension of agri-environmental schemes in 1995 to include a much wider range of landscape than had previously been the case, reinforced support for the market as the basis for valuing and protecting nature (Morris and Young 1997). Likewise, the reported success of habitat creation and restoration schemes seemed to confirm that indeed some natural assets were tradable, despite evidence to the contrary (Parker 1995). Given these kinds of pressures, planning authorities and other organisations were keen to embrace the concept but equally keen to interpret it to suit their own particular circumstances.

The confusion that followed these initial attempts to apply the concept was self-evident (CAG/LUC 1997). So, while natural capital enjoyed a brief period in the ascendant during the mid-1990s, practical experience revealed the tripartite classification of natural capital to be unworkable and an inadequate means of addressing the complexities and subtleties of how society values nature. Thus, the recent review of the concept and its usefulness sponsored by EN, the Countryside Commission, the Environment Agency and English Heritage and entitled *Environmental Capital* promotes a new approach to environmental appraisal (CAG/LUC 1997). It is striking that the revised concept draws much more strongly on the social and cultural values encompassed by the 'common good' approach outlined above. Indeed, the authors of the report comment that they would have preferred to drop the term 'capital' from their concept but felt it would cause unnecessary confusion. This might well be a mistake, for the more subtle appreciation of the qualities and characteristics of nature which are made explicit in the exposition of the concept, yet again is lost in the economic metaphor.

The concept of *environmental capital* emphasises the usefulness of recognising the services and benefits which flow from the natural environment and which contribute to an area's character. Instead of focusing on 'features' or 'objects' requiring protection, the approach recognises the importance of less tangible environmental attributes, functions and benefits. Environmental attributes such as, 'typicalness', 'distinctiveness', 'setting' and 'context', together with concerns of land, air and water quality, all contribute to the assessment of environmental capital. The approach seeks to identify explicitly those features and attributes of value in an area, and, by integrating environmental functions relating to biodiversity, land, air and water quality, heritage, amenity and recreation, the approach provides a more comprehensive evaluation of the benefits of the natural world than the earlier concept. It recommends identifying targets for each of the most highly valued attributes and an assessment of trends relating to each target. Instead of relying on expert appraisal alone to identify and assess these targets, the report also encourages a more inclusionary approach. Involving different partners and members of the public is regarded as an essential part of the whole valuation process. By encouraging a more inclusive and explicit approach to valuing environmental assets, the methodology removes the requirement to identify critical, constant and tradable capital and replaces it with a more subtle and differentiated approach.

Overall, the *Environmental Capital* report is a concerted attempt to address how common-good approaches to valuing nature can be developed whilst recognising the integrated and dynamic properties of natural systems. However, as a provisional guide only, the report holds back from recommending a preferred method for making transparent both those values on which the approach is based and the means of assessing their importance (CAG/LUC 1997). Our own work on the appraisal of environmental proposals conducted for the Environment Agency (Clark et al. 1998) is based on a decision-making process called Multi-Criteria Analysis (MCA), and shows how common-good approaches might be applied in the valuation of nature. We turn now to a brief discussion of this case study to build consensus about the criteria and value judgements which should be used to prioritise environmental issues.

Negotiating Criteria for Prioritisation of Issues in Local Environment Agency Plans (LEAPs): A Case Study of the New Forest LEAP

LEAPS are being developed by the Environment Agency to promote an integrated and sustainable approach to managing the natural environment. The purpose of a LEAP, which is a non-statutory document, is to focus attention on the environment of a specific area; involve all interested parties in planning for the future well-being of that area; agree to a vision for the area to guide Agency activities, and establish an integrated strategy and plan of action for five-year periods. LEAPs are a new addition to the arsenal of local plans and, as such, are regarded with some suspicion by local authorities and other statutory agencies charged with planning and environmental protection. Originating in the catchment plans of the National Rivers Authority, the boundaries for the LEAPs are set by geographical rather than administrative units. Thus a LEAP may cut across two or more local authorities, for example, which will inevitably increase the likelihood of conflict between the Agency and its statutory partners.

For these as well as other institutional reasons, the Agency wants to create a programme of consultation over the production of LEAPs which is inclusive of many local interests, open and transparent. At the same time, it is charged under s.39 of the Environment Act 1995 to demonstrate that it has taken into account the likely costs and benefits of its programmes, projects and plans. The case study sought to reconcile these objectives by developing a common-good approach to the valuation of the issues in the LEAP document for the New Forest. This was achieved through the recruitment of a local stakeholder group, composed of 14 representatives selected from the public, voluntary and private sectors in the area to develop criteria through which the issues in the LEAP could be discussed and prioritised.

The traditional model of public consultation is top-down, one-way dissemination of information about plans and proposals in which consultees are largely passive recipients who do no more than indicate their preference for one option or another. The new consultative practices which are emerging under the auspices of LA21 programmes (Young 1996) and often described as examples of New Democratic Structures (Wahlberg et al. 1995) are based on the idea that decisions will be more robust if based on a measure of consensus between those with a stake in what happens. Practices such as Round Table discussions, Future Search and Visioning processes stress a multi-voiced interactive process of debate and consensus building in which knowledge, values and ideas are shared among participants. We developed a procedure for economic appraisal of LEAPs which combined a standard method of policy and project appraisal – 'multi-criteria analysis' (MCA) (Nijkamp and Spronk 1981; Voogd 1983; Munda et al. 1994) – with the use of a stakeholder group to agree the prioritisation of issues in the LEAP. The project was carried out between October and December 1997 (Clark et al. 1998).

So far as we are aware, this is the first time such a project has been attempted in the environmental field. The approach combined systematic appraisal with group deliberation in a procedure where the emphasis was as much on the process as on the product. The approach to the process had three key elements. The first was to work through the stakeholder group to build coalitions and achieve a measure of consensus between different interests through the negotiation of what count as costs and benefits and how these should be appraised. The second was to facilitate enhanced dialogue between scientific and economic knowledge and other kinds of knowledges that are embedded in local places and communities. The third was to encourage networking with partners to achieve added value through increased local support and access to expertise and resources not available to the Agency in-house. The interests represented by the stakeholders and the organisation of the workshops are given in Tables 3.3 and 3.4.

Table 3.3   Members of the New Forest LEAP Group

Public sector
New Forest District Council (officer)
New Forest District Council (member)
English Nature
Environment Agency

Voluntary sector
RSPB and Hampshire Wildlife Trust
Hampshire CPRE and New Forest Association
New Forest Friends of the Earth
Brockenhurst Manor Fly Fishing Club
Calshot Sailing Club and Southampton Water Sailing Association

Private sector
NFU and CLA
Commoners Defence Association
Exxon Chemical
Southern Water
Associated British Ports

The facilitation of the stakeholder group process would be central to the success of the experiment. We could not expect automatic support from participants and nor could we expect the group simply to follow instructions. They would need persuading of the rationale and importance of the MCA method even if they were not fully convinced of its utility, and they would also need opportunities to reflect on the method and the process. The integration of deliberation and formal analysis required considered planning. The MCA was tackled in stages during the four workshops. First, the group derived a list of criteria acceptable to everyone. Second, the criteria were weighted according to their importance and the least important criteria were discarded. Third, the group 'scored' each issue against each of the criteria. Finally, a ranked list was produced from this by summing weighted scores and separating the issues into priority groups on the basis of those

Table 3.4 Workshop Tasks

Prior to Workshop 1 (individuals)	To identify costs, benefits and risks of issues in the LEAP of interest to the group member and those whom he or she was representing.
Workshop 1 (group)	To review the issues in the New Forest LEAP and produce a comprehensive, inclusive list of the costs, benefits and risks associated with the issues proposed in the New Forest LEAP.
Prior to Workshop 2 (individuals)	To think about criteria against which the issues in the New Forest LEAP might be assessed.
Workshop 2 (group)	To produce an inclusive list of criteria for assessing the issues in the New Forest LEAP.
Prior to Workshop 3 (individuals)	To score each criterion on the list produced in meeting 2 on a scale of 0 to 100.
Workshop 3 (group)	To evaluate the issues against the final list of 10 criteria.
Prior to Workshop 4 (individuals)	To review the list of issues ranked in priority groups according to the results of the MCA.
Workshop 4 (group)	To review and agree the ranked issues list and to review the process.

scores. However, it was not tackled mechanistically. The group began by reviewing the issues and discussing the costs and benefits associated with them, which provided a context for the MCA. At each stage participants had an opportunity to deliberate: in determining the criteria, in assessing the issues against the criteria and in reviewing the results. In the last session, in the presence of observers from the Environment Agency, the stakeholders reviewed and evaluated the whole process.

The Production of Negotiated, Ranked Criteria for Prioritising Issues Within the LEAP

In the first workshop, two important questions were clarified: *How could issues be prioritised if the specifics of actions proposed to solve them were not known?* Also, in the context of the specific task of prioritising issues within the LEAP, *what are criteria?* In discussion, it was agreed that some participants might find some of the proposed actions in the LEAP contentious but the group was essentially concerned with a higher-level question, that of priorities. So the ranking of issues was not concerned with whether the action proposed for a specific issue was the 'right' one to solve that problem. For example, some of the stakeholders disagreed with the assumption in the LEAP that the erection of low-flow weirs is the best way to tackle low flows in some New Forest streams. Rather, the question facing participants was whether it is more important for the Agency to address the low-flow issue, or to address, for example, reduced water quality or damaged valley mires or obstructions to the free passage of sea trout or some other issue in the LEAP.

In answer to the question *what are criteria?*, the stakeholder group were given initial guidance and then worked through the four workshop sessions to negotiate a set of criteria. The core of MCA is systematic appraisal which means comparing issues using the same criteria for each one. We defined a criterion for the stakeholders as 'a value-based standard against which each issue can be assessed', suggesting that a three-stage process could be helpful in deriving criteria. First, make a *general observation* which applies to some/all of the issues identified in the LEAP or with the costs/benefits/risks associated with them. Second, make explicit the *value judgement* involved in this observation. Finally, restate the value judgement as a *criterion* against which each issue can be qualitatively assessed. The group's choice of criteria, like the choice of any criterion, would be subjective, based on the values of those who developed them. In anticipation of a potential debate on objectivity (a debate which did not in fact materialise) this subjectivity was acknowledged and for this reason it was important that the value judgements underlying the criteria were made explicit.

Each stakeholder was asked to bring their own initial criteria – with underlying value judgements made explicit – to the second workshop. Here the group members were put into pairs, matched by their interests and experiences. Thus, the business stakeholders worked together, as did the environmentalists, and local government representatives. Once each pair had agreed their list of criteria, they moved into a larger group of combined pairs to go through the same process of discussion, sorting and evaluation of criteria. In the final stage, the whole group was brought together to evaluate all the criteria and produce a final list.

These were rich and fruitful discussions; all the members of the group participated fully, sharing the criteria they had brought to the second workshop and negotiating to produce an agreed set. Members were very willing to debate the value judgements that underpinned their criteria. A wide variety of issues were discussed as pairs of stakeholders worked to produce criteria. These included the precautionary principle and whether it could be used as a criterion; what sustainable development might mean in terms of relations between the national and local economy; problems with using the word 'traditional' in the context of local economic and social relations; the special character of the New Forest and what that meant; the relative value of private property and common goods; what constitutes irreversibility in environmental terms; relationships between economic pressures and environmental needs (the two are not always opposed); the need for adequate scientific knowledge; national and international law; cooperation and partnerships between different agencies, and between different sectors of local activities; public health and individual risk; political pressures in decision making and the need to maintain public support, and how to relate costs and benefits – who gains?

The twin devices of making value judgements explicit and asking people to consider the 'measurability' of criteria helped to focus discussion. The value judgements were particularly important in making meanings clear and helping people to see quickly where there was agreement and where there was difference. Conflict over the importance of different criteria was avoided because participants did not have to reach consensus on this, only on the validity of different criteria. The maximum number of criteria produced by any pair of stakeholders was ten, the minimum four. (See Table 3.5.)

The task of developing criteria was achievable, participants tackled it willingly and seemed to find the process stimulating and enjoyable. The atmosphere was one of cooperation rather than confrontation, with people listening to others as well as expounding their own views, and actively seeking new expressions of language and more creative ways to frame the value judgements. This creativity and collaboration was promoted by the emphasis on inclusiveness (the reassurance that all criteria would count for something) and the emphasis on making the value judgements explicit. Participants did not have to agree to endorse others' values but only the validity of the criteria that they put forward because the point at issue was whether a criterion *could* be used to assess the issues, not whether it *should* be. This meant that participants could focus on understanding, on teasing out their own and others' views, and on working out similarities and differences. In addition, all participants felt that they could contribute as the debate was perceived to turn less on specialist knowledge. At the same time, people seemed less afraid that they lacked technical expertise and more

Table 3.5 Genesis of Criteria

Criterion content	suggested by (out of 7 pairs)	number of similar criteria[1]	agreement on value judgement	suggested by (out of 3 groups)	number of similar criteria[1]	final criteria label[2]
Legal, statutory obligations	6	6[3]	yes	3	3	A
Partnership/issue involves others	6	6	no	3	5	B*
Species/habitats	4	5	yes	3	4	C*
Human health and safety	3	4	yes	2	2	G*
Local economy	3	3	yes	2[4]	2	E
Issue/problem not just local	3	3	yes	1	1	J
Level of scientific understanding/precautionary principle	3	3	no	1	1	K
Commoning/traditional activities/unique status of New Forest	2	2	yes	2	2	F*
Problem will get worse/irreversibility	2	2	yes	2	2	D*
Public amenity/nuisance	1	1	na	1	1	H
Public money leading to private gain	1	1	na	1	1	L
Anticipate future legislation	1	1[3]	na	1	1	M
Protect property	1	1	na	1	1	N**
Encourage recreation	1	1	na	1	1	P**

Notes:
1. Similar/overlapping criteria counted as having similar content, so the number of criteria may be greater than the number of pairs or groups.
2. *In this column indicates a version of one of the five criteria suggested as examples by the research team. Some pairs ignored these criteria, assuming that they would be automatically included. ** In this column indicates a criterion that was not agreed by the whole group.
3. One pair's criterion included anticipation of future legislation as well as current obligations; this criterion is counted twice.
4. Group 3 also discussed economic criteria but could not decide what criterion to use. They hoped that another group would come up with a suitable criterion.

confident of debating meanings of specialist terms such as 'ecosystem' and 'health and safety'.

The strategy of splitting the stakeholder group into compatible pairs before they moved into larger groups worked well in building consensus about the validity of criteria. The somewhat surprising lack of conflict was not because people were not willing to be disagreeable; views were often expressed trenchantly, especially in the groups. Rather, conflict was defused because people were meeting in a forum where they had to work together but were not forced to defend their interests adversarially. Putting different interests together in this situation not only made for productive discussion but also meant that the underlying politics could be acknowledged without getting in the way. Thus the process enabled people who might otherwise have been locked in fierce opposition to move out of their trenches, rather than digging in.

Participants were able to express their values clearly and cogently, but at times had problems translating a value into a criterion. This was not wholly resolved during the workshop and value judgements were at times implicit in the associated statement rather than expressed in terms of 'should' or 'ought'; for example *'threat of legal action if not delivered'* which translates into 'the Environment Agency should not risk legal action.' Some of the value judgements incorporated an argument for holding that view; for example *'economic activity should be maintained to support the rural population/maintain the social fabric of the Forest.'* However, the criteria most out on a limb, that is, pertaining to detail, complex, with an unclear value judgement, tended not to survive group scrutiny. A common problem was the provision of a statement of 'fact', rather than a value judgement, to underpin a criterion. For example, one criterion proposed was: *'To what extent is scientific knowledge limited?'* and its associated value judgement was expressed as: *'There is a need for good scientific understanding.'* Good scientific understanding is desirable but this can be argued both ways: wait for complete scientific understanding to act, or apply the precautionary principle. The way this value judgement is phrased gives little idea of what the value judgement underlying the criterion actually is. There was considerable overlap between the criteria suggested by the stakeholders, working either in pairs or in small groups, as shown in Table 3.5.

From the long list of largely overlapping criteria, we identified the key words in each criterion and value judgement to produce a single set of criteria for the stakeholders to agree and weight in terms of relative importance for each of them. This ranking procedure was important to reduce the list of criteria to a reasonable number to work with in the prioritisation of the 33 issues in the LEAP, and also to recognise that not all criteria had equal weight – some would be more important or significant than others.

Table 3.6 Weighted (Ranked) Criteria Agreed by the Group

Code	Weight	Criterion	Underlying value judgement
1	14.09	To what extent is resolution of this issue a legal requirement?	Legal obligations should be met.
2	12.77	To what extent would tackling this issue benefit non-human species and habitats?	Biodiversity should be protected and the Environment Agency should contribute to the UK Biodiversity Action Plan in line with government policy.
3	12.17	To what extent would tackling this issue maintain the unique status/international importance of the New Forest?	The Environment Agency's actions should not affect the 'New Forestness' of the area.
4	10.68	To what extent is the problem identified in this issue likely to get worse?	Issues which are likely to get worse should be tackled sooner rather than later; in particular high priority should be given to issues where delay would lead to irreversible decline.
5	10.93	To what extent would tackling this issue require the Environment Agency to work in partnership with other agencies?	The Environment Agency should work in partnership with other organisations within a cross-organisation strategic approach.
6	9.22	To what extent would tackling this issue benefit public health?	Public health should be safeguarded; danger to human life is unacceptable.
7	8.69	To what extent is the issue well understood scientifically?	Priority should be given to tackling issues which are well understood.
8	7.62	To what extent would tackling this issue benefit the quality of life for residents in the LEAP area?	Improving amenity and redressing nuisance should be given high priority.
9	7.42	To what extent would tackling this issue benefit the local economy?	Maintaining/creating employment should be given high priority.
10	6.43	To what extent are actions relating to this issue likely to be affected by potential future legislation?	Future legislation will have to be complied with so its potential impact should be considered.

Capturing Values for Nature 105

This needed to be agreed by the stakeholders. There was inevitably some rewording in the translation from contributing criterion to derived criterion through the reconciling of similar criteria. Other reasons for rewording the criteria were *assessability* (criteria needed to be framed in the form '*To what extent would tackling this issue/failure to tackle this issue ...?*) and *consistency* (criteria needed to be framed so that assessments run in the same direction). This rewording presented some difficulties, especially where suggested criteria were clearly similar but their underlying value judgements diverged, and where criteria overlapped such that there seemed to be important differences between them. In all cases, the reasoning behind the wording of the criteria was made explicit to the stakeholder group who were able to comment and suggest changes. The reworded criteria were accepted as a fair reflection of what was meant, although difficulties of interpretation emerged when they were applied to specific issues in the LEAP.

Once a long list of criteria had been agreed, this was sent to each stakeholder who was asked to rank each on a score of 0–100 on the basis of the importance they felt should be attached to the criterion in the prioritisation of actions in the LEAP. This was necessary for two reasons – one conceptual, the other practical. Conceptually, it is clear that not all criteria will have the same significance for all stakeholders and these differences needed to be both recognised and resolved. A weighted averaging of individual ranks was agreed as the fairest way of achieving this outcome. Second, the scale of the task (where the group were required to prioritise 33 issues) meant that the number of criteria needed to be reduced to a manageable number. Fourteen had been produced in the initial process. These had to be reduced to ten, and the averaged weighting provided a mechanism for discarding the four criteria which received the least points. Table 3.6 shows the weighted list of criteria.

Where the Criteria Fall in Relation to the Typology of Approaches to Valuing Nature

The typology of approaches to valuing nature explored in the first part of this chapter were drawn from existing concepts and practices in the formulation of policies for the protection and maintenance of nature conservation. As such, they represent established procedures produced mainly by academic and institutional processes. Where in the typology do the criteria produced by the New Forest stakeholder group fall? Are they concentrated in any one of the categories we identified or are they dispersed more evenly across economic, scientific, social and cultural arenas?

The intended meaning of each criterion is indicated in the value judgement associated with it. According to our typology of values, the criteria fall predominantly into two categories: 'science' and 'common-good' approaches. Legal requirements (the top-ranked criterion) includes legislation driven specifically by science such as the EC Habitats and Birds Directives, as well as other statutory requirements such as water quality and air quality which comprise the Agency's regulatory duties. Scientific knowledge is accorded a high weighting both in terms of maintaining biodiversity (2), irreversibility of changes to natural systems (4), and current levels of scientific knowledge of problems which was interpreted in terms of a measure of effectiveness (7).

The new *Environmental Capital* report's concept (CAG/LUC 1997) builds on what has become known as the 'characterisation' approach to the spatial variation of landscape and nature in the UK. In the search for what makes places, areas and regions distinctive, English Nature and the Countryside Commission have participated in the production of a Joint Character Map of England and Wales. Local character represents the synthesis of the geological, biological and physical landscape features, field and settlement patterns, vernacular building styles, and other qualities of cultural landscapes. Although difficult to pin down scientifically, the concept of local character has undoubted resonance. The stakeholders in the New Forest LEAP produced their own version of 'local distinctiveness' as an important criterion for prioritising actions (3), and also signified the importance of quality-of-life issues (8). Due regard is given to economic concerns in the list of criteria: the most highly weighted of these was in terms of due regard being given to maintaining the local economy (9), whilst holding those needs in balance with social and environmental needs. The stakeholders were clear in their rejection of financial costs and efficiency measures as the most important criteria for assessing priorities in the LEAP, preferring to leave those essentially business decisions to the Agency once the principles had been agreed by the stakeholders.

The long list of criteria produced by the stakeholders could serve as standards for assessing whether or not actions, plans and projects are sustainable or not. The criteria are independent and assess different implications of environmental actions. In the final workshop, the stakeholders were asked for their judgements about the generic value of the criteria they had produced. One of the business members commented:

> Personally I think they are quite robust. They seem generic enough to be transferable. ... There seems to be a criteria to cover each part of the community, ecological, human, in some way and it doesn't seem to be that one area of criteria is over bearing. If you had a different group putting the criteria together, I think you would have seen a similar consensus.

There was general agreement with this point of view – but considerable reluctance to see the criteria applied rigidly in all cases. The stakeholders valued the process of negotiation they had gone through to arrive at the list of criteria and stressed how important it would be for each stakeholder group to own its own set of criteria. More generally, the participants were very supportive of the MCA approach – and especially appreciative of the way in which we were able to combine a rigorous analytical process with opportunities for sharing meanings and values in non-confrontational debate.

Conclusions

A new Labour government was elected to power in 1997 with a manifesto that included greater commitment to equity and social inclusion in economic, social and political life. In this changing political climate, the environmental and countryside agencies are exploring new ways of valuing nature which reflect these new priorities. The reductive metaphor of natural capital, and determination by the neo-classical environmental economists to reduce incommensurable values for nature to a single measure of monetary value, is giving way. Recognition of the cultural significance of nature, combined with new ways of thinking about sustainability which recognise the complexities of interlocking environmental, economic *and* social systems are contributing to more sophisticated approaches to environmental management.

The LEAP case study we have recounted here demonstrates, conclusively, that individuals representing very different world views and interests can come together and debate the bases of their values. It is possible for these representatives to work amicably towards compromise and, in the New Forest case, a surprising level of consensus emerged over the principles upon which judgements about how local environmental actions should be prioritised. Such workshops will assist in the development of this more open and democratic form of decision making. In support of their more general applicability, the New Forest criteria are not dissimilar to those produced in a separate but complimentary research programme (Davos et al. 1997). We would conclude by emphasising that the process of discussing values for nature and negotiating criteria is much more significant than the actual product. Genuine participation in decision making is dependent on strong interpersonal and group relations, on maximum transparency and openness, and a commitment to share power. The Environment Agency, in supporting the New Forest work, and agreeing to take the approach we have developed into its national guidance for all the LEAPs (Clark et al. 1998), has shown itself willing to embrace the common-good approaches to valuing nature which have, for so long, been denigrated or ignored in environmental management and policy making.

Acknowledgements The LEAPs research was carried out for the Environment Agency between October and December 1997 by members of the Environment and Society Research Unit, Department of Geography, University College London.

References

Adams, W.M. (1997) 'Rationalisation and conservation: ecology and the management of nature in the United Kingdom', *Transactions of the Institute of British Geographers*, NS 22(3): 277–291.

Bateman, I.J. and Turner, R.K. (1993) 'Valuation of the environment, methods and techniques: the contingent valuation method', in Turner, R.K. (ed.) *Sustainable Environmental Economics and Management* (London: Belhaven Press: 120–191).

Billsborough, S. (1997) 'Pricing the countryside: the example of Tir Cymen', in Foster. (ed.) (1997: 89–102).

Bishop, K. and Phillips, A.D. (1993) 'Seven steps to market: the development of a market-led approach to countryside conservation and recreation', *Journal of Rural Studies* 9: 315–338.

Buckley, P. (1995) 'Critical Natural Capital: operational flaws in a valid concept', *Ecos* 16 (3/4): 13–17.

Burgess, J., Clark, J. and Harrison, C.M. (1998a) 'Respondents' evaluations of a contingent valuation survey: a case study based on an economic valuation of the wildlife enhancement scheme, Pevensey Levels in East Sussex.' *Area*, 30 (1): 19–27.

Burgess, J., Harrison, C.M. and Filius, P. (1998b) 'Environmental communication and the cultural politics of environmental citizenship', *Environment and Planning, A*, 30 (8): 1445–1460.

Burton, T. (1995) 'The Environment Act 1995: blessing or bane?', *Ecos* 16 (3/4): 7–9.

CAG/LUC (1997) *Environmental Capital: a new approach* (Cheltenham: Countryside Commission).

Clark, J., Burgess, J., Dando, N., Bhattachary, D., Heppel, K., Jones, P., Murlis, J. and Wood, P. (1998) *Prioritising the issues in Local Environment Agency Plans through Consensus Building with Stakeholder Groups*, Project Record W4/W4–002/1 (Bristol: The Environment Agency).

Comptroller and Auditor General (1994) *Protecting and Managing Sites of Special Scientific Interest in England* (London: HMSO).

Cowell, R. (1997) 'Stretching the limits: environmental compensation, habitat crea-

tion and sustainable development', *Transactions of the Institute of British Geographers*, NS 22(3): 292–306.
Department of the Environment (1996) *Indicators of Sustainable development for the United Kingdom* (London: HMSO).
Davos, C.A., Side, J.C., Jones, P.J.S., Siakavara, K., La Roca, F., Garcia, E., Burone, F. and Kerkhove, G. (1997), *The Role of Value Conflict Assessment Techniques in the Formation of Implementable and Effective Coastal Zone Management Policies: A Report to the European Commission (DG XII)*; Volume 1 – Main Report of the Study; Volume 2 – Appendices: (1) Case Study Reports; (2) The Research Instrument.
English Nature (1995) *Accessible natural greenspace in towns and cities: a review of appropriate size and distance criteria*, English Nature Research Reports No.153 (Peterborough: English Nature).
Environmental Resources Management (1995) *Environmental Capital for the Countryside – Final report* (Cheltenham: Countryside Commission).
Foster, J. (ed.) (1997) *Valuing Nature? Ethics, Economics and the Environment* (London: Routledge).
Foster, J. (1997a) 'Environment and creative value', in Foster (ed.) (1997: 232–246).
Gillespie, J. and Shepherd, P. (1995) *Establishing Criteria for Identifying Critical Natural Capital in the Terrestrial Environment – A Discussion Paper*, English Nature Research Report No. 141 (Peterborough: English Nature).
Gillespie, J. and Shepherd, P. (1996) *Developing Definitions of Natural Capital for Use within the Uplands of England*, English Nature Research Report No. 197 (Peterborough: English Nature).
Gold, J.R. and Burgess, J. (eds) (1982) *Valued Environments* (London: George Allen and Unwin).
Goldsmith, F.B. and Warren, A. (eds) (1993) *Conservation in Progress* (London: Wiley).
Harrison, C.M. (1993) 'Nature conservation, science and popular values', in Goldsmith and Warren (eds) (1993: 35–49).
Harrison, C.M. and Burgess, J. (1994) 'Social constructions of nature: a case study of conflicts over the development of Rainham Marshes SSSI', *Transactions of the Institute of British Geographers*, NS19: 291–310.
Hodgson, G. (1997) 'Economics, environmental policy and the transcendence of utilitarianism', in Foster (ed.) (1997: 48–66).
Holland, A. (1994) 'Natural capital', in R. Attfield and A. Belsey (eds) *Philosophy and the natural environment* (Cambridge: Cambridge University Press: 169–182).
Holland, A. (1997) 'Substitutability: or, why strong sustainability is weak and absurdly strong sustainability is not absurd', in Foster (ed.) (1997: 119–134).
Holland, A. and Rawles K. (1993) 'Values in conservation' *Ecos*, 14 (1): 14–17.
House of Commons Committee of Public Accounts (1995) *Protecting and Managing Sites of Special Scientific Interest* Eleventh Report, Session 1994-5 (London: HMSO).
Jacobs, M. (1994) 'The limits of neoclassicism: towards an institutional environmental economics', in Redclift, M. and Benton, T. (eds) *Social Theory and the Global Environment* (London: Routledge).

Land Use Consultants (1995) *Countryside Stewardship Monitoring and Evaluation*. Third interim report (London: Land Use Consultants).

LGMB (Local Government Management Board) (1993) *Local Agenda 21 Principles and Processes – A Step by Step Guide*, LGMB, Layden House, 76–86 Turnmill Street, London EC1M 5QU.

Lowenthal, D. (1978) 'Finding valued landscapes', *Progress in Human Geography*, 2: 373–418.

Mabey, R. (1996) *Flora Britannica* (London: Sinclair Stevenson).

Mabey, R. (ed.) with Clifford, S. and King, A. (1984) *Second Nature* (London: Jonathan Cape).

Marren, P. (1993) 'The siege of the NCC: nature conservation in the eighties', in Goldsmith and Warren (eds) (1993: 283–299).

Morris, C. and Young, C. (1997) 'Towards environmentally beneficial farming? An evaluation of the Countryside Stewardship Scheme', *Geography* 82: 305–316.

Munda, G., Nijkamp, P. and Rietveld, P. (1994) 'Qualitative multi-criteria evaluation for environmental management', *Ecological Economics*, 10: 97–112.

Nijkamp, P. and Spronk, J. (eds) (1981) *Multiple Criteria Analysis* (Basingstoke: Gower).

O'Brien, M. and Guerrier, Y. (1995) 'Values and the environment: an introduction', in Guerrier, Y., Alexander, N., Chase, J. and O'Brien, M. (eds) *Values and the environment: a social science perspective* (Chichester: Wiley).

O'Neill, J. (1993) *Ecology, policy and politics* (London: Routledge).

Parker, D.M. (1995) *Habitat creation: a critical guide*, Report prepared for English Nature by SGS Environment (Peterborough: English Nature).

Pickett, S.T.A. and White, P.S. (1985) *The ecology of natural disturbance and patch dynamics* (New York: Academic Press).

Ratcliffe, D. (1977) *A Nature Conservation Review – The Selection of Biological Sites of National Importance to Nature Conservation in Britain*, 2 volumes (Cambridge: Cambridge University Press).

Stirling, A. (1997) 'Multi-Criteria Mapping: Mitigating the Problems of Environmental Valuation?', in Foster (ed.) (1997: 186–210).

Voogd, H. (1983) *Multicriteria Evaluation for Urban and Regional Planning* (London: Methuen).

Wahlberg, M., Taylor, K. and Geddes, M. (1995) *Enhancing Local Democracy* (LGMB, Layden House, 76–86 Turnmill Street, London EC1M 5QU).

Whitby, M., Hodge, I., Lowe, P. and Saunders, C. (1996) 'Conservation options for CAP reform', *Ecos* 17(3/4): 46–54.

Wilcox, D. (1994) *The Guide to Effective Partnership* prepared for The Joseph Rowntree Foundation (London: Partnership Books).

Williams, R. (1973). *The Country and the City* (London: Chatto and Windus).

Yearley, S. (1991) *The Green Case* (London: Harper Collins).

Young, S.C. (1996) *Promoting participation and community based partnerships in the context of local agenda 21: a report for practitioners* (Manchester: The Victorian University of Manchester).

4 Private Country? Hunting, Land and Judicial Interventions

Davina Cooper[1]

Introduction

Much has been written about the public/private divide within political and legal theory, particularly by feminist scholars (O'Donovan 1985; Pateman 1989; Lacey 1993; Thornton 1995). For the courts, the dichotomy has proven a key organising framework. It shapes the character and content of judicial interventions and is reproduced, at least, ideologically in many of their practices (Blomley and Bakan 1992; Gray 1994). One area where the divide has received little academic attention is in relation to hunting law. Yet, hunting cases over the past 120 years have invoked the public/private divide in a range of forms, from property rights and the law on trespassing to revenue, local government ownership and employment practice.

On the surface, hunting may seem a good example of a private activity: property owners with the right to chase and kill animals – or permit others to do so – on land for which they possess sporting rights. However, hunting's status is far more complex; it does not remain on the private side of the divide. State regulation of field sports, the treatment of public sporting rights ownership, judicial recognition of hunting's history and value, the treatment of trespass in the course of hunting, and the refusal to constitute hunting as a nuisance illustrate the public status it possesses.

Yet I do not wish to argue that this proves hunting is public rather than private. Rather, I am interested in the interconnected relationship of public and private; and, in particular, in the role the private domain performs in the reproduction and maintenance of public activity. In this respect, I explore the 'rural' as analogous to the private domain of the 'home'. Just as the home has been identified by feminist analysts as the locus of cultural reproduction (for example, see Anthias and Yuval-Davis, 1989), so we can identify the rural as performing a similar function. In this sense, the private does not refer to non-intervention and non-accountability, but rather identifies a domain in which both 'natural' and 'essential' cultural work takes place. Thus, hunting, or at least certain forms, are defended as integral to Britain's cultural repository; a repository which protects and makes possible the collective identity that city life and nation, in turn, rely upon. In this sense, hunting is private. However, it is an association which not only allows, but requires, public policy interventions to eliminate its unacceptable elements.

To explore these issues, this chapter is divided into three parts. The first considers hunting as a private matter, and raises some problems with this representation. I then go on to explore the ways in which hunting functions as a public concern. The third, and final, section posits an alternative understanding of the private to consider the relationship between hunting and the reproduction of nationhood.

A Private Matter?

Central to the courts' portrayal of hunting is the private status of the hunt itself. This has two aspects. The first is liberty – an individual's right to participate in activities that have not been declared unlawful. The traditional link between judicial practice and liberal individualism was spelled out in *R. v. Somerset County Council, ex p. Fewings*, a case concerning the banning of hunting on publicly owned land. In referring to the 'lawful freedom' of stag hunting, Justice Laws declared: 'While, of course, it is open to Parliament to legislate so as to curtail the activities of private individuals ... such restrictions involve a very particular encroachment upon personal liberty.'[2]

The second aspect of privacy concerns landowners' rights to determine what takes place on their property (see Shoard 1987; Harrison 1991; Cox 1993). Thus, the freedom to hunt is closely linked to the law on property ownership. In other words, hunting is a lawful activity when carried out on land where permission has been granted; hunting thus becomes one of the incidental rights of property ownership. At the same time, hunting and other 'field sports' have their own distinct property status. Determining whether hunting takes place depends not on the wishes of the landowner but on the wishes of the owner of the sporting rights. Yet, like most private rights, access to sporting rights has had an entangled political history involving extensive legal intervention. As several scholars have argued, the capacity to acquire and possess hunting rights was intimately entangled with the changing character of economic and social power (Thompson 1975; Itzkowitz

1977; Manning 1993; Thomas 1993). Alongside went the attentive and punitive treatment of those who seemed to disregard its elaborate system and, hence, to challenge rural authority. In addition to poaching prosecutions, the courts have also safeguarded property rights by regulating other forms of 'uninvited' access and unlawful taking,[3] and, by determining where the right to game or hunt resides.[4]

Yet, the private-property status of hunting raises legal issues beyond that of access. A second issue that has generated judicial consideration concerns the existence of conflicting rights which may undermine the ability to hunt. The nineteenth-century covenant case of *Jeffreyes* v. *Evans*[5] illustrates some of the problems that can occur where one party has sporting rights over property another has the right to alter. In this instance, a third party, the lessee, 'cut down and carried away and destroyed divers quantities of the said furze-covers [gorse] and plantations, and thereby evicted the plaintiff from and disturbed him in the enjoyment of the said right of shooting and sporting ... .'[6] *Jeffreyes* reveals the way in which shooting and sporting rights can be conveyed as property to a party who is neither owner nor even lessee of land. This ability to separate out the property rights raises legal problems. However, they are intensified further by the capacity of owners to give permission to others to make use of their rights. Thus, people can sport over land to which they have no property entitlement providing they have permission from the sporting rights' holder (who may or may not be the owner or lessee of the land). The corollary of this is that if permission is refused, entry onto such land constitutes a trespass.

The capacity of the sporting rights' owner to deny hunts access to land has led many hunt opponents to adopt a strategy of purchasing sporting rights and then to withdraw permission from existing or would-be users.[7] The League Against Cruel Sports adopted this strategy in south-west England. In the early 1990s, as I discuss further below, several councils withdrew permission for hunts to cross their land. More recently, in 1997, the National Trust, after years of sustained and heated debate, adopted a similar position in relation to deer hunting.[8]

The efficacy of these strategies depends, however, on the courts' approach to hunts trespassing. How do the courts respond to a conflict between two private interests: the liberty to hunt and the right of owners of private property to control access and use of their land? In the main, the courts have interpreted trespass law in a manner that favours local landowners when this is compatible with hunting interests; however, there has been greater ambivalence when property interests come into conflict with the local squirearchy. One illustration of a statutory bias towards hunting is the exclusion of hunts from the poaching provisions of the Game Act 1831 providing the hunt started upon land on which it had an entitlement to hunt. This exception reflects a hunting norm that once the chase begins the deer or fox must be pursued to the bitter end; the hunt imperative thus takes precedence over the rights of landowners to deny access. A similar, judicial pro-hunt approach was adopted in the eighteenth-century case of *Gundry* v. *Feltham*.[9] There, the court declared that since fox were vermin, and it was for the public good to kill them, a person hunting might follow the fox into another's grounds.

While both of the above illustrations privilege hunting for reasons of 'ethical practice' and public policy rather than on account of individual freedoms, their bias towards hunting has been gradually superseded by an emphasis on landowners' rights. While non-permissive hunt entries onto land are rarely considered serious offences, they are deemed to harm private property interests, including the landowner's privileged entitlement to the deer.[10] In *Paul* v. *Summerhayes*,[11] Lord Coleridge declared that no right to trespass existed for hunters; fox hunting was subordinate to the ordinary rights of property, although consent could be express or 'assumed to be tacitly given'.[12] While this latter proviso may be worrying given the pressure hunts frequently place on rural residents,[13] questions also remained regarding the standard of culpability required for trespass, particularly where the entry onto private land was not by the hunt members themselves but by their hounds. Packs often run ahead in pursuit of quarry, causing the chased animal to flee; their trespass onto anti-hunt land, therefore, can seriously undermine the ability to establish deer sanctuaries regardless of whether the mounted hunt follows.

This problem was the subject of *League Against Cruel Sports* v. *Scott and Others*.[14] The League, a national organisation opposed to blood sports, owned unfenced land on Exmoor which offered sanctuary to wild deer. The local hunt were refused permission to enter, but nevertheless did so on several separate occasions. As a result, the League brought an action for an injunction against the hunt to stop them from entering their land. The question for the court was what level of intentionality was required to find the Hunt Master liable for the actions of the hounds. While Park J declared trespass had been proven, he refused to accept the League's claim that trespass in this context was a no-fault tort.[15]

From this brief outline, we can see that the courts' treatment of hunting is intimately concerned with private rights and expectations. Courts juggle the conflicting interests of hunts, landowners, sporting rights owners, and opponents according to a complex matrix of property rights and personal freedoms. Yet, while the private character of hunting tends to emerge within judicial discussion of trespass and sporting rights, it has also been articulated by the courts in other contexts. In the realm of trusts and revenue law, for instance, the promotion of fox-hunting has been held to be a valid private trust, despite the fact the courts have traditionally refused to recognise noncharitable purpose trusts.[16] More recently, the promotion of hunting was judicially declared a business activity under the VAT Act 1983. In *Customs and Excise Commissioners* v. *BFSS*,[17] the campaigning activities of the British Field Sports Society (BFSS), established in 1930 to oppose legislation against blood sports, were held to constitute business activities rather than the pursuit of ideological objectives. In this case, the court upheld the earlier decision of a value added tax tribunal which had declared, 'This is not a body ... formed to promote some object to be promoted for its own sake for the public good which solicits support from persons ... who do not, or not principally, join from any self-interested motives ... These members most certainly are self-interested.'[18] The court then went on to stress the private, non-political character of the BFSS submission:

> Mr Park [for the BFSS] submitted that the society was not the sort of society which exists to promote a cause or ideology in which its members believe as a matter of altruism. He did not put it this way, but he was arguing that it was not the sort of society whose members were not interested in the quid pro quo.[19]

In this case, the leading British pro-blood sports society gained financial benefit from portraying themselves as a private organisation bent on serving members' interests rather than as an organisation intended to benefit all supporters of field sports. This representation is an interesting one, given it is sharply at odds with the more familiar one field sports organisations promote. In this latter characterisation, their aim is not only to defend the activities of blood sport enthusiasts but to safeguard and promote the environmental, social and economic benefits of field sports (see Cooper 1997). That the BFSS dressed their argument according to members' self-interest is not surprising given the logic of litigation – one chooses the strongest legal argument, not the most effective political one. What is of perhaps more interest is that the court, reviewing the tribunal's decision, did not seriously consider the gap between the BFSS's legal characterisation and their more usual political one.

Public Interests – More than a Private Matter

In many ways, the British courts' treatment of hunting demonstrates the extent to which it exceeds private commercial rights and personal choice; indeed, the very status and protection of hunting as a 'private' activity can be seen as a public policy decision. There are three other ways in which hunting issues transcend private law. First, as Clark et al. (1994b) argue, the countryside is not a zone of pure, unadulterated freedom. People are regulated and controlled in their use of rural space, and this applies equally to field sports such as hunting. Traditionally, hunting was regulated through the state's selective confirmation of capacity to sport (Donnelly 1986; Peachey 1989: 1306; Thomas 1993: 37–38). Today, it is more constrained by restrictions on what can be hunted, how, and when. Yet, statutory protection and the involvement of the criminal law also raises other public policy questions. One case which reveals their interrelationship is *West London Magistrates' Court* v. *Royal Society for the Prevention of Cruelty to Animals*.[20] Under the Protection of Badgers Act 1992, hunts have to comply with specific rules in obstructing badger sett entrances in order not to harm badgers. In *West London Magistrates' Court*, the Master of the Beaufort Hunt had the landowner's permission to obstruct the entrance to badger setts so they could not be used by foxes escaping the hunt. The setts were blocked unlawfully and the badgers died. While the case implicitly raises questions about the degree of protection judges believe badgers should receive, the issue before the High Court concerned the *mens rea* for the offence. Henry LJ held that the Magistrates' Court was wrong to treat the Master as responsible for the actions of the 'earth stoppers' on the basis of strict liability:[21] 'The requisite mens rea, in our view, would require proof that the accused's [Master's] conduct at least encouraged the commission of the offence, whether intentionally or through conscious (advertent) recklessness.'[22]

Mere passivity by a Hunt Master in the face of previous complaints is not enough.[23] As in the *League Against Cruel Sports* case, the court in *West London Magistrates' Court* v. *RSPCA* rejected a lower standard of fault. This requirement for intentionality, knowledge or negligence reveals a judicial premise that hunting is fundamentally lawful and Hunt Masters' actions respectable. Thus, harm or damage caused by the hunt does not by itself generate a presumption of liability; indeed, injury to deer (or other animals) is an inevitable consequence of hunting. Given hunting's legal status, more than damage needs to be demonstrated; if Masters are to be 'criminalised' for hunt practices, their actions need to transgress judicially expected norms of conduct.

The second way in which judicial regulation of hunting raises policy issues beyond the 'private' domain of individual rights and liberties is in relation to hunting bans. In *League Against Cruel Sports*, the defendants questioned the right of property owners to buy sporting rights for the explicit purpose of denying hunts access to the land. The court rejected this argument stating that, regardless of the motive in purchasing the land, the League Against Cruel Sports were entitled to enjoy it without the hunt trespassing. At the same time, in *R.* v. *National Trust, ex p. Scott and others*, concerning the National Trust's controversial decision not to renew licenses for red deer hunting on land they owned in the West Country, the court did suggest 'that the Applicants had a legitimate expectation, engendered by past practice, that the licenses would be renewed, until and unless, deer hunting was outlawed' by Parliament.[24] In this case, the court declared they could not intervene for jurisdictional reasons; nevertheless Justice Tucker's words do suggest that property rights may, in some instances, be constrained by the historical expectations of hunting.

An example of where such constraints have been held to apply is in relation to state ownership. While the courts, this century, have tended to place property rights above the right or freedom to hunt where the two conflict, this approach has not been followed where the landowner is a public body. Instead of seeing this situation as involving a conflict between two parties wishing to use land in different ways, the courts have interpreted the situation as one where a public body uses unfair power to defeat private freedoms, rights and expectations. *Obiter* in the *National Trust* case in relation to a charitable body, this formed the *ratio* in the earlier case of *R. v. Somerset County Council, ex parte Fewings*[25] involving local government. *Fewings* concerned a decision by Somerset Council to ban deer hunting over land it owned in the Quantock Hills. The decision was based on several grounds, but a key factor was the majority perception within the council that hunting was not only unnecessary but also wrong due to the gratuitous cruelty it caused to deer. Both the High Court and Court of Appeal on a 2 to 1 majority held, however, that Somerset Council was *ultra vires* in attempting to ban hunting on grounds of cruelty. Local government's 'rights' as a property owner were not the same as those of an individual or private organisation.[26] While the latter could do as they wished providing the law did not say otherwise, public bodies, such as local government, could only act according to positive law.[27] The ability of a local council to regulate or restrict hunting had to be justified according to the statutory terms on which the land was held, in this case, s. 120(1)(b) Local Government Act 1972. The court held that reference in the section to the 'benefit, improvement or development of their area' meant land decisions must be made on managerial rather than ethical or political grounds (Cooper 1997).

One might argue that *Fewings* does not deny the private status of hunting, simply the private rights of public bodies. Indeed, it is arguable that the case *reinforces* hunting's private (and unaccountable) status by refusing councils the right to call hunts to account on ethical, political or moral grounds. Yet, this raises what kind of private status hunting across public land possesses. According to Justice Laws, the ban was analogous to intervening 'to regulate the morals of other people'.[28] To this extent, local government policies perceived as having an ideological orientation – the promotion of an alternative conception of the 'good life' – represent an inappropriate intrusion into private life. Alternatively, if hunting is not equivalent to private, moral activity, it can be seen as a form of private property right. Whilst hunting by itself constitutes an equivocal form of property since its lawfulness is entirely dependent on the holding of sporting rights or on receipt of permission from the holder,[29] the courts, in *Fewings*, implied that hunting's lawful status constituted it as a species of right in relation to a public body. As a form of legitimate entitlement, it could not be withdrawn except on juridically acceptable grounds.

In *Fewings*, the courts' implicit recognition of hunting's value enabled hunting to override other, 'private' practices and expectations. These included the interests and views of local councillors, as well as the right of local councils to represent (anti-hunting) majority interests within their locality:

> [The law] confers no entitlement on a local authority to impose its opinions about the morals of hunting on the neighbourhood. In the present state of the law those opinions, however sincerely felt, have their proper place only in the private conscience of those who entertain them. The council has been given no authority by Parliament to translate such views into public action ...[30]

Again, we might argue that this is simply an illustration of private hunting interests taking precedence over the majority's wishes, despite Justice Laws' characterisation of local politics as councillors' private opinions. However, not only is this preference a *public* judgment, but the differentiation between hunting and other 'private' activities suggests private status cannot alone be the reason for hunting's privileged standing.

Fewings thus goes beyond simply seeing hunting as a private activity. In so doing, it reflects wider hunting discourse. Hunt proponents and the courts, for generations, have identified positive public justifications for hunting (Cobham Resource Consultants 1992; Thomas 1993: 240–244; Cooper 1997: 675–677). Hunting is seen as leading to the removal of vermin (Itzkowitz 1977: 17). Indeed, during the First World War, officers got leave during the hunting season (Itzkowitz 1977: 21), while in the Second World War, hunters were released from military duties to cull fox cubs in order to protect lambing.[31] The need to cull in a controlled way to protect agriculture has been a repeated argument of fox and deer hunts who argue that if hunting is banned, farmers will simply kill wildlife crossing their land, thereby, in the case of deer, jeopardising the (desirable) continuation of local herds.[32] A second justification, in relation to deer hunting, is that culling maintains the good health of the deer. This argument resembles a form of eugenic biopolitics: killing in the name of the species. Hunting is also seen as developing community bonds.³³ Hunts provide a matrix of hierarchical rural community; they also organise the social and economic events that sustain community ties.

However, to understand fully the special status accorded to hunting, we have to recognise its articulation to the land.³⁴ In *Fewings*, Justice Laws, in particular, stressed hunting's historical relationship to the land: 'The hunt has been an established part of the scene in the area in question at least since the 1920s.'³⁵ In describing the land, he identified it not by name but through its relationship to the central, defining feature: 'the territory over which red deer are most regularly hunted by the staghounds'.³⁶ In this sense, hunting is more than an activity asking to be validated by the courts and public policy; it is, rather, embedded in the very conception of country(side) and soil (see Daniels and Watkins 1993: 19–20).³⁷

This does not mean, as the courts in *Fewings* recognised, that hunting cannot be legitimately restricted if shown to harm the land or its fauna, or seriously to obstruct others' enjoyment;³⁸ what it does mean, however, is that hunting is not a nuisance *a priori*. For nuisance relates to activities and people that do not belong – that can be severed from the soil.³⁹ Tim Creswell offers a useful analysis of this relationship in connection with Newbury residents' responses to Greenham Common peace camp. While many locals referred to the camp as an eyesore, the military base with its miles of barbed wire remained unproblematised:

> The air base, after all, had been part of the landscape for as long as most Newbury residents could remember – it had become part of the taken-for-granted landscape, part of the geographical doxa ... So while the air base had come to simply exist as part of the landscape, the women were perceived as intrusions. (Creswell 1996: 132)

It is this lack of belonging which allows gypsies also to be identified as a nuisance. In *Costello* v. *Dacorum D.C.*, referred to in *Fewings* for its discussion of the same statutory section, s.120(1)(b) Local Government Act 1972, Lord Justice Lawton declared:

> [The council] were clearly alive to the need to ensure that people living in the area were not offended by or caused nuisance by gypsy sites ... The site had long been ... an eyesore. It gave offence, because of what was done on it, to large numbers of people living in the neighbourhood. The council were under pressure from the ratepayers to do something about the site ...⁴⁰

In this judgment, gypsies and travellers are juxtaposed against local people. The former are not considered residents of the area; their rights therefore are limited to narrow statutory protection rather than included within a wider interpretation of local benefit. Gypsies are, thus, disarticulated from the soil. While their nomadic lifestyle could be seen as a basis for linking them to the land, it is used here as the grounds for their extrication (cf. Sibley 1997: 228). Perceived as ethnically and culturally other, they are identified as parasitic, sullying the land for those who *do* belong. By contrast, hunting, far from being parasitic, is treated as productive of the countryside landscape. Any harm caused by hunting to the rural environment − for instance, soil erosion, damage to plants, and to wildlife from the mounted hunt or followers in four-wheel drives − is seen as capable of being separated from the essence of the hunt. While gypsies and travellers are perceived as intrinsically damaging to the rural environment and therefore incapable of reform, the hunt at its purist form is in tune with, rather than at odds with, nature.

The final way in which hunting cases have exceeded private law that I wish to discuss concerns saboteuring. On the one hand, saboteuring raises private law issues in the form of trespass. However, 'sabing' also raises public concerns, particularly in the way it has been constituted as a public order matter involving (likely) breaches of the peace,[41] and, more recently, as aggravated trespass.[42] Several commentators have discussed the detrimental impact of the Criminal Justice and Public Order Act 1994 on saboteurs and other civil trespassers, such as New Age Travellers (see Allen and Cooper 1995; Halfacree 1996; Sibley 1997). Sibley (1997: 221) also highlights the symbolic meaning of trespass − city people intruding where they are unwanted; thus the criminal trespass laws provide a symbolic way of fortifying the rural against urban encroachment.

The use of the criminal law in this context also has a further function: to fortify order − private ownership, discipline, and traditional activities − against the disregard and challenge travellers and saboteurs pose to conservative norms and values. A similar approach is evident in the case of *R. v. Coventry City Council, ex p. Phoenix Aviation and others*.[43] Involving a series of three interlinked applications, the case concerned whether public authorities could ban the flight and shipment of livestock in order to avoid the disruptive actions of animal rights protesters. The court held that they could not. Simon Brown LJ, in giving his decision, declared that authorities should not surrender to 'the dictates of unlawful pressure groups' or 'mob rule'.[44] The 'rule of law', the 'legitimate interests' of 'lawful trade', and the 'historic role' of Dover port[45] are all threatened by public action that appears to acquiesce to protest. In his judgment, animal rights activists are not only perceived as dis-ordered, they are also constituted as extraneous to the community. According to Simon Brown LJ, activists are mobile, migrating to the places where their activities appear likely to generate success; in contrast local landscapes are defined by their relationship to historical continuity, trade and legality. Thus order, tradition and community are articulated together to define the outsider as inherently disruptive. The same approach is apparent in judicial responses to saboteurs. Hunting's relationship to order – its role in sustaining and reflecting traditional social forms – means it is the opponents of hunting, rather than hunters, who are equated with disorder. It is they who disrupt the 'healthy' workings of the rural body politic, and are thus subject to the criminalising effects of public order legislation.[46]

The Private Reproduction of Culture and Nation

I have explored so far the ways in which the courts treat hunting as both a private freedom and a public good. To what extent is this inconsistent and incoherent? Within the terms of liberal discourse, it might be argued that this kind of tension is not unusual. Freedoms and property rights are always bounded; within a modern polity, the private invariably intersects public agendas and forms of regulation. What does it mean then to talk about a private domain? If its existence, distribution and boundaries are determined by the public – if it can be penetrated at any time in pursuit of public concerns – to what extent does it constitute a domain of freedom and non-accountability?

In this discussion, I wish to adopt a different approach, to shift our understanding of juridical conceptions of the private away from a focus on non-regulation, non-intervention and non-accountability. Instead, I wish to consider the private as the domain of 'naturalised' nation-work. However, before discussing the rural's relationship to cultural reproduction further, let me make three initial points. First, my focus is less on *actual* rural practices than on the symbolic role the rural plays within liberal nation-state discourse.[47] Second, the courts do not always interpret the rural as the domain of 'natural' cultural reproduction; however, this interpretation does underlie many of their responses to deer hunting. Third, the private – or rural – domain is not the only place in which cultural reproduction occurs. However, what is important for my analysis is the specific role the rural plays within liberal discourse.

Identifying the domestic private domain as a place of reproduction is not new. Drawing on Marxist perspectives, feminists in the 1970s and early 1980s explored the role women and the domestic realm play in reproducing a labour force. Subsequently, feminists extended this analysis to encompass the role of the home and family within processes of cultural reproduction, for instance in relation to sustaining ethnic identities (Anthias and Yuval-Davis, 1989).[48] Not only is the private a place where norms, customs, and conventions can be reproduced, but the private's articulation to affectivity, the non-political, and the normal allows these norms and rituals – as well as the wider social practices to which they are linked – to appear natural and uncontestable. For instance, the traditional celebration of Christian festivals not only reproduces ethnic cultural-religious practices, but also conservative kinship norms.[49]

Equivalent practices occur in the analogous private realm of the rural. At first glance, it may seem as if the rural would be better understood as public in contrast to the privatised city. After all, the city is the presumed place of anomie and alienation compared to the communal ties of rural life. This is not, however, the approach I am adopting.[50] The symbolic analogy between the rural and the domestic domain are evident in several ways. First, both rural and home are imagined as historically static, past places – subjects of romantic idealising as well as ridicule. There is a gendered dimension to this too, since in both cases men symbolically leave the private behind for the ostensibly impartial, detached, cultivated character of public (city) life.[51] Second, both rural and home are rhetorically linked to the propagation of conservative religious and traditional values (see Ramet 1996). Third, access to both are predicated on affective qualities of belonging. While the public domain is formally open to all, private space allows users to regulate access according to non-rational criteria. Linked to this is the fact that both home and rural are perceived as bearing and reproducing national identity (Cloke and Park 1985; Lowenthal 1991; Miller 1995; Ramet 1996): the place where race and ethnic essence is protected and sustained. In this sense, despite the rhetorical linking of the countryside to the people – our heritage and national treasure – the rural is, in many ways, far less open. As those arguing for a right to roam repeatedly rediscover, the countryside is not 'public' space. More symbolically, it also does not belong to us all equally. Rather, it is structured around a homogenous ethnicity which is tied to a historic relationship to the soil. Within this context, cities may be culturally pluralistic; they can even be encouraged as such. National identity remains untroubled, so long as rural areas remain predominantly White and Anglo-Protestant.[52]

Thus, just as the workplace and public life is dependent on the cultural reproduction that takes place within the home, so cities are dependent on the racialised, cultural reproduction symbolically associated with the countryside. In other words, the urban and rural cannot be reduced to a conflictual relationship (cf. Ramet 1996: 72), despite the symbolic threat the uncontainable city poses to the continuity of country 'traditions' such as hunting (Sibley 1997: 220). Urban and rural are culturally interdependent; they take their meanings from each other. Not only does the countryside define city life by constituting its antithesis, but the rural safeguarding of a national essence allows the urban to express cosmopolitan values with safety.

The countryside also helps purify the cities, like blood purified through filtration. This can take a practical form – people leave congested centres for the countryside's fresh air. However, even this carries a cultural and racial subtext: for dirt, decay and city pollution have historically signified, within discourses of nation and race, immigration and ethnic diversity. Within this set of meanings, visiting or moving to the countryside represents city-dwellers' attempts to re-establish links with the blood and soil of the land, to find themselves once more – away from hybridity and difference – in the archetypal national subject.

The association between the rural and national identity does not mean the city plays no part in attempting to reproduce national identity. Urban nation-work also takes place; closely linked to state action, it tends to be the product of direct or midway governing, through legislation, funding and institutional negotiations (cf. Rose 1996; Cooper 1998a). The difference with the rural is that it, the countryside, appears to reproduce national identity non-juridically, in other words, not through state diktat but through duty, love and honour (Everett 1994; Lash and Urry 1994: 293–295) – through the affective emotions people in proximity feel for their land and soil. The *conscious* deployment, management and commodification of the country-side to reflect 'national' values (Lowenthal 1991: 215–217, 218; Everett 1994: 38, 45) is thus shrouded within dominant legal and political discourse. Instead, the rural is perceived to operate through feeling, emotion and the unquestioning repetition of traditional practices.[53]

So where does hunting fit within this picture? My argument is that, with some minor exceptions, the courts protect hunting because it is deemed integral to the role performed by the symbolic rural. Hunting, as both ritual, landscape and socio-economic organisation, facilitates the cultural functioning of the country(side). At this level, despite its association with community, tradition and visibility, hunting is a private not public activity. Its participation within the processes of racialised, cultural reproduction takes the self-governing form associated with nature, emotion and partiality in contrast to the impersonal, rational, instrumentalist reproduction of the city.

At the same time, the maintenance of our national identity, in a context of ever-growing pluralist, public spaces, depends upon the capacity of hunting and other traditions to link 'us' to a past. In this sense it is a *public* good. The role of hunting in the maintenance and protection of a national essence explains why hunting by different people receives differential treatment. It is not the culling of animals *per se* which is significant, but that the country-side remain 'true' to itself – continuing the 'reproductive'[54] activities and social relations practised for generations. Thus, hunting consists of more than culling and physical exercise, it also offers a hierarchical, conservative structure, a capacity to identify and determine community borders, and a romanticist picture of a countryside that has not changed despite the increasing pace of transformation within city life.

Conclusion

1997 was not a good year for hunting. First, the National Trust decided, after years of debate, to withdraw deer hunting licences across its land; then, a private member's bill came before Parliament proposing the outlawing of hunting. The long-term effects of these actions – and the 'countryside's subsequent fight-back'[55] – remain to be seen. However, one thing is clear. In the face of attacks on hunting from the voluntary sector, MPs and local government over the past decade, the courts have remained broadly sympathetic to hunting's continuation. We might identify reasons for this in the judiciary's own involvement,[56] despite their professions of neutrality; however, my analysis in this chapter has focused not on personal practice but on judicial reasoning and discourse. From this perspective, the courts defended hunting on the grounds of individual liberty and private property rights. At the same time, underlying their emphasis on personal autonomy were public policy considerations. Hunting has never been a freedom for all but regulated in a range of complex ways.

Yet, my focus on the judiciary's capacity to safeguard traditional, elite hunting forms does not invariably mean the courts possess a high degree of autonomy. The cases discussed in this paper scarcely stand out as juridical anomalies. The principles used to defend hunting from political and civil attack are embedded within the English common law. At the same time, the judiciary have skewed conventional notions of property rights, individual liberty, limited state authority, and public order, to protect hunting. With some exceptions, this has occurred in three main ways. First, in cases involving hunting interests, judicial reasoning tends to favour pro-hunt arguments. Second, principles such as trespass and *mens rea* have been interpreted and developed in ways that reflect a belief in the basic legitimacy of hunting and other blood sports. Third, at a discursive level, concepts such as liberty, hunting, nuisance, cruelty, harm and public order have been judicially imagined in ways that identify hunting as essentially benign, in contrast to the activities of, for instance, saboteurs and traveller communities.

My focus in this chapter has been on the way discourses of public and private became interwoven in the course of judicial reasoning. This process goes beyond the cases that directly address hunting's legitimacy and authority, such as *League Against Cruel Sports* and *Fewings*, to include the range of other cases that raise blood sport issues in the context of company law, taxation, employment rights, conveyances and public order.

In addition, I have explored the role of hunting within the symbolical private domain of the rural. We might see hunting, here, as analogous to family Christmases – a cultural anchor that diffuses the threat posed by urban multiculturalism. Yet, to the extent that hunting performs this functional role within the rural, it is also vulnerable to changing requirements. The rural may be depicted, like the home, as constant and unchanging; nevertheless, the symbolic meanings required of it do vary.

The contested character of what counts as hunting can be seen in the early twentieth-century case of *Rodgers* v. *Pickersgill* concerning deer cruelty.[57] The decision turned on whether the cruelty occurred during the course of hunting or on its completion, the former, interestingly, being exempted from the Act. While one judge held that cruelty had taken place in an endeavour to make the deer run and thus was part of the hunt, the majority decision questioned whether dragging a deer out of a yard, where it had taken shelter, into a road, and then along the road could be defined as occurring in the course of hunting. Lord Coleridge declared, 'To make s.4 [the hunting exemption] cover any such acts would enable persons to perpetrate any form of torture, or any form of cruelty, in order to make an animal run which had taken refuge.'[58] This case illustrates the extent to which the courts will police the boundaries of acceptable hunting. For by distancing the 'normal' from more excessive versions, they thereby define cruelty as outside the parameters of the regular hunting experience.

It is possible, however, that hunting's downfall will come when it no longer fits within the symbolic performance required of rural life. Despite hunting's hard work to sustain its legitimacy according to ever-changing requirements – for instance, in recent years, according to norms of egalitarianism, conservationism, responsibility and economic productivity – its ability to adapt continually, while still sustaining the legitimacy that comes from consistency, is doubtful. Yet, while hunting may eventually prove unable to keep up with the symbolic requirements made upon the private rural domain, to what extent is it helpful to think of the rural as private? When feminists have powerfully critiqued the existence of a public/private divide for years, is it wise to resurrect it in this context?

It should be clear from my analysis that I am not using the term 'private' in connection with the countryside to mean non-accountability or non-regulation; rather I use it to refer to the rural as a domain in which cultural reproduction is *perceived* to occur according to 'natural' processes. This symbolic rural function thus raises wider issues than simply whether hunting should or should not continue. It goes to the heart of broader questions about the nature of British identity. Just as feminists have argued that the reproductive work of the home needs transforming if wider social relations are to change, radical multiculturalism requires that the reproductive work of the rural be dismantled. For it is one thing to promote multiculturalism in the cities while the rural domain, the symbolic anchor of White, Anglo-Christianity, remains untouched. It is another to take cultural pluralism and equality into the heart of the country(side).

Notes

1   Thanks to Didi Herman and the editors of this volume for their useful comments.
2   [1995] 1 All ER 513 at 530.
3   See for instance, *Beckwith* v. *Shoardike and Hutch* 4 BURR. 2093 (1767); *R.* v. *Pratt* 4 EL. & BL. 856 (1855) for a case concerning criminal trespass which distinguishes it from civil trespass; see also *Pratt* v. *Martin* JP vol. 85 (1911) 328; and *Jemmison* v. *Priddle* [1972] 1 QB 489 concerning the shooting of deer over another's land where no permission has been granted contrary to s. 4 Game Licenses Act 1860.
4   In *Inglewood Investment Company* v. *Forestry Commissioners* [1989] 1 All ER 1, for instance, the court had to decide whether a reservation using the term 'game' included deer.
5   S.C. 34 L.J.C.P. 261 (1865).
6   19 C.B. (N.S.) 248.
7   Pro-hunt forces have adopted a similar strategy of buying up sporting rights. In some instances this has meant hunting takes place across the land of people opposed to hunting. On the work of such a pro-hunt body, see Bonham Carter 1991: 118.
8   *The Guardian*, 11 April 1997; *The Observer*, 13 April 1997; *The Times*, 22 August 1997. According to press reports, the NT refusal to reissue licences to local hunts has impacted significantly on deer hunting and culling in Exmoor and the Quantocks, see *The Guardian*, 3 October 1997; *The Independent*, 25 November 1997.
9   (1786) I.T.R. 334.
10 See for instance *Jemmison* v. *Priddle* [1972] 1 QB 489.
11 (1878) 4 QBD 9.
12 See also *Essex* v. *Capel* (1809); *Baker* v. *Berkeley* 3 CAR. & P. 32 (1827).
13 At the same time, it is important to recognise the power of rural authority which may supersede the formal legal position. For instance, traditionally pressure was placed on farmers to allow hunts to ride over their land, to acquiesce to property damage such as to fences, and to avoid measures that hindered or endangered the pursuit of prey. See Itzkowitz (1977: 69, 122–125).
14 [1985] 2 All ER 489. See also *Calvert* v. *Gosling* (1889) 5 TLR 185, DC where Lord Coleridge CJ said at 186, 'That was an undertaking [that is, to refrain from going on the plaintiffs' lands] which it was impossible to keep literally, for no one could keep the fox from going in any direction or the hounds from following it ... Under those circumstances it was not a case for an interim injunction, for no case was shown of an *intention to trespass* on the lands of the plaintiffs' (emphasis added).
15 Park J held trespass existed where a Master of the Hunt deliberately took a pack of hounds in pursuit of a quarry knowing there was a real risk of hounds entering the prohibited grounds and either intended them to enter the land or, through failing to exercise proper control of them, caused them to enter the land.

See also *Read* v. *Edwards* (1864) [S.C. 34 L.J.C.P. 31] where an owner was held liable for the action of his dog in entering another's wood and destroying young pheasants. Willes J held that liability was based on the fact the owner knew the dog was of 'peculiarly mischievous disposition ... and the destruction of the game, was the natural and immediate result of the animal's peculiarly mischievous disposition, which his owner knew of, and did not control'. Does this case hold the dog owner to a higher standard than in the *League Against Cruel Sports* case, reflecting, perhaps, more sympathy for the pheasant owner than for those running a deer sanctuary?

16 In *Re Thompson, Public Trustee* v. *Lloyd* [1934] 1 Ch. 342. In general, only charitable trusts can exist as purpose trusts where there is no human beneficiary.
17 *Customs and Excise Commissioners* v. *British Field Sports Society* QBD [1997] STC 746.
18 Ibid.
19 Ibid.
20 14 December 1994, QBD, lexis.
21 Ibid.
22 Henry LJ, ibid.
23 Ibid.
24 Tucker J, *R.* v. *National Trust, ex p. Scott and Others*, QBD 16 July 1997, lexis, of *Scott and others* v. *National Trust* [1998] 2 All ER 705 at 715, where the court recognised that the hunt's active involvement in management of the deer, inter alia, gave them a sufficient interest to bring charity proceedings.
25 [1995] 1 All ER 513, upheld [1995] 3 All Er 20.
26 [1995] 3 All ER 20, Bingham LJ at 25, 28.
27 [1995] 1 All ER 513, Laws J at 524.
28 Ibid. Laws J at 530.
29 For the law on this point, see *Palmer* v. *Fletcher* (1663) 1 Lev 122; *Thomas* v. *Sorrell* (1672) Vaugh. 330; *Muskett* v. *Hill* (1839) 5 Bing NC 694; *Wood* v. *Leadbitter* (1845) 13 M. & W. 838; *Winter Garden Theatre (London) Ltd.* v. *Millennium Productions Ltd.* [1948] AC 173; see also Gray (1993, ch. 19); Rogers (1994: 390–392); Stanton (1994: 378–379); Smith (1996: 439–446).
30 *R.* v. *Somerset County Council, ex p. Fewings* [1995] 1 All ER 513, Laws J at 529–530. Though cf *R.* v. *Reading BC, ex p. Quietlynn Ltd* (1986) 85 LGR 387, in relation to the licensing of a sex shop, where it was held that one role for local councillors was to express their views on subjects of local interest.
31 See *Plas Machynlleth Fox Destruction Society* v. *MAFF* 4 ITR 364 (1969).
32 There is some suggestion that this has occurred since the introduction of the National Trust ban on hunting in the Quantocks and Exmoor.
33 See the Savage Report to the National Trust Council, March 1993, para 12.11.
34 Hunting is perceived by proponents as having shaped the land – its needs have structured the organisation of rural flora; in addition, through its close scrutiny and traversing of the soil, through its management of wild animals in the name of the species, hunts apply a form of governance and stewardship (see Cooper 1998a). They are thus more than a private activity or civic group.
35 Laws J [1995] 1 All ER 513 at 516.
36 Ibid.
37 See also *Forster and Another* v. *Simpson, Bailey* v. *Same* [1984] RA 85, Lands Tribunal referring to *Manton Stables Rating Case* (1930) – if a man is a hunting man with a long string of horses, can anyone suppose that exercising them for the coming hunting season is using land other than as a meadow or pasture land.
38 Laws J [1995] 1 All ER 513 at 525.
39 For instance, the use of mountain bikes on rural land does not have the same status within a dominant imagery as does hunting; they are defined as incompatible with more 'natural' activities, see G. Clark et al., 1994a: 14.

40 (1982) 81 LGR 1 at 5, 10.
41 See for instance, *Pease and Another* v. *Chief Constable of the Avon and Somerset Constabulary* QBD, 10 July 1986, lexis; *R.* v. *Blandford Magistrates' Court, ex p. Pamment* [1991] 1 All ER 218.
42 See *Winder and Others* v. *DPP*, *The Times*, 14 August 1996.
43 [1995] 3 All ER 37.
44 Ibid. pp. 62, 63.
45 See the interlinked application, *R.* v. *Dover Harbour Board, ex p. Peter Gilder & Sons and anor* [1995] 3 All ER 37.
46 In *R.* v. *Kirkham and Another*, 26 March 1996, lexis, hunt supporters were prosecuted for violent disorder; however, this was a case where a saboteur was attacked.
47 For useful discussion of the former, see Mansfield (1995); Cloke and Little (1997). See also Sibley (1997: 219) who argues that dominant visions of the rural are not static but change according to context, for instance, whether the historical juncture is one of crisis or not.
48 In Britain, these processes may be most apparent in relation to minority communities, however they also occur in relation to the White, Anglo majority.
49 For example, Christmas is a time when people are supposed to *be* with their (biological) families. Thus, social families and ties of friendship are demoted as people 'return to' core (authentic) kinship structures.
50 Elsewhere, I have argued for a normative conception of public space as the places where people come together positively as equal strangers (Cooper 1998b). I would argue that this is more likely to occur in cities than in the rural where positive regard and inclusion are dependent on a process of becoming known or familiar that may also take generations.
51 Hunting plays a role here in that, during the early period of industrialisation, it was seen as a way of keeping the gentry from spending all their time in the cities.
52 For a critique of the symbolic notion of the rural as White, see Agyeman and Spooner (1997). However, despite their perceptive analysis of the exclusionary and racialised effects of rural life and discourse, their analysis ignores the religious dimension of this identification. In other words, the place of the church and Christian traditions within the (symbolic) rural generate their own particular forms of exclusion.
53 Does this make the rural feminine in a way that is analogous to the ideological feminisation of hearth and home? On the one hand, the rural is associated with the feminine attributes of nature, irrationality and passion in contrast to the masculine city; on the other, its links with nature – 'red in tooth and claw' etc. – render it a place of essential violence. According to Itzkowitz (1977: 20, 22) in the mid-nineteenth century, the countryside was associated with hardy, masculine values in contrast to the softer, effeminate, and foreign character of the city. For a useful discussion of the contradictory role of women within discourses of city, rural and nation, in the context of Ireland, see Nash (1996: 70–74).

Hunting itself relies on an opposition between wild, feminised nature and the cultivated chase of man which nearly always prevails, see Cartmill (1995: 784). However, the stag is also gendered in contradictory ways, Aldin (1935), for instance, refers to the (implicitly masculine) nobility of the stag, while describing hinds as the perfect mother.
54 By this I mean those forms of field sports that are seen within liberal discourse as beneficial and sustaining, rather than those perceived as anomalous, gratuitous and cruel.
55 On 1 March 1998, a national demonstration was held in London in defence of country-

side interests. While the pro-hunting lobby was a major participant, mobilisation also related to other perceived attacks on rural interests, such as restrictions on the sale of British beef, closure of village schools, the 'right to roam', and new residential developments on 'green-field' sites.

56 For one example of this, see 'Groom takes Judge to Tribunal', *Daily Telegraph* 6 January 1998. Sir John Chadwick claimed he had to give up hunting because of time constraints on being appointed an appellate judge. The case concerned unfair dismissal of a former groom.
57 This case concerned s. 2 of the Wild Animals in Captivity Protection Act 1900, see [KBD] Justice of the Peace (Reports) 13 August 1910, vol. 74: 324–326.
58 Ibid., Lord Coleridge J at 326.

References

Agyeman, J. and Spooner, R. (1997) 'Ethnicity and the Rural Environment', in Cloke and Little (eds) (1997).
Aldin, C. (1935) *Exmoor: The Riding Playground of England* (London: HF and G Witherby).
Allen, M. and Cooper, S. (1995) 'Howard's Way – A Farewell to Freedom?' *Modern Law Review*, 58: 364–388.
Anthias, F. and N. Yuval-Davis (1989), 'Introduction', in Yuval-Davis, N. and Anthias, F. (eds), *Woman – Nation – State* (Basingstoke: Macmillan).
Blomley, N. and Bakan, J. (1992) 'Spacing Out: Towards a Critical Geography of Law', *Osgoode Hall Law Journal*, 30: 661–690.
Bonham Carter, V. (1991) *The Essence of Exmoor* (Somerset: Exmoor Press).
Broad, J. (1988) 'Whigs and Deer-stealers in other Guises: A Return to the Origins of the Black Act', *Past and Present*, 119: 56–72.
Cartmill, M. (1995) 'Hunting and Humanity in Western Thought', *Social Research*, 62: 773–786.
Clark, G. et al. (1994a) *Leisure Landscapes: Leisure, Culture and the English Countryside: Challenges and Conflicts* (Lancaster: Lancaster University).
Clark, G. et al. (1994b) *Leisure Landscapes. Leisure, Culture and the English Countryside: Challenges and Conflicts* (London: CPRE).
Cloke, P. and Park, C. (1985) *Rural Resource Management* (Beckenham: Croom Helm).
Cloke, P. and Little, J. (eds) (1997) *Contested Countryside Cultures* (London: Routledge).
Cobham Resource Consultants (1992) *Country Sports: Their Economic and Conservation Significance* (Reading: Standing Conference on Countryside Sports).
Cooper, D. (1994) *Sexing the City; Lesbian and Gay Politics within the Activist State* (London: Rivers Oram).
Cooper, D. (1997) '"For the Sake of the Deer": Land, Local Government and the Hunt', *Sociological Review*, 45: 668–689.
Cooper, D. (1998a) *Governing Out of Order: Space, Law and the Politics of Belonging* (London: Rivers Oram).

Cooper, D. (1998b) 'Regard between Strangers: Diversity, Equality and the Reconstruction of Public Space', *Critical Social Policy*, 57: 463–491.
Cox, G. (1993) 'Shooting a Line?: Field Sports and Access Struggles in Britain', *Journal of Rural Studies*, 9: 267–276.
Creswell, T. (1996) *In Place/Out of Place* (Minneapolis: University of Minnesota Press).
Daniels, S. and Watkins, C. (1993) 'Friends of the Earth?' *Geographical*, November: 16–20.
Donnelly, P. (1986) 'The Paradox of Parks: Politics of Recreational Land Use before and after the Mass Trespass', *Leisure Studies*, 5: 211–231.
Everett, N. (1994) *The Tory View of Landscape* (New Haven: Yale University Press).
Gray, K. (1993) *Elements of Land Law* 2nd edn (London: Butterworths).
Gray, K. (1994) 'Equitable Property', *Current Legal Problems*, 47: 157–214.
Halfacree, K. (1996) 'Out of Place in the Country: Travellers and the "Rural Idyll"', *Antipode*, 28: 42–73.
Harrison, G. (1991) *Countryside Recreation in a Changing Society* (Bristol: TMS Partnership).
Itzkowitz, D. (1977) *Peculiar Privilege: A Social History of English Foxhunting, 1753–1885* (Hassocks, Sussex: Harvester Press).
Lacey, N. (1993) 'Theory into Practice? Pornography and the Public/Private Dichotomy', *Journal of Law and Society*, 20: 93–113.
Lash, S. and Urry, J. (1994) *Economies of Signs and Space* (London: Sage).
Lowenthal, D. (1991) 'British National Identity and the English Landscape', *Rural History*, 2: 205–230.
Manning, R. (1993) *Hunters and Poachers: A Social and Cultural History of Unlawful Hunting* (Oxford: Clarendon).
Mansfield, N. (1995) 'Class Conflict and Village War Memorials, 1914–24', *Rural History*, 6: 67–87.
Miller, S. (1995) 'Land, Landscape and the Question of Culture: English Urban Hegemony and Research Needs', *Journal of Historical Sociology*, 8: 94–107.
Nash, C. (1996) 'Looking Commonplace: Gender, Modernity and National Identity', *Renaissance and Modern Studies*, 39: 61–77.
O'Donovan, K. (1985) *Sexual Divisions in Law* (London: Weidenfeld and Nicolson).
Pateman, C. (1989) *The Disorder of Women* (Cambridge: Polity).
Peachey, B. (1989) 'Game Poaching Law (1)', *Solicitors Journal*, 133: 1306–1310.
Ramet, S. (1996) 'Nationalism and the "Idiocy" of the Countryside: The Case of Serbia', *Ethnic and Racial Studies*, 19: 70–87.
Rogers, W. (1994) *Winfield and Jolowicz on Tort*, 14th edn (London: Sweet and Maxwell).
Rose, N. (1996) 'Governing "Advanced" Liberal Democracies', in Barry, A. et al. (eds) *Foucault and Political Reason* (London: UCL Press).
Shoard, M. (1987) *This Land is Our Land* (London: Paladin).
Sibley, D. (1997) 'Endangering the Sacred: Nomads, Youth Cultures and the English Countryside', in Cloke and Little (eds) (1997).
Smith, R. (1996) *Property Law* (London: Longman).

Stanton, K. (1994) *The Modern Law of Tort* (London: Sweet and Maxwell).
Thomas, R. (1993) *The Politics of Hunting* (Aldershot: Gower).
Thompson, E.P. (1975) *Whigs and Hunters: The Origins of the Black Act* (London: Allen Lane).
Thornton, M. (1995) *Public and Private: Feminist Legal Debates* (Melbourne: Oxford University Press).

5 Hedgerows, Laws and Cultural Landscape

Jane Holder

Introduction

The relationship between law and landscape is generally considered in terms of the legal regulation of land use and development. This is to tell an incomplete story: law has left enduring marks on the landscape and continues to shape the physical environment. As links between the critical traditions in law and geography are made, so this relationship between law and landscape becomes a little clearer (Blomley and Balkan 1992; Cooper 1998).

'Landscape' has many meanings.[1] At least two might be mentioned here in order to provide a schema by which law's relationship with landscape may be explored. The first refers to the surface features of an area, including both natural elements (for example, landform, water, soil, flora and fauna) and artificial objects (for example, settlements, roads, dams, canals) shaped by natural processes and human activities. The second meaning is that landscape is the group of visible features of an area from an observer's viewpoint, defined by forms, lines, colours and textures, which provide a framework for the interpretation of nature and culture ('the inner landscape'). The latter recognises that landscape stimulates the visual senses and may alter according to individuals' differing perspectives, histories and experiences. In this sense, landscape is inseparable from human perception; it is 'the work of the mind' (Schama 1996: 7).

The indivisibility of landscape and people was expressed in the Dutch word *landschap* which entered the English language as 'landskip' at the end of the sixteenth century, meaning, pragmatically, a unit or jurisdiction of human occupation (Schama 1996: 10). Human use and habitation of land was therefore at the core of the original meaning of the word. This prevails in the idea of cultural landscapes, that is, landscape as a product of the interaction between people and nature. Very few landscapes have not been touched by people: some have been artifically created, others transformed and shaped by human practices and land uses (Bennett 1996). Thinking more imaginatively, rather than landscapes representing or being shaped by cultural influences, the set of values and ideas held by a social group at a particular time and place, landscape may be thought to be culture. This understanding is a development of the second meaning of landscape. Because observation or perception makes the difference between raw matter and landscape, differentiating between a natural landscape and a cultural landscape makes little sense, unless non-human values and interests are at issue. The cultural power of landscape is such that it has accordingly been used to invoke the major concerns of modernity – nation, freedom, liberty and state – in ways which may be idealised, and dangerous when abused[2] (see also Coates 1993).

Using the case of the hedgerow, the aim of this chapter is to show that law conceives of landscape only in the first sense of surface features of an area. This means that a sense of landscape as perspective, and cultural signifier, is absent in legal regimes for its protection. This feeds into current debates on the state of the environment and its protection. First, using the case of the hedgerow to trace the legal protection of landscape reveals law's part in defining what is meant by 'nature'. I examine the way in which law considers hedgerows to be little more than the sum of their parts – trees, fauna and flora – and 'nature' as constitutive of these. The cultural significance of the hedgerow, as an essential part of an idealised rural picture, and as representative of a particular locality is not registered. The main argument is that by failing to take account of the social and cultural importance of the hedgerow, law can take only a narrow view of the meanings of 'natural' attributed to them, and thereby ignores that nature may be created by culture, the categories of the natural always being open (Evernden 1993).

The second issue raised by this chapter is the status of hedgerows as commons. Strikingly, although many hedgerows were planted to give effect to enclosure by excluding peasants from common lands and demarcating the boundaries of property, they are now considered to be 'commons' themselves, part of the shared natural heritage (Countryside Commission 1994a). There is therefore considerable continuity between the issues and problems which arose from their planting and those which arise from their loss in modern times: the meaning and nature of threats to the commons, the exclusion of groups from decisions about the future of land, and the capability of law, typically concerned with the protection of individual property rights, to protect 'commons'.

I discuss law's shaping and protection of the physical environment and the issues outlined above in three parts. First, I locate the hedgerow in the landscape by considering its historical, ecological and cultural importance.

Second, I examine legal mechanisms for the protection of landscape. Using the case of hedgerows, I review the main, but belated, legislative response to their loss, The Hedgerows Regulations 1997.[3] This pursues a crude approach to the protection of 'important' hedgerows through the counting of species and features. The law therefore fails to capture the social and cultural importance of hedgerows for particular localities. I consider that this approach typifies the narrowness of legal definitions and conceptions of landscape, particularly when compared with non-legal meanings and understandings which emphasise the relationships between people, nature and landscape. Even before the Regulations were made, however, the recognition of the conservation value of the hedgerow meant that laws, some ancient, were employed by individuals. In the final section of this chapter, I compare this piecemeal, but creative, use of law with the protection accorded by the current legislation.

The Hedgerow in Landscape

As ancient forests began to be cleared for agriculture in prehistoric Britain, hedges were left as the skeletons of these woods, their edges creating field boundaries. In late Saxon and Norman times (c.440–1066), more woodland was removed to clear space for open field strip farming, leaving hedges as barriers to control the movement of livestock (Elworthy 1990). Beyond the open fields was common land subject to shared rights by villagers to gather wood and berries, and to mow grass for hay to feed their stock and for grazing. Many of these open fields and commons were enclosed by hedges which followed the lie of the land and trackways. Some hedgerows also developed naturally at the edges of fields when a fence, ditch or bank near a source of tree seed was neglected for a few years. Hedgerows were the normal furniture of the rural landscape. They provide evidence of centuries-old farming systems, particularly the mixed farming of lowland Britain, and a link with past rural traditions and crafts.

As discussed in more detail elsewhere (Holder 1999), the mass planting of hedgerows occurred to give effect to the enclosure movement by demarcating the enclosed land (the old open fields) and fencing off the 'waste' or common lands (Rackham 1996: 190). Enclosure of land began roughly in 1450 and reached a peak between 1750 and 1850,[4] leading to the abolition of common land rights and husbandry practices and large tenanted farms (Beckett 1990: 35). There were many reasons for enclosure, mainly of an economic nature, including the need to secure more commercially oriented farms so as to provide for an increasing urban population. It is possible also that enclosure was a response to environmental degradation caused by the open field system which exhausted the arable land, and led to depopulation in rural areas (Bradley 1968).

Local and Parliamentary Enclosure Acts, of which there were approximately 4,000, were therefore used to confirm existing arrangements and extend landlords' control over the land and its inhabitants. This was generally arranged among large landowners and its acceptability determined in Parliament by other members of that class. In this way, law operated as a legitimating device for decisions already taken about the restructuring of land and property relations. The Enclosure Acts therefore provide the main example of how law has borne upon the landscape and shaped it.

In ecological terms, hedgerows have traditionally supported a dense and diverse fauna and flora, acting as a reservoir of wildlife. Elder, blackthorn, privet, roses, barberry, crab apple, bullace, sloe, oak, ash, willow, wild cherry, beech, sycamore and field maple are some of the plants and trees which adapted and survived in the hedgerows which grew up as woodland was cleared for human settlements. For birds (blackbird, skylark, hedge sparrow, chaffinch, whitethroat, song thrush, yellowhammer and wren), animals (common rat, fox, stoat, badger, stoat, weasel, hedgehog, mole, rodents and shrew) and invertebrates (butterflies, earthworms, centipedes, beetles, arachnids and aphids), hedgerows similarly provided an extension of the ecological conditions of woodland. By providing corridors of habitat linking woodland that would otherwise be isolated, hedgerows allowed them to extend their range and so avoid the pressures of competition (Dowdeswell 1987).

The ecology of the hedgerow is closely related to its cultural importance, for example by the associations which may be made with its produce – the berries (barberries, blackberries, elderberries, raspberries and strawberries) and weeds, fungi, herbs, greens, flowers and nuts, and also the identification with particular local styles of hedgerow or the species found in them. In this respect, the cultural landscape of fields and hedgerows might give meaning to ideas of the 'rootedness' of a community (Cotterrell 1995; de Sousa Santos 1987) not necessarily in a geographical sense but in terms of people's aesthetic and material experiences of landscape as a sense of place (Hepburn 1996; Hannum 1997), for example, of planting or foraging a hedgerow. In turn, cultural influences may be seen to determine the ecology of hedgerows. The 'management' of hedgerows by those living and working in the landscape is crucial to the survival of the hedgerow and its inhabitants, particularly given the rate at which 'traditional', or rural ways of life have adapted or succumbed to modern, industrialised society (Bennett, 1996; Elworthy and Holder 1997: Ch. 11). This suggests that the issue of conservation should be logically extended to include consideration of human cultural diversity also (Thorne and Huang 1991: 61–63).

The hedgerow is commonly portrayed as a quintessential, natural, feature of the *English* landscape in literature, poetry, paintings and maps (Schama 1996; Lowenthal 1991) even though there is nothing distinctly English or even British about hedgerows. The idea of Elysian rural England has been taken up by English socialists and liberals, but mostly conservatives. For example, towards the end of the nineteenth century a group of Tory poets created in their work a picture of unchanging England to set against rising social unrest and foreign threats (Weiner 1981: 55–56). Amongst this group, Poet Laureate Alfred Austin idealised rustic, old England in his 'Return to England' which, typically, is entirely about hedgerows, cottages and village spires.[5] By the First World War, nostalgic and utopian visions centred on the country and encouraged patriotism. An anthology of writing, *England, the Old Country*, was distributed to soldiers which evoked the England of Alfred Austin and Rupert Brooke. For example, 'O England', E.V. Lucas' poem sentimentalised 'country of my heart's desire, land of the hedgerow and the village spire'. Hedges and fields still form an essential part of an idealised, rural myth or 'national essence' which serves to uphold certain social hierarchies and practices, most obviously hunting (see Chapter 4).

The cultural associations of the hedgerow with 'nature' are particularly complex. John Stuart Mill bemoaned the widespread uprooting of hedgerows in the name of agriculture, which he saw as part of farming's master plan to tame nature:

> Solitude in the presence of natural beauty and grandeur, is the cradle of thoughts and aspirations which are not only good for the individual, but which society could ill do without. Nor is there much satisfaction in contemplating the world with nothing left to the spontaneous activity of nature; with every foot of land brought into cultivation ... every hedgerow or superfluous tree rooted out, and scarcely a place left where a wild shrub or flower could grow without being eradicated as a weed in the name of agriculture. (Mill 1848: 58)

But such a portrayal belies the artificiality and ambiguity of hedgerows. Although some hedgerows are naturally occurring, most were originally planted to divide fields and mark the boundaries of property. Confusingly, even these tended to be rooted on ancient boundaries. Hedgerows have also shown a capacity for attracting flora other than those planted, so that they take on different ecological characters, a propensity now greatly limited by modern farming practices. When originally planted in great numbers in the eighteenth century, hedgerows were seen as monotonous and unnatural, an indication that agriculture, like the towns, was moving further away from nature (Evans 1992: 27). Expressing this sentiment, William Gilpin wrote: 'Wherever man appears with his tools, deformity follows his steps. His spade and his plough, his hedge and his furrow, make shocking encroachments on the simplicity and elegance of landscape' (1808: 38). Representing both the domination and presence of nature, the hedgerow exposes the transience of 'nature'; that it is shaped by culture and time.

Conserving the Hedgerow

Following the Enclosure Acts, the rural landscape was relatively stable: the majority of hedges which existed in 1870 were still there in 1950 (Rackham 1986: 191). All then changes. The economics of agriculture, responsible in the main for the enclosure movement centuries earlier, led to a greater emphasis on arable farming rather than rotational farming which had relied on hedgerows to prevent livestock straying onto crops. The focus on high production levels to maximise subsidies resulted in increased use of fertilisers and pesticides and large farm machinery such as combine harvesters with wide turning circles. Small fields that had previously housed livestock were no longer economic and so it became common practice for the size of these fields to be increased by grubbing out hedges. Such technological farming was encouraged by the Ministry of Agriculture, Fisheries and Food which, until 1992, gave grant aid to farmers to remove their hedges. This practice reached a peak in the mid-1960s, with the loss of about 10,000 miles of hedgerows per year (Countryside Commission 1977: para. 9). The rate of loss has since slowed but hedgerow removal continues, causing loss of species and making the large fields vulnerable to wind erosion of the fertile topsoil as well as water erosion.[6]

Although the removal of hedgerows has been brutal, the greater threat to the hedgerow is from dieback, caused by local environmental factors arising from modern agricultural practices. For example, ploughing close to trees damages root systems, compaction of soil by farm vehicles results in a breakdown in soil structure and reduced root function and heavy application of fertilisers leads to growth abnormalities (Forestry Commission 1991). The declining standard of hedgerow management also bears some responsibility for dieback. Mechanised flails bring a 'short back and sides' look to the hedgerow, which fails to protect saplings. This compares with a time when hedges were cut manually with billhooks into intricate patterns that provided for new growth and allowed for the tailoring of hedgerows to the local landscape – Welsh, Midlands and West Country hedgerows all differed.

In response to these influences, law has traditionally upheld, not conservation of the landscape, but rather good husbandry and estate management. The Agriculture Act 1947 which laid the basis for the post-war agricultural arrangements required that the necessary work of maintenance and repair of hedgerows was to be carried out, for example hedges were to be cut and laid rather than left to become overgrown.[7] The 1947 Act was the product of the Report of the Committee on Land Utilisation in Rural Areas (the Scott Committee) (1943) which proposed that farmers should, by virtue of their ordinary agricultural practices, continue to be custodians of the landscape, holding it in trust for the whole nation (1943: para. 160). In the event, the 1947 Act was too weak to control the direction of agriculture.

The Town and Country Planning Act 1947 was similarly a response to the approach adopted by the majority of the Scott committee. As a consequence, agricultural and forestry (rural) land uses, including those affecting hedgerows, did not come within the ambit of the British development control system,[8] this urban bias suggesting that the Act's title was something of a misnomer as well as contributing to a perception that threat to the rural environment was coming from the town (see Shoard 1980). The removal of hedges in particular illustrated the limitations of planning law and led to arguments that the planning system should protect hedgerows in the same way as it does certain trees.[9] Instead, protection of hedgerows has (until recently) been advanced by aid for their management, utilising economic measures such as the Hedgerow Incentive Scheme[10] (which replaced the grant aid given to farmers for removing hedges) with its provision for the negotiation of management agreements between farmers and the Countryside Commission for planting, restoring and maintaining hedges.

The part to be played by law in protecting landscape has been slowly recognised, as illustrated by the formulation of statutory duties which, variously, require public bodies to have regard to the beauty and amenity of the landscape.[11] Such duties are generally not combined with compulsory powers to support landscape protection, grant-aided management agreements with owners remaining the main means of achieving this aim.

More specifically, the law lagged behind the reality of the loss of hedgerows. As farming came to be seen as increasingly problematic in conservation terms, several private members' bills were brought to introduce specific protection regimes for hedgerows. These failed to be enacted, as did a government proposal that farmers be paid to preserve rather than remove hedgerows.[12] Taking the opportunity offered by the passage of the Environment Act 1995, the government finally gave itself powers to make regulations to protect hedgerows.[13] The result, The Hedgerows Regulations 1997,[14] prohibit their removal unless a procedure is followed,[15] thus finally separating arrangements for the protection of hedgerows from aid for their management. Owners must give notice to the local planning authority that they wish to remove a hedgerow. Should the planning authority consider that the threatened hedgerow is 'important', according to centrally set criteria, it may issue a hedgerow retention notice stating that the works are not to be carried out. The system is reinforced by criminal sanctions and the requirement that hedgerows removed in contravention of the Regulations must be restored. The 1997 Regulations represent a new direction for conservation law. The legal regime – of notification, license and sanction – is the familiar 'command and control' model pursued for development control, but is here invoked for the purposes of protecting hedgerows as part of the rural landscape. This legal form usurps the tradition of governing the countryside via 'management' by farmers, backed up by voluntary systems of financial incentives, grants and subsidies (Bell 1997: Ch. 16).

Defining 'important' hedgerows is the key to the operation of the Regulations. These are considered to be hedgerows which have existed for 30 years or more and which satisfy at least one of two sets of criteria.[16] The first set relates to archaeological and historical matters, for example, that the hedgerow marks the boundary of at least one historic parish or township existing before 1850. The second set relates to wildlife and landscape considerations and includes lists of woodland species (bluebell, oxlip, toothwort, etc.), woody species (rowan, alder, wild cotoneaster, etc.), endangered or vulnerable animals and birds species,[17] and various hedgerow features. The criteria are complex, precise and technical and offer ample opportunity for disputes.

The general approach of the 1997 Regulations of very closely defining the type of hedgerow deserving legal protection is flawed in several respects. First, only the proposed *removal* of a hedgerow triggers legal protection. This includes within its scope acts that result in the destruction of the hedgerow, for example, a deliberate act carried out on nearby land. Slow dieback, caused by less direct and obvious acts such as the over-application of chemicals, which poses the main threat to hedgerows, is not captured by the Regulations. Second, the central concept of the Regulations, the protection of 'important' hedgerows, might be questioned on the ground that this secures protection for the 'fittest' hedgerows in terms of species inhabiting them and the features that they boast. However, once hedges have deteriorated to the point that they are of very poor quality, there are no farming reasons to keep them. And a grubbed-out hedgerow stands no chance of becoming an 'important' hedgerow over time.

The most significant flaw is that the criteria by which hedgerows are judged to be important are very narrow. This is best illustrated by the factors to be considered when judging the wildlife and landscape importance of a hedgerow, particularly that the criteria are couched in quantifiable terms. A hedgerow is defined as important if it includes at least seven woody species listed in the Regulations. This need only be six species where at least three specified features exist. These features are listed as a ditch along at least one half of the length of the hedgerow, a standard tree for each 50 metres of hedge, or certain connections with other natural features, particularly other hedgerows (hedgerows forming part of a continuous network are recognised as having special value).[18] In the case of the last: '... a connection with another hedgerow scores one point and a connection with a pond or a woodland in which the majority of trees are broad leaved trees scores 2 points.'[19] Connections 'scoring 4 points or more' constitute a 'feature' of the hedgerow.[20]

The operation of these criteria presupposes a scientific assessment of the number and the type of species present in a measured stretch of hedgerow. The underlying premise is that 'importance' *can* be quantified in this manner; it does not appear that the criteria act as a proxy for more subjective considerations. This corresponds to an approach to conservation by which values are attributed to natural resources or 'capital' by quantifiable terms, for example, through individuals' willingness to pay money to protect or enhance nature (Pearce et al. 1989). The focus of this approach is on 'features' or 'objects' requiring protection rather than the recognition of less tangible attributes such as typicalness, distinctiveness, setting and context (see Chapter 3). The adoption of quantitative criteria in the 1997 Regulations may be seen as forming part of the more general incorporation of economic valuing techniques in environmental law.[21]

The narrowness of the criteria to determine 'important' hedgerows can also be seen by the failure of the Regulations to acknowledge the cultural significance of hedgerows. For example, no mention is made of the significance of the differing appearance of hedgerows in various regions, and hence their representativeness of locality.[22] It is perhaps considered that their cultural significance stems from their historical or ecological importance. This is the case in part. However, the absence of discrete cultural criteria means that no regard may be had to local feeling about a hedgerow by means of public consultation.[23] Instead, the Regulations advance conducting a uniform audit of the species and features of the hedgerow and surrounding area. Such weak protection for culturally significant, particularly locally representative, hedgerows which might not fulfil the existing ecological, wildlife and historical criteria, underlines a need for national law to be more locally applicable and adaptable. From this perspective, the management agreement, allowing for some degree of negotiation between parties and variability according to local conditions, might be a more appropriate mechanism for protecting landscape.

The treatment of hedgerows in the 1997 Regulations suggests that law conceives of hedgerows in terms of the first meaning of landscape outlined in the introduction to this chapter – the surface features of an area, the easily definable and quantifiable characteristics. In contrast, the second meaning of landscape, the *observer's* intuitive perspective of features of an area – the landscape as culturally defined – is absent from the legal regime for protecting hedgerows. The general picture of law derived from the Regulations is of a set of complex and technical rules which are simultaneously simplistic and superficial, the preoccupation being with counting (of species, length and features) rather than the meanings to be attributed to hedgerows, and deriving from them. Underlying this is scant understanding of the place of people in the protection of landscape, the connections between hedgerows counting for more than the connections between people, nature and landscape. The hallmarks of modern law are all present in the 1997 Regulations: universalism, disembeddedness (from the social and cultural milieu of a particular community), universalism and instrumentalism (Banuria and Marglin 1993).

Law has proved itself not entirely incapable of taking account of cultural, or intangible, values.[24] Nevertheless, the main advances in the incorporation of cultural values in decision making processes are being made outside law, the general aim of which is to develop more deliberative and inclusionary methods of valuing nature, in particular involving the public. These developments might be located within 'common good' approaches to valuing nature which implies embracing ethical and moral concerns as well as popular values for particular places, features or their attributes (see Chapter 3). For example, the Countryside Commission has developed a new map of the English landscape with the aim of defining discrete regional character areas. Alongside such attributes as geology and soils, cultural associations were also drawn upon by exploring the public's perception of the local landscape. The new map of landscape, viewed from a regional perspective, will be used to identify local priorities and develop a series of regional landscape conservation strategies (Countryside Commission 1994b).

This is not to say that the incorporation of cultural values (those held by a community or locality) *in law* for the protection of hedgerows would not be unproblematic. Since the cultural appreciation of hedgerows has changed considerably over time, there is some danger in protecting hedgerows as one detail of the 'romance of the countryside' at the cost of failing to recognise the potential significance of new forms in landscape such as the motorway verge. Defining 'locality' or 'community' in law is also difficult since these concepts are subject to change. More significantly, giving legal expression to local and community cultural values might contribute to the safeguarding of a rural culture which may be exclusionary (see Chapter 4).

The limitations of law in accommodating cultural values may be attributed to the possibly undesirable goal of trying to take account of the incalculable in law. This view is held by Harte who considers that no system of law can by itself create an attractive landscape or control land so as to satisfy everyone in society. He argues that the more that legislators try to trap elusive and subjective qualities such as beauty or amenity in a framework of rules, the less clear the law becomes and the more initiative is stifled (Harte 1985). In contrast, 'elusive' might be taken to mean cultural values – knowledge and aesthetic experience – which may, in jurisprudential terms, be regarded as 'basic goods' (Finnis 1980). From this perspective, it is the detailed knowledge and 'management' practices of people which preserves and sustains a landscape, not the scientific recording of its calculable features. Conservation law and policy which fails to take account of this is inevitably half-hearted. It might even be questioned whether, by writing culture out of the story of landscape protection, law is producing an 'anti-landscape', so closely tied are cultural values and landscape (Schama 1996: 61).

More practically, the Regulations demonstrate a regulatory paradox: the prospect of legislation encouraged landowners to hasten destruction of hedgerows prior to the legislation taking effect.[25] The tenor of the accompanying 'good practice' guide for local planning authorities charged with administering the system is inauspicious (DoE/MAFF 1997). This emphasises that the retention of important countryside hedgerows is most likely to be met by adopting a common-sense approach, based on cooperation rather than confrontation with farmers. The Guide therefore neatly incorporates the 'business friendly enforcement procedures' set out in the Deregulation and Contracting Out Act 1994,[26] echoing the sentiments of the Scott Report some fifty years earlier.

In the long wait for legislation in this area, some individuals responded to the loss of hedgerows by creatively using existing law. In *Seymour v. Flamborough Parish Council* (1997),[27] this law hailed from the eighteenth-century enclosure movement. The subject of the dispute, which caught the collective legal imagination because of the remarkable successes of its legally untrained protagonist, was a 56-yard stretch of ancient hedge, threatened by the Council's plans to uproot it to extend a bowling green. Cracknell J ordered the Council to preserve the 'undistinguished, badly maintained, straggly and unkempt' hawthorn hedge on the grounds that it was still bound by the Flamborough Enclosure Act 1765 which required the parish council 'to maintain forever' the hedge. This successful reliance on a local Enclosure Act demonstrates an alliance between the protection of property interests (the broad aim of the local Act) and conservatory interests, mediated through law, and in this case spanning time and purpose. The judge stressed that the judgment did not set a precedent and that each of the thousands of eighteenth- and nineteenth-century Enclosure Acts must be judged on their merits. But he underlined the general principle that 'the courts cannot and do not strike down a statute merely because it is old or passed by a Parliament that was very far from being elected by universal suffrage.' The implication of the judgment is that protection may be granted to hedgerows which are the subject of arcane Enclosure Acts. But those which predate such Acts still require legal protection, a point emphasised by the judge in his consideration of the then forthcoming Hedgerows Regulations.

Conclusions

The hedgerows planted to give effect to the Enclosure Acts are physical representations of the social and legal history of enclosure, particularly patterns of land ownership, and rejection of common land rights. Although law has shaped the physical form of land, the current legal protection of landscape is tenuous. The legislative measures remain oblique, setting out duties of taking the conservation of amenity and beauty of land into account in decision making, but imposing few specific legal obligations. In its protection of hedgerows, law pursues a one-dimensional view of landscape as no more than the sum of its surface features, so that measurement, rather than memory or understanding, is the absolute arbiter of value. Landscape is, in this case, legally understood in scientific, objective and narrowly historical terms, less so in social, popular, or cultural terms. Unlike in the tradition of critical geography, law has still to appreciate that landscape, like space, is socially constructed and to reflect this in its representations.

The legal recognition of hedgerows as part of a richer, extended landscape, as 'commons', may be furthered in the future by European environmental law. For example the EC Habitats Directive[28] imposes a duty on Member States to encourage the management of 'the traditional systems for marking field boundaries', or 'green corridors', which are deemed essential for the migration, dispersal and genetic exchange of wild species.[29] Such features have been described by the Court of Justice as forming part of the 'common heritage of the Community',[30] and thus capable of subjugating the subjective or national interest element of land use to 'common responsibilities'.[31] This development of a concept of a common natural heritage parallels that of European citizenship (MacCormick 1997), raising similar difficulties of definition, competence and enforcement.

In the absence of law which is capable of appreciating landscape beyond the sum of its surface features, as the accoutrements or marks of property, greater reliance might perhaps be placed on such developments. Even more imaginative is the current grassroots plan to plant a 150-mile-long, cross-Britain Millennial hedgerow ('The Great Hedge'), across private property, common lands, and linking existing hedgerows.[32]

Notes

1. For a discussion of these and other meanings, see Kiss and Shelton 1997: Ch. 11.
2. For example, following the deportation and killing of Jews in southern Lithuanian woodland villages, the landscape was to be altered so that it became something unmistakably German, organised by the Reichskommissar for the Affirmation of German Culture. This was to be coupled with the expansion of forest in Lithuania, stocked with Teutonic species, some of which, such as the Bison, were reclassified for the purpose. This amounted to a plan to carve German identity from a quite different topography (Schama 1996: 70–71).
3. SI 1997 No. 1160.
4. Rackham (1996) estimates that 200,000 miles of hedge were planted between 1750 and 1850. Enclosure hedging became commercialised, so that hedge plants were raised in nurseries rather than being taken from woods. According to Turne 'Buie quicker at market, new gathered and small/buie bushes and willow, to fence it withall', quoted in Rackham 1996: 190.
5. *Lyrical Poems* (London, 1891).
6. A report by the Institute of Terrestrial Ecology on hedgerow changes in Great Britain between 1984 and 1990 revealed that the total hedgerow length in England had fallen in the period by over 20 per cent and in Wales by 25 per cent (Barr et al. 1991).
7. S. 11(2)(d) of the Agriculture Act 1947. The cutting and laying of hedges by hand means that saplings are protected by the old growth. See Elworthy 1990.
8. S. 55(1)(e) Town and Country Planning Act 1990, as amended, excludes forestry and agricultural land uses from the scope of development control.
9. For example, under s. 197 of the Town and Country Planning Act 1990 the local planning authority must ensure that in granting planning permission for development adequate provision is made by the imposition of conditions for the preservation or planting of trees. Under s. 198 of the 1990 Act the local planning authority may make a tree preservation order which may prohibit the cutting down, topping, lopping, uprooting or destruction of trees.
10. Introduced in 1992, and now part of the Countryside Stewardship Scheme, administered by the Ministry of Agriculture, Fisheries and Food.
11. S. 4 of the Wildlife and Countryside (Amendment) Act 1985 required that the Forestry Commission take account of such features by inserting s. 1(3A) into the Forestry Act 1967. Similar aims were introduced into planning legislation which required that development plans include policies on 'the conservation of natural beauty and amenity of the land' (ss. 12(3A), 31(3), 36(3) of the Town and Country Planning Act 1990, as amended). S. 61 of the Environment Act 1995 substitutes a new s. 5 in the National Parks and Access to Countryside Act 1949 which requires all public authorities to have regard to 'conserving and enhancing the natural beauty, wildlife and cultural heritage of the areas'.
12. Planning and Compensation Bill, Official Report, Hs L, Vol. 54, Issue 1514 WA 85–87.
13. S. 97 of the Environment Act 1995.
14. SI 1997 No. 1160.
15. Reg. 5.
16. Reg. 4. The criteria are set out in Part II of Schedule 1 to the Regulations.
17. These include birds and animals protected by the Wildlife and Countryside Act 1981, or categorised as a declining breeder or endangered, extinct, rare or vulnerable in various lists drawn up by the Royal Society for the Protection of Birds or the Nature Conservancy Council.

18 Sched. 7(1)(a) and (b) of Schedule 1, Part II, to be read in conjunction with Schedule 7(4)(h).
19 Sched. 7(5) of Schedule 1, Part II.
20 Sched. 7(4)(h) of Schedule 1, Part II.
21 For example, the introduction of cost-benefit analysis as a legal requirement by ss. 4 and 39 of the Environment Act 1995, and the concept of Best Available Techniques Not Entailing Excessive Cost (BATNEEC) in s. 7(7) of the Environmental Protection Act 1990.
22 Interestingly, the proposed amendment to the Planning and Compensation Bill for the legal protection of hedgerows did include a reference to 'having regard to local custom and practice'.
23 Such 'local feeling' might be determined by consultation. However the provisions in the Regulations on consultation are very narrow: Reg. 5(3) requires that the local planning authority consult the relevant parish council on hedgerow notices, but this is to determine the importance of certain hedgerows in terms of the criteria listed.
24 For example, in international law the Convention for the Protection of the World Cultural and Natural Heritage aspires to safeguard that 'unique and irreplaceable property which is part of the cultural heritage'. However, in the case of *enforceable* procedural rules, the status of interests of a cultural character rank lower than interests of a more tangible character, such as the protection of the individual and the material value of property (Riley 1997).
25 Since legislation was promised in 1990, at least 60,000 miles have been grubbed up or have degenerated through neglect, Leader article, *The Guardian*, 3.1.1997.
26 S. 5 and Schedule 1 of the Deregulation and Contracting Out Act 1994.
27 Not yet reported, see *The Times*, 3.1.1997.
28 Council Directive 92/43/EEC on the conservation of natural habitats and of wild fauna and flora, OJL 206/7, 21.5.1992.
29 Article 10(2) of Directive 92/43/EEC, *Id*.
30 Case C-44/95, *R* v. *Secretary of State for the Environment, ex parte Royal Society for the Protection of Birds ('Lappel Bank')* [1996] 3 CMLR 411, para. 24.
31 See, for example, Opinion of Advocate General Fennelly in Case C-44/95, '*Lappel Bank*' [1996] 3 CMLR 411, paras. 72–75.
32 Organised by Plantlife, Natural History Museum, see J. Theobald, 'Getting Close to the Hedge', *The Guardian*, 22.1.1993, p. 18.

References

Banuria, T. and Marglin, F. (1993) *Who Shall Save the Forests? Knowledge, Power and Environmental Destruction* (London: Zed Books).
Barr, C.J. et al. (1991) *Changes in Hedgerows in Britain 1984–1990*, Department of the Environment/Institute of Terrestrial Ecology (London: HMSO).
Beckett, J.V. (1990) *The Agricultural Revolution* (Oxford: Blackwell).
Bell, S. (1997) *Ball and Bell on Environmental Law*, 4th edn (London: Blackstone Press).
Bennett, G. (1996) *Cultural Landscapes: the Cultural Challenge in a Changing Europe* (London: Institute for European Environmental Policy).

Blomley, N. and Balkan, J. (1992) 'Spacing Out: Towards a Critical Geography of Law', *Osgoode Hall Law Journal*, 30: 661.
Bradley, H. (1968) *The Enclosures in England: An Economic Reconstruction* (New York: AMS).
Coates, I. (1993) 'A Cuckoo in the Nest: the National Front and Green Ideology', in Holder, J. et al. (eds) *Perspectives on the Environment* (Aldershot: Avebury).
Committee on Land Utilisation in Rural Areas (the Scott Committee), (1943) *Report on Land Use in Rural Areas*, Cmn. 6378 (London: HMSO).
Cooper, D. (1998) *Governing Out of Order: Space, Law and the Politics of Belonging* (London: Rivers Oram).
Countryside Commission (1977) *New Agricultural Landscapes* (Cheltenham: Countryside Commission).
Countryside Commission (1994a) *Views From the Past: Historic Landscape Character in the English Countryside* (Cheltenham: Countryside Commission).
Countryside Commission (1994b) *The New Map of England: A Celebration of the South Western Landscape* (Cheltenham: Countryside Commission).
Cotterrell, R. (1995) *Law's Community: Law's Theory in Sociological Perspective* (Oxford: Clarendon).
de Sousa Santos, B. (1987) 'Law: A Map of Misreading: Towards a Post Modern Conception of Law', *Journal of Law and Society* 14: 279.
DoE/MAFF (Department of the Environment/Ministry of Agriculture, Fisheries and Food) (1997) *The Hedgerows Regulations 1997: A Guide to the Law and Good Practice* (London: HMSO).
Dowdeswell, W.H. (1987) *Hedgerows and Verges* (London: Allen and Unwin).
Elworthy, S. (1990) *Farming in Britain and its Relationship with the Environment* (unpub. LL M dissertation) University of Warwick.
Elworthy, S. and Holder, J. (1997) *Environmental Protection: Law in Context* (London: Butterworths).
Evans, D.A. (1992) A *History of Nature Conservation in Britain* (London: Routledge).
Evernden, N. (1993) *The Social Creation of Nature* (Baltimore: Johns Hopkins University Press).
Finnis, J. (1980) *Natural Law and Natural Rights* (Oxford: Clarendon Press).
Forestry Commission (1991) *Ash Dieback*, Bulletin 93 (London: HMSO).
Gilpin, W. (1808) *Remarks on Forest Scenery and Other Woodland Views (Related Chiefly to Picturesque Beauty), in Three Books* (London: R. Blamire, 3rd edn; reprinted by Richmond Publishing Co Ltd. Surrey, 1973).
Hannum, H. (ed.) (1997) *People, Land and Community* (New Haven/London: Yale University Press).
Harte, J.D.C. (1985) *Landscape, Land Use and Law* (London/New York: Spon).
Hepburn, P. (1996) 'Landscape and the Metaphysical Imagination', *Environmental Values*, 5 (3).
Holder, J.B. (1999) 'Law and Landscape: The Legal Construction and Protection of the Hedgerow', *Modern Law Review*, 62 (1): 100–114.
Kiss, A. and Shelton, D. (1997) *Manual of European Environmental Law*, 2nd edn (Cambridge: Cambridge University Press).

Lowenthal, D. (1991) 'British National Identity and the English Landscape', *Rural History*, 2: 205.
MacCormick, N. (1997) 'Democracy, Subsidiarity, and Citizenship in the "European Commonwealth"', *Law and Philosophy*, 16: 331, at 340–342.
Mill, J.S. (1848) *Principles of Political Economy* (London: Penguin, reprinted in 1970).
Pearce, D.W., Markandya, A. and Barbier, E. (1989) *Blueprint for a Green Economy* (London: Earthscan).
Rackham, O. (1986) *The History of the Countryside* (London: Dent).
Rackham, O. (1996) *Trees and Woodlands in the British Landscape: the Complete History of Britain's Trees, Woods and Hedgerows* (London: Routledge).
Riley, J. (1997) '*Locus Standi* and Cultural Interests', *Journal of Planning and Environmental Law*, 20.
Schama, S. (1996) *Landscape and Memory* (London: Fontana).
Shoard, M. (1980) *The Theft of the Countryside* (London: Temple Smith).
Thorne, J.F. and Huang, C.S. (1991) 'Toward a Landscape Ecology Aesthetic: Methodologies for Designers and Planners', *Landscape and Urban Planning* 21: 61.
Weiner, M. (1981) *English Culture and the Decline of the Industrial Spirit 1850–1980* (Cambridge: Cambridge University Press).

PART III
ENVIRONMENTAL JUSTICE

6 The Grassroots at Risk: Local Perceptions and Environmental Injustice

*Angela C. Halfacre and Albert R. Matheny**

Introduction

Environmental justice has become a key concept in analysing the legitimation of environmental regulation, both in the United States – specifically addressing the objections of those disenfranchised from the domestic policy-making arena – and also internationally among those in developing countries who resist the exportation of hazards from industrialised nations. Sometimes referred to as 'environmental injustice' or 'environmental racism', the phenomenon has been documented for well over a decade[1] and explored academically since at least 1990 (Bullard 1990, 1993; Hofrichter 1993; Szasz 1994).

Grassroots environmental activists have used the environmental justice theme as a rallying cry to mobilise local citizens in protest of industrial or governmental policies which might impose new environmental risks upon communities. In the United States, particularly the Citizens Clearinghouse for Hazardous Waste (CCHW) has articulated this criticism to great effect, as have non-governmental organisations (NGOs) worldwide.[2] Their protests centre around an essential component of all environmental regulation: the redistribution of risks, costs, and benefits associated with hazardous industrial practices.

In this chapter, we identify the underlying legitimacy issues in hazard regulation, especially as they occur in a federal system and as they affect local under-represented populations. To do so, we use a theory of policy dialogue developed by Williams and Matheny which suggests that the politics of environmental disputes are incompletely articulated by three different and competing 'languages' of regulation: managerial language, pluralist language and communitarian language (Williams and Matheny 1995). We apply this theory to data analysed by Halfacre (1997), and we sample the comments of citizens in two contaminated localities – not citizen activists, but 'average' citizens, previously uninvolved in politics or environmental protest.

Risk Redistribution and Regulatory Legitimation

Regulating the hazards produced by siting factories or waste facilities, or by cleaning up the toxic remains of defence operations, for example, is part of 'the new social regulation',[3] precisely because it attempts to redress externalities, that is, the consequences of unrecognised risk production – a new type of 'market failure' in which risk producers avoid paying the full price of their 'product' in the short run by shifting safety costs, and the attendant long-term risks, to the general public. The intent of this type of environmental regulation then is redistributive, aimed at forcing producers to absorb the (concentrated) cost of safe containment in order to benefit (diffusely) the general public.[4]

Typically, the redistributive consequences of such regulation require an environmental crisis and a strong dose of entrepreneurial politics to overcome governmental reluctance to act against the organised interests of risk producers. However, entrepreneurial politics also has its disadvantages: while it can inspire regulatory activity in a time of environmental crisis, the inspiration often wanes in the enduring efforts necessary to implement and enforce its mandates. The result is often a distortion of the original initiative. At worst, the effort may become a mere symbol with no real impact upon the regulatory target.

The redistributive consequences of hazard regulation make it exceptional in other ways, too. It asks not only that those producing risks bear the costs of their management; but it also redistributes the risks, costs and benefits disparately among the general population. The impact of hazard policies is local as well as national. When federal and state investigators identify previously unknown hazardous waste sites for clean-up, for example, residents nearby become aware of increased health risks and often endure the very real costs of declining property values. When government sites a hazardous facility, the decision concentrates risks and costs borne by a small, identifiable group of people and institutions (typically residents near the site and local governments providing services for the site) and diffuses benefits broadly among the general public.

Hazard regulation, then, is a form of social regulation that dramatically affects geographically-bounded communities. The intensely local nature of this redistribution finds local political institutions completely unprepared. Their political capacity is no match for the redistributive conflict which hazard regulation engenders. Local governments find it difficult to reconcile the general benefits of hazard management with the local resistance to its consequences in the targeted community. As a result, local politics routinely defaults to the local veto: a well-worn but effective resistance toward any and all redistributive policies (Peterson 1981).

This veto is likely to be effective where targeted communities have the political and economic wherewithal to resist. So the risk to be redistributed then begins a journey down the path of least resistance, and ends up targeting communities less capable of resisting – typically rural, economically depressed or minority locales; hence the concerns raised about environmental injustice. There is irony in hazard policy having such a political bottom line, when the problems it addresses are generally defined in scientific terms. This irony is not lost on those who eventually absorb the risks at the local level.

Indeed, the scientific and technical content of hazard policy can also contribute to its delegitimation. While being a central ingredient of hazard regulation, its presence also permits policy makers to discount the importance of public participation in the discussion of hazard regulation. An elite of so-called experts typically emerges to dominate the regulatory arena (Covello et al. 1989). As a result, the locally redistributive impact of regulatory policy is also defined exclusively as scientific and technical, with two consequences. First, the barrier of expertise excludes the general public, particularly at the local level, from entering into official debate or having any meaningful impact on the consequences they will bear, thus violating a fundamental sense of democratic fair play. Second, because the data and assumptions of the scientific and technical arguments about hazards are often tentative and controversial, the debate itself is characterised by uncertainty and challenge rather than scientific consensus, thus undermining the credibility of expert decision making – credibility essential to legitimate regulation.

The resulting policies and their redistributive impact are seen by those affected as arbitrary because the presumption of objectivity cannot be maintained in an environment of uncertainty. Experts confronted with uncertain factual information inevitably fall back upon value judgements to fill in the gaps. 'Science' cannot disguise the fact that these judgements are innately political; yet value judgements typically remain unacknowledged when experts make policy.

Ultimately, and despite the importance of scientific input, the regulation of hazards becomes political because it is redistributive and because it involves political judgements as well as factual determinations. The combination of these characteristics cannot be legitimated in the conventional policy-making process; none the less, the conventions of policy making have established the existing boundaries for understanding and structuring that process. The resulting mismatch between politics and process produces a crisis of legitimacy in social regulation.

Exacerbating this crisis is that hazard regulation must be implemented within a federal system. States and localities are often ill-equipped to confront well-organised risk producers, so they default in their regulatory responsibilities by transforming the redistributive burdens on producers into social costs, either by funding hazard regulation from general revenues (thus diffusing the fiscal burden to the tax base of the general population) or by neglecting to regulate effectively or at all (thus allowing the social costs – and industry profits – of unsafe practices to accumulate).

The crisis in hazard regulation manifests itself in several ways. Policies unfairly target less resistant communities, and these communities and others like them learn from the experience. Everywhere citizens become less willing to bear a part of the redistributive burden. Because their substantive input is ignored in shaping policy in the first place, and because they are asked to bear burdens which their experience in political participation does not prepare them for, citizens resist decisions which affect them in predominantly negative ways. They mobilise to protest their 'consumption' of hazards, often producing what their critics label the 'Not In My Back Yard,' or NIMBY, response to hazard regulation. Among other things, NIMBY symbolises the public's deep distrust of the regulatory apparatus charged with managing risk production safely and fairly.

The Languages of Regulation

In earlier research, one of the authors and Bruce Williams characterised this crisis in regulatory legitimacy as a product of friction along the political frontier which divides market forces from the power of the state and from democratic influence. The boundary defining that frontier may be characterised contingently as 'the public interest'. But the public interest is an elusive (and, some would say, illusive) subject, so much so that the research distinguished three separate and contested 'languages'[5] of the public interest, all pretending to capture its essence exclusively, and yet each failing ultimately in its expression.

Each language of the public interest deals differently with the challenges to the conventional relationships among government, market and democracy posed in particular by the new social regulation. The 'managerial' language, drawing from its Progressive heritage and its commitment to an objective and calculable public interest, supports the presence of expertise at the centre of the regulatory process, but balks at the issue of public participation. The 'pluralist' language, as the name implies, prefers a public interest emerging, not from expert calculation, but from the adversarial representation of interests in the arena of group competition, a competition undergirded by procedural protections and a commitment on the part of the participants to abide by 'the rules of the game'. The 'communitarian' language has its roots in the underappreciated, but nevertheless powerful, notion that citizens in a democracy are the best source of the public interest, if they are only allowed to speak for themselves in a voice undistorted by distant political representatives or the technicalities of expertise. The communitarian has suspicions that government mainly protects itself, and those interests closest to it, rather than the people it was called to protect.[6]

Because of the tendency of different parties in the regulatory process to 'talk past one another' in these three competing languages, misunderstanding and distrust on all sides are the inevitable consequence. For legitimate policy to emerge, the process should provide for a dialogue which forces each party to consider the facts relevant to, and values implied by, the opposing languages in a free and equal exchange. Of course, this means reordering the existing status of regulatory experts, industry, organised interests and ordinary citizens in the policy process.[7] In particular, citizens must be able to engage in policy dialogue in an empowered way – with access to autonomous expertise and on an equal footing with government and industry experts and organised interests.[8]

Because this has not happened in the past, the more conventional regulatory discourses – the managerial and pluralist languages – have tended to dominate the policy process, thus excluding important communitarian concerns. Its exclusion from the policy process obscures the contours of the communitarian language, and a summary of its content is useful here. First, the communitarian voice gives expression to the commonality – rather than the individuality – of our existence. Thus, for example, private property rights are less important in communitarian terms than are the larger consequences of the exercise of those rights for the community as a whole. This concern for community well-being and for responsibilities over rights is related to the second characteristic of the communitarian language – its parochial emphasis, that is, a focus on local rather than regional or national politics. Finally, the communitarian language speaks of common-sense judgement – instinctively suspicious of complex scientific and technical argumentation – and of a self-reliant approach to governance which reinforces the parochialism of its political frame of reference. The ability of grassroots protesters to transcend their local interests and to embrace the complexities of hazard regulation in general is an important indicator, first, of the capacity of citizens to become full participants in regulatory policy making and, second, of real shortcomings in the existing regulatory process.

The Williams and Matheny research explored the potential for inclusion of the communitarian voice in policy making and found that organised grassroots interests did indeed move citizen concerns for their own backyard to a higher level of awareness about the larger implications of their local protests. As phrased by the CCHW, mobilised citizens were moving from 'NIMBY to NIABY – Not In Anyone's Back Yard'. That research was based upon interviews of grassroots activists who were mobilising local citizens to resist policies which they felt were too dangerous or unjust for their communities to bear.

But what about the citizens themselves, particularly those less likely to be politically involved? When confronted with hazards, are they aware of the environmental risks facing them? If so, how do they interpret these risks? Are they aware of, or willing to deal with, the scientific essentials of these risks? Do they address the equity issues involved in the introduction of these risks into their communities, for example, the economic opportunity/environmental safety tradeoffs? Are they concerned only about their own 'back yards', or do they appreciate the larger consequences of hazard policy? Finally, do they indicate a potential for meaningful participation in hazard policy formation? These are all crucial issues for assessing the potential of 'democratic' solutions to the crisis of legitimate regulation and particularly for gauging the relevance of mobilisation to the maturation of communitarian dialogue. In essence, they provide us with pieces to the puzzle of environmental justice and its place in the policy process.

The DOE/CERE Study

In pursuit of congressional legislation passed in 1993, directing the US Department of Energy (DOE) to provide Congress with a status report on risks to public safety and health caused by the nuclear weapons facilities around the nation, DOE arranged with the Consortium for Environmental Risk Evaluation (CERE) to gather data on risks from around each of the six facilities in question. CERE is made up of Tulane and Xavier Universities and a collection of other universities and consulting firms, most of which are located near the sites. Rather than pursue the conventional public hearing mode of gathering input, CERE used a variety of innovative means for collecting data – in particular, focus groups involving local people who were actively involved with the hazard issues at each facility and local people who were uninvolved until that time.

CERE was careful to construct its focus groups[9] to reflect a variety of demographic variables such as age, gender, race or ethnicity, income and education levels, rural residence, downwind or downgradient location, etc. The focus groups were guided by trained moderators instructed to provoke discussion within the groups using more than two dozen questions, beginning with broad enquiries about social problems and gradually narrowing down to the environmental risks associated with the nuclear facilities. Each focus group was made up of around 12 participants and had a specific selection profile, for example an African American group or a seniors (age 65 and above) group. There was typically equal gender representation across all groups. Tapes and transcripts of more than forty focus groups were made in early 1995, and these are what we obtained for analysis.

In previous research, one of the authors of this chapter investigated more broadly all of the information associated with CERE's data collection as they apply to risk characterisation (Halfacre 1997). Here, we concentrate exclusively upon the uninvolved 'stakeholders' at two facilities – Oak Ridge in Tennessee (OR) and Savannah River in South Carolina (SR) – as a rare opportunity to get real feedback from people who might never have a voice in the debate over risks in their communities. This opportunity is all the more intriguing because the focus groups target under-represented citizens, for whom the issue of environmental injustice may be relevant.

Typically, the only citizens heard from in environmental disputes are those who are already mobilised, and so it is empirically interesting to examine whether the discourse already encountered among grassroots activists exists in a latent form in the voices of those not yet mobilised. In short, does communitarian discourse emerge only through the social process of grassroots activity, or is it part of the everyday lives of non-activists as well? What follows are summaries and relevant quotations from the 14 focus groups' transcripts – six from OR (72 participants) and eight from SR (86 participants).

Focus Groups: Residents and Risks

In analysing the dialogue from the various focus groups, we were particularly interested in whether or not communitarian sentiments existed, and, if so, whether these sentiments went beyond the limitations of the communitarian language noted in Williams and Matheny (1995: Chapter 7). Those limitations are:

- temporal/local – the tendency for a self-absorbed and nostalgic return to a better, simpler past;

- technical – an aversion to or distrust of modern science as a solution for their problems; and
- organisational – a parochial concern for local problems only, with no grasp of the institutional necessities for sustaining an agenda in the political arena.

For the communitarian voice to contribute to policy making in a meaningful way, it must overcome these limitations, as the activists' articulation of it did in the Williams and Matheny research. Specifically, their use of the language was strongly future oriented, readily embraced scientific and technical input, and constantly stressed solutions and strategies beyond the local level of the community.

What we found in our analysis of the CERE 'uninvolved stakeholders' focus group data supported transcendent tendency in the activist use of communitarian dialogue. On both the temporal limitations, the members of the focus groups were, across the board, sensitive to the NIMBY issue and were concerned about the effects of radiation from the sites on future generations. As to the technical limitation, they were consistently adamant that more information was needed, that they had a 'right to know' – from trustworthy, independent and scientific sources – about the nature of the hazards they face in their communities. The organisational limitation, in contrast, was revealed repeatedly in statements from virtually all the groups. Along with the lack of strategies for acting effectively on their concerns, explicit references to issues of environmental justice as a political issue were few and far between. There was a general consensus that politics was part of the problem rather than part of the solution.

With this introduction in mind, we now share some of the flavour of their comments along with our own notes about how the focus groups generally proceeded. (For a discussion of the more general findings from the focus group sessions, see Halfacre 1997.) First, group members were asked to list three problems facing their communities. Despite the fact that these people lived in close proximity to sites with serious nuclear pollution problems, in almost every case, other issues such as crime, poor schools and the lack of jobs consistently ranked above environmental concerns. In only one group, African Americans from the Savannah River Site (SR), did members consistently emphasise environmental issues up front.

It became clear, however, as the focus group moderators began to target first the environment and then specific problems related to the nuclear sites and their clean-up, that the members had well-considered responses to the questions raised. One African American from Oak Ridge (OR) surprised himself when he spoke up:

Man: Yeah, I often think about it, it is pollution, and everything is going bad, and then we'll – but what we going to do? Are we set in, are we cooked in, because what you going to do if Martin Marietta [the site contractor] close up? Then you're going to cry again ... So we just stuck, or what you going to do? You don't want Martin Marietta to close down, so you've got two problems here, so obviously you've got to work on it. I don't believe I said that, because I meant to come to be quiet, because I was too dumb to get up here in it. But you got a problem here, you know.

In some cases, people knew useful information about the pollution problems in and around their communities, but reacted to this knowledge in very different ways. This white OR woman was very concerned about pollution effects on her and others' children, but seemed overwhelmed by a sort of cognitive dissonance:

Woman: But you go down to the park ... There is a little stream that runs through a park over by UT [Tyson Park]. There's a playground. There's tennis courts, softball field. There is all of these wonderful things for your enjoyment for your children, little picnic areas and a little pretty stream that runs through with signs that say, do not touch this water. Stay out. No wading, or swimming, or fishing, no anything, right beside the little park that's supposed to be so wonderful. I don't want to know what's in it. I don't.

Others were able to assemble information from a remarkable variety of sources and digest it so that it made sense in their understanding of the problems. This SR African American had a particularly gruesome story:

Man: I heard of an incidence with – I was talking about the chemical plant – this had to do with the water level where you fish, but I heard that some gentlemen hunting behind the chemical plant and they shot a deer from behind the chemical plant and when they got ready to skin it, when they cut it open, it was all black inside. And I would suppose that was from whatever paths are running off from the chemical plant.

Or this SR commercial fisherman's appreciation of wetlands:

Man: [You've got golf courses] instead of having, you know, like swamp areas where that water used to run off and go into a swamp, where that water re-purifies itself after a certain period of time. But all they does is do systems of canals with it. All the runoff goes into a canal or a ditch, then it all runs into a creek at one time instead of sitting in a swampy area, and then filtering into the rivers and creeks and everything. And I think we're getting a bunch of it [pesticide and fertiliser runoff]. Every time they get a big rain, we get all of it at one time instead of a little bit along. So they need to – I mean, like I say, every time they destroy a swamp or a wetland and dig a canal that holds all that water, they're taking away from what is natural ... By passing the ecological process by – the swamps are a biological filter, you know, a natural filter.

This OR white man took his information a step further and began to form strongly communitarian judgements about the pollution in his area:

Man: Well, I moved here twenty-something years ago. The reason I moved here, I moved from Ohio, was because this was supposed to be a real clean and pristine area. Then what happens, they find selenium at the bottom of the lake ... Selenium from Oak Ridge and the responsibility doesn't go back to the people who did it. Responsibility should be traced back to the person that was responsible for it. Not put on the population to make up these differences. The stockholders who had stock in that company, that stock should be devalued and sold to pay for these clean-ups. It shouldn't go on other people. It seems like time, and time, and time again, the government decides that a bunch of people are going to be responsible for the actions of a few because they don't want to enforce the law ...

Seniors especially were often more trusting of the federal government's regulatory efforts at monitoring and clean-up, but, at the same time, these seniors consistently expressed distrust of elected officials and private owners. Compare these quotes from the same focus group of SR seniors:

Man: I think [water pollution is] caused from neglect of the factories, and they're doing another one until ... the EPA[10] actually got into it. And there were lawsuits brought by the people. This place smelled so bad, and the water was getting so bad you couldn't drink it. But since the EPA got into it a few years back and started taking ... cases to court, it's cleaned up a lot ... But there's still, I'd say, 65 per cent to go even with the EPA back here to getting onto them. It's just ridiculous.

Woman: I think the danger of it. I don't think that we really know just how dangerous it is. Like he said, all we see is on TV or what some politician tell us when he's trying to get re-elected.

[Comparing government-owned operations to privately-owned ones]

Man: Because those people, from what I've always heard, read, and been told, they do just exactly what they can get away with, and no less and no more.

Moderator: 'Those people', meaning who?

Man: The owners of the factories down there.

It is clear that group members were thinking about what they were hearing, and starting to share opinions as well as information. But what emerged in nearly every group was a strong desire for more information about the hazards they face, from reliable, independent scientific sources. This desire for honest information was overwhelmingly the issue uniting all the focus groups. The OR downgradient rural focus group put it best:

> Man: Roger brings up a good point [about the safety of disposal]. We don't know. We don't know what they're doing. I've got an uncle that works at Oak Ridge, and you can start talking about his work, and it becomes the most vague generality you've ever heard of in your life. The government knows a whole lot more about this than we do. I mean what we're fed through the media.
>
> [later]
>
> Moderator: ... Who would you trust to give you that information [about hazards and cancer] and say, 'I believe that's true'? ...
>
> Man: Privately funded groups of people that know what to look for and know what they're talking about that aren't receiving any government monies whatsoever ... .
>
> Woman: I wouldn't touch the ones that work for them at the plant, 'cause they ain't going to come out and tell you the truth, I mean working there.
>
> Moderator: Who else would you not trust?
>
> Woman: The EPA.
>
> Man: THE EPA.
>
> [later still]
>
> Man: Yeah, I agree with them as far as the education part. And to bring it one step further, I would say that maybe somehow, some sort of group of the civilians, you know, the people who live around the area, and bring them out on a periodic basis and let them see exactly what's going on, like those tours you were talking; get some people who are engineers and that kind of stuff, who understand the terms. And get them in there and see – let them make the reports. Someone who has no bias there whatsoever. I mean, that supposedly what the national – the EPA is all about, but that's not always the case, because they have their own national interest in it ...
>
> Moderator: Andrew?
>
> Man: Getting your local congressman and push for an educated group. By 'educated', I mean know what they're looking for, where. Compensate them for their work and have it checked on a periodic basis, and have the study made public. And it probably best be done by getting professionals that are in the area that have a reason to be concerned about it.
>
> Moderator: Roger?

> Man: [agrees with previous speakers] ... To educate the public and inform them of the disposal procedures, and general safety procedures at the plant. Because, you know, just around this discussion we're having here today, we don't know a whole lot about what's going on with nuclear. I will be the first to admit that myself. And the fact that none of us really know except what we kind of heard from other people, typifies the idea that we're not getting accurate information, meaningful information.
>
> Moderator: Any other recommendations?
>
> Man: And, based on those recommendations, hold a body responsible, a body of individuals responsible for seeing that whatever the community wants done in their area about that particular problem, gets done. And by somebody that can do something about it. Somebody in position with accountability act on it instead of just having another committee run by the state.

The OR downgradient rural focus group was remarkably 'focused' on this communitarian issue, with its dimensions of 'the right to know,' accountability and equal power with industry and government. Their articulation of these points was repeated by the SR commercial fishermen (with a different moderator):

> Man: Well, I would call the governor and tell him to train, or let someone go to school to learn about the stuff they handle there, for the public, you know, that this person or this group were going in with knowledge, and monitor these things, and release this information to the public, you know. And they'll know if something is going wrong, or whatever, you know.

Note here that in both of these focus groups there is no deep cynicism about science itself, but rather the sources of information – government and industry – which they feel are being corrupted by their 'interests' in the problem and their disregard for local concerns or input. They are willing to engage scientific issues as long as those issues are addressed disinterestedly and by scientists who have the power and the responsibility to pursue their communities' interests on an equal footing with industry and government.

Nearly as striking as the 'right to know' sentiment is the absence of NIMBYism in nearly all the focus group comments. The moderators specifically asked their groups whether the sites should be shut down or left open with the waste hauled off or treated on site – a clever way of getting at both the NIMBY and jobs versus environmental issues. The responses were interesting and indicated a definite transcendence of the limitations of communitarianism. This SR African American statement is representative of the consensus of all the focus groups:

Man: Clean it up but I don't want them to close it, even if they don't make whatever they make anymore. I don't want to see it close because I think there should be enough people there from now on forever working there to monitor that stuff. No matter how much they clean it up, or how much they tell us they have cleaned it up ...

Several group members mentioned that it would be much more dangerous to move it than to treat it on site because of the potential for accidents in transport, and, in several instances, group members felt it would be hypocritical to take their problem and make it someone else's problem.

Despite the obvious frustration with the government's role in the clean-up of the two sites, none of the groups came up with any sort of organisational strategy for rallying local citizens around political recourse. In fact, the SR seniors actually admitted to being puzzled by the presence of activists at the SR site:

Man: You would be surprised that we local people have very little concern about that plant. Now, they have demonstrations out there that the environmentalists come in from all over the world, and picket, and get on the roads ... and say, 'No more bombs', and 'No more radioactive materials'. But they come from all over the world. It's not the local people.

Man: The local people don't demonstrate. Those people do ...

Man: These people don't demonstrate. The northern people come down here and demonstrate for us. We stay home and watch.

This sort of bemused attitude toward political activity often turned to a sort of fatalism or anger at being trapped into having to live near or work at a dangerous facility. While revealing this anger, the following quote by a SR African American was one of the few to make a connection between industry's benefits and the community's risks:

Man: Well dealing with the chemicals, I don't [know] too much about the plant, but I'm just saying, if it dealing with the chemicals that your have announced when you speaking on it, it's like a concern what do they need it for. I mean they [chemicals] being made and the waste is going one way. I mean, what is their benefit from what they're making for this waste to go out. I mean, is it really something that's helping the whole country or they just doing something that's benefiting themself. And if they are benefiting themself, what is the outcome from it because there's lot of people that's getting hurt from them [chemical wastes] that's around them.

Conclusions

While the environmental justice concerns reflected in the last quotation are not often repeated within the focus groups, there are plenty of statements which allow us to have a better appreciation of the 'latent' attitudes of local people who are not yet inspired to be active in pursuit of political goals. Several things are clear. First, these individuals are willing to handle scientific and technical information, and they realise its importance in solving their sites' problems. Second, they are frustrated by the lack of responsiveness of both government and industry to their concerns. Third, they are willing to share in the responsibility for cleaning up the sites.

If nothing else, this makes these people constructive participants in the policy process, and without their participation, that process, as it is being applied in the sites studied here, is likely to lead to nothing more than unacceptable, illegitimate results. If these people can be brought into a meaningful dialogue with policy makers (not just in focus groups), accompanied by independent scientific experts, then democratically acceptable outcomes might emerge.

Perhaps the findings gathered from these focus groups helps to explain why grassroots activists are so successful at mobilising residents to pursue communitarian agendas. If these group members are in any way representative of the larger population of 'uninvolved stakeholders', then the only thing missing is political activism, which grassroots organisers like the CCHW provide. The success of that organisation in blocking 'Locally Undesirable Land Uses' or 'LULUs' has been remarkable, and its philosophy of activism has always been to facilitate rather than to dictate what the locals should do in fighting their own fights, a perfect match for the voice studied here.

In closing, it is interesting to note that the two focus groups with the most cogent discussions and the most articulate proposals were the OR downgradient rurals and the SR commercial fishermen. These groups were, by comparison and on average, the least educated and least wealthy of any of the groups studied here. Perhaps this explains their reluctance to become politically active, but it also offers no excuse for their input to be ignored in the policy process. For regulation to be legitimate, it must be an inclusive process which recognises that everyone – regardless of his or her station in life – has something to add to the regulatory dialogue.

Our data permit us to hear the voices of people who have never spoken in the policy process. We have found that these voices often speak in communitarian terms, that language most often overwhelmed by managerial and pluralist deliberation. If these people are not encouraged to add their voice to the making of regulatory policy, then their discontents will surface later as activists mobilise them to protest policies developed without their input. What they say and the way they say it needs to be taken into account before policies are made, so that regulations will address their concerns, as well as the technical or procedural concerns of the competing languages. Regulation will be different as a result, and may face a more positive reception when it is implemented.

Notes

* The authors wish to thank the US Department of Energy and the Consortium for Environmental Risk Evaluation of Tulane and Xavier Universities for the focus-group data used in this study.
1 In 1983, the General Accounting Office (GAO) documented that three out of four hazardous waste dumps were located in predominantly poor and minority communities. See GAO (1983).
2 See, for example, CCHW (1986). The CCHW is now known as the Center for Health, Environment, and Justice. The extensive media coverage of the execution of an environmental activist at the behest of petroleum interests in Nigeria is a bleak recent example of international environmental agitation in this vein.
3 Social regulation in general often refers to programmes aimed at establishing equitable goals in society not necessarily provided for by market operations, such as social security or civil rights regulation The 'new social regulation' refers to the mass of regulatory legislation which Congress passed at the end of the 1960s and in the early 1970s which aimed at correcting such non-obvious 'market failures' as environmental pollution and occupational safety and health. Further, the new social regulation also attempted to correct so-called 'government failures' caused by a lack of public access to administrative decision making processes. See Vogel (1981).
4 J.Q. Wilson's now classic taxonomy of regulation emphasises the difficulty of redistributing concentrated costs to organised intensely held interests, while diffusing benefits to an amorphous and unorganised 'general public'. See his 'Politics of Regulation', in Wilson (1980).
5 Williams and Matheny (1995). These languages were inspired in part by the three 'home domains' of social theory laid out in Alford and Friedland (1985) and 'the democratic wish,' based upon Morone (1990), Nedelsky (1990), and many other sources.
6 Although the communitarian language as a means of expressing local protest has not been documented extensively in previous literature, the communitarian ideology has attracted recent scholarly attention as a critique of the welfare state and as an alternative to the liberal emphasis on individual rights. See Etzioni (1995).
7 Especially in the case of the latter, a new sort of citizenship is required, along the lines suggested in Barber (1984). See also Mansbridge (1980) and J. Dewey's many works on democratic participation.
8 This understanding is based upon Williams and Matheny (1995: Chapter 3). The idea that unconstrained communication can achieve a 'true' public interest is drawn from Jurgen Habermas's 'ideal speech situation' and the American pragmatism of John Dewey. In the dialogic model, the three languages can interact in ways that the shortcomings of one may be compensated for by the strengths of the others. The model serves as a critical template for assessing the adequacy of actual policy communication. See Habermas (1975) and Dewey (1927).

9 CERE assembled the focus groups by randomly choosing names from zip codes around the sites, then screened residents by phone survey to fit the various group profiles required for their study.
10 The EPA is the Environmental Protection Agency – the federal agency charged with protecting the environment as well as citizens from environmental health risks in the United States.

References

Alford, R.R. and Friedland, R. (1985) *Powers of Theory* (Cambridge: Cambridge University Press).
Barber, B. (1984) *Strong Democracy: Participatory Politics For A New Age* (Berkeley: University of California Press).
Bullard, R. (1990) *Dumping in Dixie: Race, Class, and Environmental Quality* (Boulder, CO: Westview Press).
Bullard, R. (ed.) (1993) *Confronting Environmental Racism: Voices from the Grassroots* (Boston, MA: Southend Press).
CCHW (1986) *CCHW, Five Years of Progress 1981–1986* (Arlington, VA: CCHW).
Covello, V.T., McCallum, D.B. and Pavlova, M.T. (eds) (1989) *Effective Risk Communication: The Role and Responsibility of Government and Nongovernment Organizations* (New York: Plenum Press).
Dewey, J. (1927) *The Public and its Problems* (Chicago: Swallow Press).
Etzioni, A. (ed.) (1995) *New Communitarian Thinking: Persons, Virtues, Institutions, and Communities* (Charlottesville: University Press of Virginia).
GAO (General Accounting Office) (1983) *Siting of Hazardous Waste Landfills and Their Correlation with Racial and Economic Status of Surrounding Communities* (Washington, DC: US General Accounting Office).
Habermas, J. (1975) *Legitimation Crisis* (trans. T. McCarthy) (Boston: Beacon Press).
Halfacre, A.C. (1997) *Risk, Trust, and Group Identity: Ethnic and Racial Perceptions of Environmental Hazards* Ph.D. Dissertation, University of Florida.
Hofrichter, R. (ed.) (1993) *Toxic Struggles: the Theory and Practice of Environmental Justice* (Philadelphia: New Society).
Mansbridge, J.J. (1980) *Beyond Adversarial Democracy* (Chicago: University of Chicago Press).
Morone, J.A. (1990) *The Democratic Wish: Popular Participation and The Limits of American Government* (New York: Basic Books).
Nedelsky, J. (1990) *Private Property and The Limits of American Constitutionalism: The Madisonian Framework and Its Legacy* (Chicago: University of Chicago Press).
Peterson, P.E. (1981) *City Limits* (Chicago: University of Chicago Press).
Szasz, A. (1994) *EcoPopulism: Toxic Waste and the Movement for Environmental Justice* (Minneapolis: University of Minnesota Press).
Vogel, D. (1981) 'The "New" Social Regulation in Historical and Comparative

Perspective', in McCraw, T.K. (ed.) *Regulation in Perspective* (Cambridge, MA: Harvard University Press).

Williams, B.A. and Matheny, A.R. (1995) *Democracy, Dialogue, and Environmental Disputes: The Contested Languages of Social Regulations* Ph.D. Dissertation, University of Florida.

Wilson, J.Q. (1980) 'Politics of Regulation', in Wilson (ed.) *The Politics of Regulation* (New York: Basic Books).

7 Environmental Justice: The American Experience and its Possible Application to the United Kingdom

Antonia Layard[1]

Introduction

This chapter will look at spatial environmental justice in a domestic setting, focusing particularly on the effects of pollution on human health. It examines how we, in the United Kingdom, might implement one set of policies embodied in the 1994 US Executive Order on Environmental Justice and the subsequent US Environmental Protection Agency (EPA) Environmental Justice Strategy. These policies require regulators to identify disproportionately high and adverse human health or environmental effects on minority and low-income populations and to address these 'injustices'. Given that health is affected by pollution,[2] and presuming both that technology is currently not geared up to eliminating these effects entirely and that the overall gain from these polluting activities is desirable, it is important to assess how we are to respond to these effects on health both in theory and in practice. In particular we must consider, if pollution is to be legal (albeit at very low limits), how, and in this context, where, to infringe interests (or rights) in life and health if regulators deem that some infringement is 'worth' the burden (or the risk of the burden). And although we may conclude that a more precautionary approach should be enshrined, we cannot ignore the *status quo*. If these effects not only occur, but are also thought to be reasonable, tolerable or acceptable, how are we to respond? In particular how are we to address the spatial distributions of such potentially or actually harmful activities?

Recent discussions of domestic environmental justice have received their widest audience, and the greatest government response, in the United States, where two strands have intertwined. The first is rooted in the critical legal studies movement of the 1960s, concerning itself with questions of ideology and power, while the other proceeds within more traditional confines of political theory, discussing questions of 'justice', 'equality' and 'rights'.[3] This latter discourse is of little interest to many critics whose 'theory of social change convinces them that legal or policy arguments are not likely to be effective in achieving social change' (Binder 1987: 31) yet it is this more traditional discussion which will form the basis of this chapter. Before moving on, though, it is worth noting that in practice it has been the critical approach which has been closely linked to activists charging 'environmental racism', a concept which has emerged as a potent political tool.[4] This term, coined by the Reverend Benjamin Chavis,[5] alleges that racial minorities bear greater exposure to pollution than racial majorities. Thus it is said that:

> ... people of colour throughout the United States are receiving more than their fair share of the poisonous fruits of industrial production. They live cheek by jowl with waste dumps, incinerators, landfills, smelters, factories, chemical plants and oil refineries whose operations make them sick and kill them young. (Austin and Schill 1994: 53)

While academics have critiqued and refined the methodology used in these empirical surveys, in particular focusing on the boundaries that have been chosen in individual pieces of research (Baden and Coursey 1997: 1), the activism, led by a formidable array of clerics, activists and academics, integrated the might of the civil rights movement with environmental campaigns, to become extremely influential.

Yet though racism may provide one explanation for differentiated treatment in some instances, not all commentators pursue this line. For some, it is 'an insufficient reason for those problems because the poor, regardless of race, are also disproportionately impacted' (Gunn 1996: 1248); it is residential location which is the primary focus of the Executive Order 12898 *Federal Actions to Address Environmental Justice in Minority Populations and Low-Income Populations* introduced by the Clinton Administration in 1994. In this context, as in its focus on action within the existing policy framework, the Executive Order does not meet all the concerns of the critics. Even though it is not representative, the Executive Order and the principles it presents will provide the subject for analysis in this first section. In the environmental justice discussion, it is illustrative rather than conclusive.

The Executive Order requires each federal agency to identify and address 'disproportionately high and adverse human health or environmental effects of its programs, policies and activities' on minority and low-income populations. Each agency is required to develop an environmental justice strategy, and that prepared by the US Environmental Protection Agency (EPA) has two goals. First:

> No segment of the population, regardless of race, color, national origin, or income, as a result of EPA's policies, programs, and activities, suffers disproportionately from adverse human health or environmental effects, and all people live in clean, healthy, and sustainable communities. (EPA 1996)

And second:

> Those who live with environmental decisions – community residents, State, Tribal, and local governments, environmental groups, businesses – must have every opportunity for public participation in the making of those decisions. An informed and involved community is a necessary and integral part of the process to protect the environment. (EPA 1996)

This chapter will concentrate on the first, substantive, aspect of the US environmental justice programme. Clearly both legislative and common law attempts to deal with issues of environmental risk are, like many other policy choices, inescapably value laden. Both are attempting to respond to the creation of burdens (or social costs) by certain activities by which an entire nation state benefits, as citizens of a wealthy, prosperous country, while the risk of health-affecting pollution from these productive and profitable activities is borne by a smaller group and in the last resort the actual effects are felt by an even smaller group still. In order to explore these issues in detail, it is necessary first to consider the 1994 Executive Order and its key provisions, as one example of an attempt to address environmental injustice. In particular, it is important to assess how the key concepts of equality and a substantive interest in environmental protection that the Executive Order and the EPA's environmental justice strategy apparently identify might be implemented in the United Kingdom. In both countries two approaches have so far been tried to implement equality in environmental risk distribution: market mechanisms and regulatory decision making. Both are considered briefly and one key issue, the distinction between inter- and intra-community justice, is examined in both contexts.

The Theory Behind the US Environmental Justice Executive Order and EPA Strategy

It is a commonplace that justice is a highly contested concept. Since Aristotle submitted that 'justice is equality', even though he, like Plato and others before him, 'believed firmly that a just distribution is in general an unequal one' (Vlastos 1984: 41), theorists continue to debate the possible underlying principles. Recently, one prominent theorist concluded that 'the best general definition is still Justinian's: justice is the constant and perpetual will to render to everyone his due' so that 'people, as separate individuals, receive the treatment that is proper or fitting for them' (Miller 1991: 260). Yet this still begs the question in many cases. Despite this, outside the critical legal school, the theoretical basis of the environmental justice movement is rarely discussed by activists in the US. Indeed, as Been notes, 'calls for "fair" siting may be deliberately vague because the rhetorical force of the calls may be compromised by attempts to specify their content' (Been 1993: 1027). Certainly the Executive Order itself does not define what it is that is just and an early EPA workgroup went so far as to reject the term 'environmental justice' in favour of 'environmental equity', arguing that this is a term that lends itself more readily to specific measurement than either environmental racism or environmental justice (Gunn 1996: 1235). Yet such a quantitative assessment of justice is clearly difficult to square with more traditional conceptions.[6]

The first point to be made here then is important, though this chapter is equally charged with ignoring it. For it is clear that to the extent that the Executive Order invokes principles of justice, interests or equality, it is calling on unarticulated assumptions or beliefs of political theory. A close examination of the substantive objectives of the EPA Strategy reveals two aspects: first, the interest individuals (or communities) have in not having their health harmed by pollution, to live in a clean and sustainable environment, and second, that any pollution which is to be sanctioned should be distributed proportionately. Both elements could clearly be espoused within a theory of justice and while such vagueness is perhaps inevitable against a background of political expediency, it poses difficulties for analysis. To see whether the aims of the Executive Order have been properly fulfilled, it is first necessary to articulate them. It of course follows that were we to introduce concepts of environmental justice into the United Kingdom, there would be strong reasons to consider the underlying philosophical concerns here as well.

Despite the lack of articulation, it is perhaps unsurprising to see these two elements of a substantive interest and proportion or equality appear within the Executive Order and EPA Strategy. Philosophers have long argued that arguments on equality frequently mask prior arguments about interests, where the interest does much of the work. Thus despite the initial focus of the Executive Order and Strategy being on distribution, it is in fact the interest which may claim more of our attention in the long run. In Hart's words: '[t]he evil is the denial of liberty or respect: not *equal* liberty or *equal* respect' (Hart 1979: 453) and Raz has similarly argued that 'there is no reason to care about inequalities in the distribution of grains of sand, unless there is some other reason to wish to have or avoid sand.' Certainly, if egalitarianism is the only spur, this has unappealing consequences – either all Fs who have G are deprived of it, or all Fs are given G (Raz 1986: 235). Thus it is irrelevant whether all communities are subjected to those pollution risks now considered disproportionate, or none at all. This need not set the principle of interests at loggerheads with notions of equality, for it is possible that we are only concerned about equality when the interest is sufficiently important to warrant it.

Certainly there is wide agreement that such environmental interests, or rights, are to exist in some form. Thus Principle 1 of the 1972 Stockholm Declaration asserts that,

> ... man has the fundamental right to freedom, equality, and adequate conditions of life, in an environment of a quality that permits a life of dignity and well-being, and he bears a solemn responsibility to protect and improve the environment for present and future generations.

A 1992 review found similar versions of such a right and state duties for environmental protection in over 44 national constitutions, in those of a dozen state members of federal states, and in the general laws of several countries (Brown Weiss 1992: 297). Yet two key limitations remain. The first is that such versions of a 'fundamental right' both at Stockholm and in subsequent formulations are no more than 'soft law' in the international sphere, that is, they are not legally binding. The second limitation, and one applicable to international and domestic formulations alike, is that 'the international community has not ... defined in practical terms the threshold below which the level of environmental quality must fall before a breach of the individuals' human rights will have occurred' (Sands 1995: 222). Thus, for example, Article 24 of the recent South African Constitution provides that '[e]veryone has the right – (a) to an environment that is not harmful to their health or well-being; and (b) to have the environment protected, for the benefit of present and future generations, through reasonable legislative and other measures ...'.[7] Similarly in Europe, though the European Court of Human Rights held in *Lopez Ostra* v. *Spain* that pollution contravened the applicant's right to an undisturbed home life, it did so on the basis that the

Lorca Town Council had not succeeded 'in striking a fair balance between the interest of the town's economic well-being – that of having a waste-treatment plant – and the applicant's effective enjoyment of her right to respect for her home and her private life'.[8]

In this context, there seem to be strong arguments that if individuals have an interest in life and/or health (whether or not it may reasonably or tolerably be infringed) that this interest should be equally observed. Rawls has famously distinguished between two main types of social good: basic liberties, to which each individual has an equal entitlement; and material resources, which he recommends distributing according to the 'difference principle'. Though he includes the right to life as a basic liberty, Rawls does not include a right to health in that category (Rawls 1972). This is thought by some to be an oversight. Thus Hayward argues that '[t]hinking of the right to an adequate environment as a right to freedom from environmental harms is to put it on a par with the other basic liberties according to which each person has, in the Rawlsian schema, an equal right' (Hayward 1998: 10). If we then have an interest (or a liberty) to environmental health, this might be conceived as an interest in remaining free from health-harming pollution, which is capable of being equally observed.

This seems to be what the substantive aspect of the EPA environmental justice strategy is saying: no segment of the population is to suffer disproportionately from adverse health effects of pollution, and all people should live in clean, healthy and sustainable communities. The initial difficulty with this formulation is that it seems to be putting the disproportionate distribution before the protection of the interest itself, when the only reason we appear to care about the distribution is that we value the interest. Our main priority, if we follow in the footsteps of these US policy makers, is to ensure that all people live in clean, healthy and sustainable communities. Certainly if all we are concerned about is the interest itself, the solution is simple. Stop the pollution, do not violate the interests and equality will be irrelevant.

The next point of importance here is that inherent in questions of pollution is the notion of a trade-off, familiar to many instances of rights infringements. We do not just 'stop the pollution' because we believe (mistakenly perhaps) that to do so would be to bring modern society and its moderately technologically advanced ways to a screeching halt. We permit pollution, and the rights infringements it apparently entails, because of the benefits that cars, factories and hospital incinerators bring. Evading pollution entirely is neither feasible nor (according to many) desirable. Thus while in the United Kingdom pollution is defined as being 'due to the release from any process of substances which are capable of causing harm to man or any other living organisms supported by the environment' where the definition of harm 'includes offence caused to any of [man's] senses or harm to his property; and "harmless" has a corresponding meaning',[9] a recent collaborative guide between Her Majesty's Inspectorate of Pollution (HMIP) and industry noted that 'there is no straightforward definition of harm and so deciding on the combination of circumstances in which a release may be regarded as insignificant is a matter of judgement' (Environmental Analysis Co-operative 1996: 8). Environmental legislators may attempt to do what industrialists and regulators alike believe is not possible − to legislate in such a way to avoid harm. Our current processes enable us to minimise pollution in many cases, but it is still permitted at 'tolerable' levels.[10] And so the focus on distribution and spatial 'justice' is not misplaced. For the claim of the environmental justice movement (to the extent that such cohesiveness can be attributed to it) was, and remains, that some communities are more polluted than others and that this is 'unjust' (however this is defined). This is an issue so far not addressed by conventional interpretations of environmental rights.

And so the issue which policy makers consider under the heading of 'tolerability' and which lawyers formulate into questions of reasonableness and due diligence is frequently considered by theorists as relating to the 'force' of rights. Again this is contested. Thus Rothbard writes: 'the remedy is simply to enjoin anyone from injecting pollutants in the air, and thereby invading the rights of persons and property. Period' (Wenz 1995: 63), while Nozick, a (then) fellow libertarian, disagrees: '... it would exclude too much to forbid all polluting activities' (Nozick 1974: 149). He assumes, without further explanation, that the compromises required to live in a pollution-free state would be too much to ask. Certainly restricting all risky activities would significantly curtail individual liberty to act. Theories on how to resolve rights clashes, or the clashes between rights and other interests, are clearly not confined to the pollution sphere. But they do raise particular issues where 'the events of complexity, surprise and interdependence are governing characteristics of technological hazards' (Cutter 1993: 2). Some flexibility here is essential, as well as a readiness to accept change, innovation and unpredictability (Freeden 1991: 37). In this context it appears plausible that rights or interests should be capable of being infringed, justifiably, at tolerable levels of pollution and that they are not thereby extinguished or violated. But this does not end the debate.

Having decided that interests cannot be absolutely protected, we need some mechanism to decide which interests will be infringed. In this context we also need to decide *whose* interests are to be infringed. In pollution terms, do we place all the actually or potentially harmful activities in one corner of a town, region or country, exposing the residents or employees there to a very high risk of harm but minimising the risks for other residents, or do we try to locate them 'justly', 'equally' or 'equitably' throughout the area? In other words, if, as it appears, some areas of the country are healthier than others, for example, when natural radiation seeps into parts of Cornwall and Devon, or cities located in valleys experience increased air pollution, and low-income populations have greater health problems than high-income groups,[11] does this mean that some communities *should* bear greater health risks by design, simply because it is economically efficient to do so? For we are presented with a number of choices. We could either infringe as few interests as possible (by exposing some individuals as much as possible) or we could choose to expose all individuals 'equally' if this is what environmental justice is thought to require. It is this second approach that is embodied in the US initiative on environmental justice.

The answer the Executive Order and Strategy thus presents is that any infringements, if and when they occur, should be proportionately distributed. In philosophical terms, this appears to be akin to the proposals for the fate of interests in conditions of scarcity if it is impossible to satisfy all the justified claims in full (Raz 1986: 223). The reason we infringe interests equally rather than protecting as many as possible by infringing some to the hilt (for example, by locating all the actually or potentially harmful polluting activities in one end of town) appears to be because these interests are so important that we believe they should be equally protected. In the Rawlsian scheme of things they are not subject to the difference principle. Our first objective thus appears to be to respect interests (or liberties) to health. This is the best solution. However, if these interests cannot be observed, on grounds of reasonableness, cost or design limitations in the relevant technology, how then should we infringe them? Having decided on proportionality (or equality) the next task is then how to achieve this in practice. Is it possible to formulate schemes for proportionate interest infringement in this context?

Inter-community Justice[12]

In addressing these issues of inter-community justice (though they have not been formulated as such), US policy makers have proposed a number of possible options. In general these are *ex ante* solutions, anticipating environmental problems and inequity before they occur. Thus the US Executive Order and Departmental environmental justice strategies require environmental justice concerns to be taken on board early in the policy planning process by requiring *inter alia* each federal agency to focus attention on the human health and environmental conditions in minority and low-income communities and fostering non-discrimination in federal programmes that substantially affect human health or the environment. To implement some of these objectives, or to distribute 'locally undesirable land uses' as they are known, two key approaches have been employed: a market-based approach and regulatory decision making. Market transactions leave the choice (such as it is) to communities themselves, and if all communities have equal access to this bidding process, equality might be ensured in this way. Alternatively, decisions could be freely made by decision-making bodies. This could either occur at the national level, with centralised bodies distributing 'proportionate' risks, though in a largely decentralised system this might prove difficult. Conversely, local decision makers could be empowered to make their own siting decisions, on a similar basis to market transactions, but this would need to occur without outside interference. One difference between the two mechanisms is that in this economic paradigm, communities make choices they perceive as 'rational' which may differ from the 'reasonable' conclusions reached by regulators and the common law. Both concepts are of course controversial in their definition. These will now be considered in turn.

Market Transactions

If market transactions are explicit, a developer or public agency enters into a public bargaining position with a potential host community, offering them benefits – be they roads, tax rebates or community leisure facilities – in an effort to persuade them to host the site. Some schemes are remarkably explicit. Thus the US Department of Energy has an established Monitored Retrieval Storage (MRS) programme to provide temporary storage facilities for spent nuclear fuel rods. This programme typically pays communities for each stage of the discussions they enter into. The Skull Valley Goshute Tribe, for example, received $100,000 to study feasibility, $200,000 for Phase IIA, and $300,000 for Phase IIB (Skull Valley Goshute Tribe 1995: 65). While some such exchanges have occurred, primarily in the United States, Rabe's survey leads him to suggest that these efforts are often unsuccessful. He concludes that:

> ... market approaches to siting have failed in large part because of their near exclusive emphasis on the attractiveness of compensation packages. In the absence of extended dialogue and other trust-building measures, compensation is frequently dismissed as bribery and fuels public animosity towards site proponents (Rabe 1994: 76).

A key question in this context is whether we sanction the trade in the first place. Perhaps inevitably the practice has attracted many critics who argue that a policy perhaps not intended to be discriminatory has this effect, particularly when advocates of compensation and bidding procedures readily admit that many North American exchanges have targeted poorer communities (Kunreuther and Easterling 1992: 179). Where wealth inequality is accepted, the appeal of a pure market is limited in tragic situations (Calabresi and Bobbit 1978: 25) even though it is merely that 'when societal balances of power are inequitable, risk negotiation will reflect those institutional imbalances. It cannot correct injustices already sanctioned by society' (Schrader-Frechette 1991: 213). Yet unless there are clear normative restrictions to the trade itself (in particular, if we reject, for whatever reasons, the notion of market-traded risk in this context), this argument may lose its force, for it may inhibit separate communities from choosing what is best for them. Precedents (for individuals at least) do exist, for though the *in vivo* sale of human organs for financial reward are now prohibited in the United Kingdom,[13] in the occupational sphere fire fighters, miners and soldiers all receive an inflated premium to reflect the greater risks of accidents or disease they face. This is the premise of market-traded risk. Certainly, Mason argues that no coherent philosophical basis underlies the prohibition on market trades of *in vivo* organ transplantation, submitting that it presents 'little more than a rather hurried and intuitive recoil from what appears to be a fundamentally degrading process which is likely to have adverse effects on society's values as a whole' (Mason 1992: 125). In both situations, as in instances of market-traded pollution risks, individuals accept additional pecuniary rewards for facing greater risks to health.[14]

Clearly, in both situations, individuals consent (whether or not that consent is truly 'free') and it is possible that the occupational trades are permitted because they benefit the community, whereas the former is not because it benefits a sole individual and there is something distasteful about one human being bearing risks for another.[15] As in the pollution context communal benefit overrides individual burden. Perhaps as citizens in a community we collectively benefit from the work of the police, fire fighters and miners, and the risks these employees face. If one employee is harmed they cushion the blow the community would otherwise take. It may be that by analogy we accept that a community, and ultimately an individual, should accept additional risks for the benefit of others. It is arguably the 'price' for living in a moderately technologically advanced community. However, when these risks are not equitably distributed, the identity and role of the community in whose name these risks are born might need to be more closely examined. In practice, many of these arguments hinge upon whether consent is in fact 'free', in both a market and a regulatory context. Engels was one famous critic of the theory of market-traded risk, pointing to the inadequacy of compensation for injured workers, the lack of worker education and knowledge concerning the risks and the falsification of accident records by mill owners to present an over-optimistic portrayal of conditions at their firm (Engels 1987). Where markets do operate efficiently however, some individuals may prefer to accept the additional risk for increased pay. Thus many may benefit from their work even if they bear the burden, because they as individuals receive a benefit *ex ante*.

Certainly the Skull Valley Goshute Tribe reject regulatory intervention which inhibits their choice: 'the charges of "environmental racism" and the need to "protect" and "save" us smack of patronism. This attitude implies we are not intelligent enough to make our own business and environmental decisions' (Skull Valley Goshute Tribe 1995: 67). Where unemployment is endemic and options limited, many Native American tribes are accepting payment merely to engage in discussions on sitings of radioactive or toxic waste. These disputes are complex, primarily because they require prior agreement on the nature of the trade. If this is acceptable, then freedom to choose it may well follow if, and this is clearly key, such prior consent is informed and the precise nature of the risks are understood by all parties engaged in the negotiations. A more difficult question, and one affecting individuals as well (and so discussed below) is the validity of any community's consent where risks are borne collectively, but actual harm is borne individually.

In this scenario (just as much as in instances of regulatory decision making), consensus cannot always be achieved. Thus in 1995 'after some remarkable tribal political acrobatics' the Apache of the Mescalero reservation in southern New Mexico agreed to store 2,000 tons of radioactive waste in the grounds of the Sacred Mountain, the Sierra Blanca, for 40 years and $250 million, causing great controversy. Even though the Mescalero Apache Indians are said to live well, for the Sacred Mountain is now New Mexico's largest ski resort and the tax-free Apache Casino a great success, the community still has 34 per cent unemployment and half of their 3,000 people live on or below the poverty line.[16] Yet after losing a first vote to accept the radioactive waste by 490 to 362, the tribal leadership eventually secured consent for the project by 593 to 372, amidst claims by New Mexico's attorney-general Tom Udall that leaders 'strong-armed members of the tribe'. Even if no cogent arguments can be made against the nature of the trade, nor the mechanisms for obtaining consent, closer examination of the interrelationship between communities and individuals may lead us to conclude that community market-traded risks still face significant theoretical and practical objections. Certainly even if the community acts freely, and is equal in pursuing the trade *ex ante*, the way in which decisions are reached and strategies of participation may have important implications for democratic claims.

Siting through Regulatory Decision-Making

In theory it might be possible for centralised planning or land use authorities to distribute an equal or proportionate distribution of risky exposures throughout the country. Yet in practice a number of objections make such a policy unfeasible. For even if such proportionate exposures could be assessed in principle (and presumably summed across different spheres equating natural and human-made pollution risks, traffic concerns and/or occupational exposures), the actual implementation would be extraordinarily difficult. And in a decentralised planning system where applications for planning permission are generally made by private developers rather than centralised stage agencies, distribution will in most instances almost certainly be practically impossible.

Moreover, this institutional, regulatory approach may again assume the very equality policy makers are seeking to create if environmental justice is then implemented from on high. This is a difficulty facing all egalitarian theories of distribution. For 'given that people exhibit a wide variety of tastes and wishes (over and above those inherent in their different plans of life), in what does an equal distribution of resources exist?' (Miller 1976: 144). Different communities may well have different preferences, and might prefer incinerators to new roads. One partial solution to this dilemma is proposed by Popper. He suggests implementing a point system to share and trade unwanted facilities, where a waste dump might be equivalent to six halfway houses, or a coal-fired power plant might be 'worth' five trailer parks. Popper submits that regional bodies could first negotiate point values and then each community would be required to absorb an equal number of points. As he concludes 'the point system merely brings out into the open and routinizes [what has been] done covertly, semi-randomly, often unfairly and corruptly' (Popper, cited in Piller 1993: 193). Nevertheless, problems of imposition may still rise in developing a scale, particularly if social, political and health effects cannot be metrically assessed (Rappaport 1994: 159) and if an institutionalised exchange rate again imposes the very equality it aims to seek.

Thus on many occasions a new potentially or actually polluting activity will be accepted in an area without great debate. By their very nature, the majority of these situations will not make the headlines or end in litigation and will thus be of low visibility. However, in the US, Rabe notes that 'a community is highly unlikely to volunteer unilaterally to host a treatment or disposal facility in the absence of tangible economic rewards or clear assurances of long-term safety in facility management' (Rabe 1994: 76). A similar point is made by Szasz, who cites a study prepared for the California Waste Management Board. It concluded that:

The overriding conclusion of survey research on public attitudes towards [Waste-to-Energy] facilities is that opposition to the local siting of such a facility cuts across all subgroups. Regardless of socio-economic status or residence, specific cases can be found in which even the subgroup least likely to form an opposition movement became intimately involved in the opposition struggle. (Szasz 1994: 107)

Certainly in these circumstances there does not appear at this stage to be any great conflict between communities. If local representatives approve the planning application and no local protest occurs, it seems that it is not perceived as being unjust. But with greater awareness of the issues (or perceived issues), a truly voluntary acceptance of a potential or actual hazard, without some form of inducement, whether express or implied, is unlikely to occur.

In any case, decisions can be made by local communities through existing planning mechanisms. Here again each local authority is to some extent 'sovereign', that is, it can reach the planning decisions it prefers, sanctioning trade-offs if they appear to be in their interest. The difficulty here is that on occasion decisions might be rejected by local authorities and still imposed by the centre. In the UK, for example, local decision makers (in the planning context, elected councillors) might reject an application by a developer or public body to host an actually or potentially hazardous facility in their locality only to have it overturned by central authorities (and such overturning approved by the High Court).[17] The increasing centralisation of the planning process, and is implications for pollution, has been noted with concern by some commentators, for certainly in the 1980s more planning decisions were taken at a central level and central policy becoming pervasive particularly through increasing reliance on Planning Policy Guidance Notes or PPGs (Bell 1997: 225). In recent years, this focus has been mitigated somewhat, yet the system is still frequently 'developer-friendly' with central regulators on occasion intervening to permit development where local regulators had refused it.

One such conflict formed the basis of the 1993 decision in *Gateshead Metropolitan Borough Council* v. *Secretary of State for the Environment*[18] where it was confirmed that local regulators could not disregard central pollution control measures and reject a planning application on pollution grounds alone. As the judge, Jeremy Sullivan QC, held:

> ... it is clear beyond any doubt that the environmental impact of emissions to atmosphere is a material consideration at the planning stage ... But, just as the environmental impact of such emissions is a material planning consideration, so also is the existence of a stringent regime under the EPA for preventing or mitigating that impact and for rendering any emission harmless. It is too sim-

plistic to say that 'the Secretary of State cannot leave the question of pollution to the EPA'.

Here the Minister had concluded that there would be no unacceptable impact on adjacent land, a conclusion the judge held had not been unlawful.[19]

Despite the fact that some overlap, either procedurally or substantively, may occur between the pollution and planning systems, one key difference, and one that affects the allocation of burdens and benefits in society, is the centralisation of pollution regulation and the decentralisation of planning law.[20] Thus though neighbourhoods may wish to reject proposed developments, they are not entitled to over-emphasise the possible effects of pollution with the test of 'over-'emphasis left to central institutional decision makers. By insisting that pollution is a question to be left to a centralised agency, regulators may attempt to and will frequently succeed in quashing the NIMBY phenomenon.[21] In these circumstances local authorities are not truly sovereign and their choices are not free. As the judge noted in *Gateshead*:

> Reasonable people might well differ as to whether the proper course in a particular case would be to refuse planning permission, or whether it would be to grant planning permission on the basis that one could be satisfied that the problems could and would be resolved by the EPA process. But that decision is for the Secretary of State to take as a matter of planning judgement, subject, of course, to challenge on normal *Wednesbury* principles.[22]

On these occasions, control lies firmly in the hands of central government.

This centralisation of pollution regulation might be seen as one way to impose equality – with people everywhere being exposed to equal levels (however defined), but of course this is not the case. And so this control is particularly contentious when trade-offs are to be made and one of the key concerns of Gateshead MBC was HMIP's determination of BATNEEC criteria. This test, the cornerstone of the Environmental Protection Act of 1990 (EPA), requires regulators to mandate the 'best available technology not exceeding excessive cost'. Simply put, Gateshead (MBC) were concerned that NEEC would be more influential than BAT so that:

> HMIP might not impose the maximum levels of emission control on the basis that, in their view, the cost would not be justified. The result could be a difference between what HMIP would consider acceptable and what the local authority would consider acceptable in terms of emission levels. (Mylrea 1994: 103)[23]

As with the UK's regime on integrated pollution control, regulation is pragmatic and therefore accepts that emissions and effluents are regularly permitted even though they present a risk of harm.

Consequently, although Jeremy Sullivan QC held that the Council should fail *inter alia* because HMIP would not be *required* to authorise a plant even if harmful air pollution were to result, the regulators are clearly *permitted* to authorise a plant even though pollution will result. In practice the Department of the Environment has made it very clear that as all risks cannot be reduced to zero, they 'need to be considered alongside the costs, consequences and benefits in order to decide whether the risks are tolerable' (Department of the Environment 1995: 35).[24] It is this broader debate which occurs once these risks have been judged to be tolerable[25] and it is here that local and central authorities may have radically different agendas. Burnett-Hall concludes:

> ... though few would argue in principle against this division of responsibility, there is room for argument, to put it no higher, that HMIP does not invariably impose standards as stringent as it might in setting conditions for processes subject to Integrated Pollution Control. (Burnett-Hall 1995: 116)

By leaving these decisions to centralised regulators, local people may have little control over the pollution to which they are exposed. This raises important issues of trust, particularly in cases of scientific uncertainty. For though the pollution regulation decision can (and arguably should be) made independently of planning approval,[26] local councillors may be unwilling to make the planning decision if they do not know precisely what they will be consenting to. Placing faith in a centralised agency is plausible if pollution will be eliminated as a result of the regulation; where it is merely controlled and sanctioned, these decisions will be far more contentious.

In light of these issues, one way to protect an individual's interest in rejecting additional insults to life and health might be to institute the mechanism of an environmental challenge. In the United States, such an approach was taken by the proposed Environmental Equal Rights Act of 1993[27] which would have allowed citizens to challenge and prohibit the construction of waste facilities in 'environmentally disadvantaged communities', defined as those containing a higher than average percentage of low-income or minority residents already hosting at least one waste facility, Superfund site, or facility which releases toxics. A challenge would have been granted and the proposed facility's construction and operating permits denied unless the facility proponent could demonstrate that no alternative location posing fewer risks existed in the State and that the proposed facility would neither release contaminants nor increase the impact of present contaminants. Analogously, the proposed Environmental Justice Act of 1993,[28] first introduced by then Senator Al Gore in 1992, called for a comprehensive survey of every county, attempting to rank the 100 counties most severely contaminated by toxic chemical releases and then prohibiting new industrial activity in those areas determined to receive toxic discharge in quantities found to adversely impact human health. Ultimately both proposals were defeated in the 103rd Congress, generally unsympathetic to extending environmental regulation. A similar policy could be implemented in the UK, perhaps through the system of individual challenges to decisions by the Secretary of State.[29] But were a Secretary of State to be compelled to dismiss the application on the ground of environmental inequity alone,[30] new potentially or actually hazardous facilities might not be sited in environmentally disadvantaged areas no matter how high the unemployment rate or other factors persuading individuals to argue in favour of the facility. Were a community of one mind, this might be thought acceptable but in the majority of cases such consensus may be difficult to achieve.

Despite the difficulties in the UK, it might be possible to temper the current system to help promote equality. One possibility might be to rely on s.106 agreements.[31] These obligations enable payments – which need have no link to the land itself – to be made directly to the local planning authority, and it is these funds which could be used to implement mechanisms to promote environmental justice.[32] One proposal might then be to conceive of interests in health as a package or variegated interest. This requires accepting that whilst potentially or actually hazardous facilities present a risk of harm which may well materialise, these might be compensated for. Since pollution is just one of many factors impacting on human health, both harm and improvement can occur in a myriad of ways. If a proposed facility is expected to impose health risks, even so-called 'tolerable risks', this can be mitigated by providing additional health services or facilities, designed to off-set this additional risk of harm. Such a proposal does require that we talk openly and clearly about the risks involved even when the exposure risks are ostensibly 'quite minor' (Boerner and Lambert 1995: 94). If health effects are occurring, and government research indicates that they are, then this is an issue that should be squarely addressed.

This last proposal may be seen as insufficiently radical to take on board the systematic criticisms of the critics, particularly in the US, yet it would certainly require closer cooperation between local planning authorities and pollution regulators, estimating risks *ex ante* and mandating the nature and scope of the research required to discover whether adverse health effects exist and how best to mitigate them. The proposal may also be politically unrealistic, since it requires great candour and transparency over the levels of environmental risks communities are currently facing, or, given the state of scientific uncertainty on certain issues, environmental risks communities may be facing. Were then a health centre to prescribe, for instance, free vitamin pills for residents living near facilities apparently emitting electromagnetic fields in an attempt to mitigate the increase in anthropogenic risk it might either (a) engender community panic about the risk or (b) appear to support claims that are currently scientifically uncertain. Yet it would attempt to integrate the two concepts of equality and entitlement, enabling affected communities to benefit from the prosperity and employment that potentially or actually hazardous facilities bring, while not descending into the dualism of pitting prosperity against environmental health. Perhaps a more realistic option than providing mitigating health services to an affected community, though still through the s.106 mechanism, is to require long-term health monitoring and surveys in the community, perhaps using the site to conduct epidemiological case-control studies to assess whether, or to what extent, citizens in this community are exposed to greater than average health effects. Monitoring has two advantages: first, it may help in compensating communities or individuals *ex post* if the harm is greater than first envisaged and second, amassing reliable scientific evidence will provide valuable information for regulators and planners authorising plants in the future.

The first advantage, assisting with compensating *ex post*, may inspire fear in developers and authorities alike. Though reasons of space prohibit further exploration of this notion here, it is arguable that if entitlements to a clean environment are believed to be desirable (as the US environmental justice approach appears to imply) then these could be litigated either in tort or before a human rights body.[33] One of the greatest difficulties in these cases is the question of causation, since information gaps and latent harm make the occurrence or guaranteed absence of environmental hazards notoriously difficult to prove. Though this requires further analysis, it is plausible that this could constitute part of a rectificatory environmental justice strategy *ex post*. It is this mechanism which might redress the balance between individual and community harm, if additional health resources did not mitigate an individual's exposure to harmful pollutants. The second objective is less contentious as it would provide an attempt to assess whether or not environmental inequity exists, a lacuna for which the Environment Agency has been so robustly criticised in England and Wales.[34] Given the need for independent scientific advice one commentator has suggested empowering the Agency for Toxic Disease (ATSDR) to take on this role in the US (Crawford 1996: 860), while in the UK financial contributions from developers under s.106 agreements could be used to fund university research projects in the absence of centralised scientific research programmes. Even with such programmes, we may be exposing communities, with or without their consent, to uncertain harm. It may be that none of the proposals outlined in this chapter meet the needs of any given situation or are politically feasible. Yet they are presented as a reminder that environmental justice, if it embodies principles that are felt to be compelling, must ultimately be implemented in a practical way.

Once again, if communities are to be the arbiters of what risks they are willing to accept and on what basis, this still leaves the question of the role for individual consent. For it is individuals who ultimately bear the harm of pollution effects, even though this is frequently only realised *ex post*. As Wenz provocatively writes: 'a child dying of cancer receives little benefit from the community's new swimming pool' (1995: 67). In such cases, the most difficult situation to resolve is when a community cannot act with 'one mind' and individuals differ within a community as to what is best. Thus, for example, plans by UK NIREX Ltd, the nuclear waste agency, to construct a rock characterisation facility (RCF) at Longlands Farm in Cumbria were challenged at a public inquiry running from September 1995 to February 1996 (Sheate 1996: 80). Here the challengers included local people (including Cumbrians Opposed to Radioactive Environment, Gosforth Action Group and Friends of the Lake District), national organisations including Greenpeace and Friends of the Earth, and, unusually, another EC Member State, Ireland. Their supporters were similarly both local and national. Similar activism was shown at the proposal for the thermal reprocessing plant (THORP) at Sellafield in Cumbria[35] and in an increasing number of road protests and opposition to development on protected land.[36]

These protests in general combine objections by both local and 'outsiders' against the views of both locals and outsiders. For the purpose of this analysis, it is the views of the former that are of interest and the question becomes how to resolve a dispute when an individual or group objects to a community's decision, whether it is reached by administrative or judicial diktat or as a result of market transactions. This might be labelled a concept of 'intra-community justice'. If in practice compensation is difficult or impossible to award, the arguments presented by the environmental justice movement might be extended to claim that if individuals are required to give up their interests in life and health, on occasion with knowledge and without consent, then this should not be in vain. We should not rest on our scientific laurels overwhelmed by technological complacency. If individual interests cannot be adequately consulted and compensated, a collective paradigm shift may be required to organise our societies on less polluting lines. That this can be done is, it is true, a claim of optimists, but if the claims of justice and individual interests are to be taken seriously, a more precautionary approach may need to be enshrined well before the design stage.

Conclusion

This chapter has suggested that though largely unarticulated, two key theoretical concepts appear to underlie the US Environmental Justice Executive Order and EPA Strategy: the interest in being free of pollution and the proportionate distribution of risks if that cannot (on current thinking) be achieved. If we believe these interests to be important the key question is how they should be implemented and in this chapter two alternatives, markets and regulatory decisions, have been considered. One scheme, where a central authority allocated pollution equally, would be almost impossible to implement, even if normatively desirable despite its initial attraction. For the number of public projects which could be allocated in this way are dwarfed by the influx of private projects allocated through decentralised means. In addition, problems of precise quantification and different perceptions of relative goods and bads would be almost impossible to circumvent.

Alternatively, therefore, this chapter has considered the suggestion that it might be possible to use market or regulatory mechanisms to promote a community's set of choices. This could empower communities to decide for themselves on the trade-off to be made between explicit or implicit economic or infrastructure advantages borne against actual or potential increased risks to life and health. As each community would have access to this procedure (unless specific geological or geographical features rendered some communities better suited for some ultra-hazardous activities than others), this might be an attempt to respond to the entitlement and equality issues the Executive Order and Strategy have identified as important. Issues of consent would remain difficult, unless existing democratic structures, presumably the system of voting by councillors, remained. Further, if pollution inequality followed in the wake of economic inequality, then although this latter concern might be the real focus of our interest, if we take no measures to alleviate it, then although purely subsidiary, pollution inequality by design may be exacerbating an already difficult situation by prompting poorer communities to make trade-offs richer ones have no need to consider.

Yet even if it is possible to promote proportionality or equality between communities, as a form of intra-community justice, we are left with the far greater problem of individual entitlements, which might be distinguished as concerning intra-community justice. This latter concept recognises that we need to examine the inter-relationship between communities and individuals, ultimately perhaps formulating concepts of environmental rights. This second concept may hold far greater potential for truly coming to grips with issues of environmental justice, both distributive and rectificatory, particularly as the interests and rights formulated thus far have been developed on the individual level. To address these we could compensate *ex post*, but the ultimate solution, if we hold these interests dear and are reluctant to fall for the perceived dualism between broader societal goals and harming health, is perhaps to change our polluting ways *ex ante*.

Notes

1. I would like to thank Robin Malloy, Paul Craig and Tim Hayward for their insights and help with the structure of this chapter, Maurie Cohen for the generous loan of books and materials and the editors for their comments, both procedural and substantive. Any errors which remain are of course my own.
2. For example, traffic pollution is believed to be a major cause for several thousand advanced deaths a year, 10–20,000 hospital admissions and many thousands of instances of illness, reduced activity, distress and discomfort (Department of the Environment 1996: 26).
3. I am grateful to Robin Malloy for this point.
4. Thus the health effects of pollution may be differently manifested, racial minorities may have fewer opportunities to 'vote with their feet' and access to services may be more difficult. In a US context, Robert Bullard has argued that 'White racism helped create our current separate and unequal communities. It defines the boundaries of the urban ghetto, *barrio* and reservation, and influences the provision of environmental protection and other public services. Apartheid-type housing, and development policies reduce neighbourhood options, limit mobility, diminish job opportunities and decrease environmental choices for millions of Americans' (Bullard 1997: 107).
5. At the press release accompanying the launch of the famous 1982 United Church of Christ Commission for Racial Justice Report: *Toxic Wastes and Race in the United States*, see Baden and Coursey 1997: 1.
6. This focus on empirical studies rather than principle may again serve the critics better than traditional theorists and many critics may be unwilling to acknowledge the conceptual issues with which this paper concerns itself. As Binder notes of the critics (whom he supports): 'The ideological beliefs [the critics] attack reassure members of the ruling class that oppressed groups can achieve "equality", "justice" or "freedom" in American society without a massive redistribution of power. Their aim is to persuade people in power that violent protest by underprivileged people in America is rational, justifiable, inevitable. Their hope is that this may erode the resolve of America's rulers to use repressive force against oppressed people; and their further hope, perhaps utopian, is that this will embolden such people to take their cause into their own hands' (Binder 1987: 35).
7. See http://www.constitution.org.za for the Constitutional website for South Africa.
8. *Lopez Ostra* v. *Spain* (1994) 20 European Human Rights Reports 227. The Court held that there had been a violation of Article 8 of the Convention.
9. Section 1(4) of the Environmental Protection Act 1990.
10. The Tolerability of Risk (TOR) Framework, developed by the Health and Safety Executive (HSE) in its 1988 Report into the proposed development at Sizewell B, encapsulates the willingness to accept the risks industrialisation brings. It concluded that 'a risk of death of 1 in 1000 per annum is about the most that is ordinarily accepted for workers in the U.K. and it seems reasonable to adopt it as the dividing line between what is just tolerable and what is intolerable' (Health and Safety Executive 1988: 23).

A modified version of this framework is incorporated into Integrated Pollution Control regulation used in the UK (HMIP 1994: 24).

11 It is well documented that income affects health. Recent research has indicated that it is not so much the absolute level of poverty that matters as the size of the gap between rich and poor. As a recent editorial in the *British Medical Journal* noted: 'What matters in determining mortality and health in a society is less the overall wealth of that society and more how evenly wealth is distributed. The more equally wealth is distributed the better the health of the society' (BMJ 1996).

12 The issue of *inter-community* justice can be distinguished from *intra-community* justice. This latter concept examines the interrelationship between individuals and their communities, ultimately relating to the concept of environmental rights. It is the former which is relevant here, but the latter which may hold far greater potential for analysing issues of environmental justice and rights, particularly as the interests or rights have so far largely been formulated on the individual level.

13 S. 1(1) of the Human Organ Transplants Act of 1989 prohibits the commercial dealings in human organs, restricting the transplanting of organs between persons not genetically related and it is now an offence to make or receive payment of an offer to supply an organ, or to seek to find a person willing to sell an organ.

14 As Munzer notes, proponents of a free market in body parts 'are proposing more than just a market for blood, semen, ova, hair, placentas or diseased organs removed during surgery – the sale of which many readers may accept. Debate centres chiefly on organs that are non-vital but whose surgical removal involves significant risk or causes morbidity – such as the sale of a cornea, kidney or skin' (Munzer 1994: 261). Blood donation is widely condoned and essential to maintain current levels of medical care and it appears that we are concerned about possible sickness or harm, rather than with the act of donation itself (Titmuss 1970).

15 When this exchange is bilateral (rather than allocating organs held on trust by a public body), and it is for cash, the stark reality affronts our sensibilities (the fraternal implications of a donation are applauded for this very reason in Titmuss (1970)) particularly if one party is poor and the other (comparatively) rich. As Thomson writes: 'it is morally indecent that anyone in a moderately well-off society should be faced with such a choice ... a choice between starving on one hand, and running a risk of an incompensable harm on the other' (cited in Schrader-Frechette 1991: 213).

16 'Nothing is sacred in the Apache nuclear feud', *The Observer*, 21 May 1995: 19.

17 Under s.288 of the Town and Country Planning Act 1990 (as amended). For the detail on these provisions in an environmental context see Bell 1997: Ch. 9 and Hughes 1996: Ch. 5.

18 [1994] Env LR 11 upheld [1995] Env LR 37.

19 The challenge was brought under s.288 of the Town and Country Planning Act 1990 where the grounds for appeal approximate to grounds for judicial review. A decision can be challenged either if it is not within the powers of the Act, or if substantial prejudice has been caused by a failure to comply with the relevant procedures. These will cover bad faith, perverse decisions, failure to take account of relevant factors, taking into account irrelevant factors, mistakes of law, acting on no evidence, giving inadequate reasons or a want of natural justice.

20 Though the Environment Agency operates in distinct regions, the standards and requirements to be applied are the same.

21 The acronym stands for 'not in my backyard' and though North American in origin has come into widespread use in the UK as well. It implies that residents will resist any

potentially or harmful activities in their neighbourhoods. An interesting account of three NIMBY scenarios is provided by Piller 1993.
22 As Lord Scarman has explained in *R. v. Secretary of State for the Environment ex p Nottinghamshire CC* [1986] AC 240 at 249, ' "*Wednesbury* principles" is a convenient legal "shorthand" used by lawyers to refer to the classical review by Lord Greene MR in the *Wednesbury* case of the circumstances in which the courts will intervene to quash as being illegal the exercise of administrative discretion'. See *Associated Provincial Picture Houses Ltd. v. Wednesbury Corporation* [1948] 1 KB 223.
23 It is worth noting that a second integral test of the integrated pollution control system, the best practicable environmental option (BPEO) has been under review by the DoE which recently published its long-awaited guidance for assessment. 'The final version of the guidance was slipped out quietly in April. Indeed, a spokesman told *ENDS* that "we're not publishing that it's been published".' *ENDS Report* 267, April 1997: 32. Given that it is local communities who live with the effects of the pollution BPEO and BATNEEC permit, it is perhaps unsurprising that local authorities feel the need to exert some control over the pollution regulation process.
24 This statement echoes that by the Royal Society Study Group which held that 'decisions on what risks are tolerable and what are not should be taken with consideration of the consequent benefits gained or foregone and the risks of alternative courses of action. The belief that regulation or other actions can exclude all risk, leaving pure benefit, is a delusion.'
25 In the language of the HSE, that *ambient* risks do not exceed 1×10^6 (that is, 1 in 1,000,000). For an explanation of these assumptions see the (unpublished but publicly available) document by HM Treasury 1996: 11.
26 Per Glidewell LJ in *Gateshead* in the Court of Appeal [1995] Env LR 37.
27 HR 1924 introduced by Representative Cardiss Collins (D-Ill) seeking to amend the Solid Waste Disposal Act.
28 HR 2105 re-introduced by Representative John Lewis (D-GA).
29 Objectors are entitled to attend Council meetings (where planning applications are discussed) and, as long as they have *locus standi*, the third party retains their right to pursue a costly and time consuming action for judicial review against the local authority. More importantly however, the Town and Country Planning Act 1990 permits individuals to challenge the Secretary of State's decision (after he or she has 'called in' an application) by means of statutory appeal, on grounds which are similar to those under judicial review, under s.288. A decision can be challenged either if it is not within the powers of the Act or if substantial prejudice has been caused by a failure to comply with the relevant procedures. Any 'person aggrieved' by the decision can institute an appeal including all the parties who appeared at a planning inquiry or made representations, as well as the appellant, the local planning authority, and owners and occupiers of the site. But even if the High Court quashes the Secretary of State's decision, the case is merely remitted to the Minister. And it should be noted that the breadth of s.288 is such that is does not give third parties substantive appeal rights questioning the merits of planning decisions; these are possessed by developers only, on appeal to the Minister. See generally Bell 1997: Ch. 9 and Hughes 1996: Ch. 5.
30 Though no legislative power currently exists to require the Secretary of State to call in an application this could be compulsory if a facility were to be sited in an 'environmentally disadvantaged area' (however defined). The Secretary of State might be empowered to reject the application for planning permission on that basis. Environmentally sensitive areas could either be defined by statute, as the Environmental Equal Rights Act attempted to do, or the Department of the Environment could collaborate

with local planning authorities to identify particularly disadvantaged areas as Al Gore's Environmental Justice Act proposed.
31 Though planning agreements have been in operation since 1932 (s.34 of the Town and Country Planning Act 1932) since 1991 developers are able to enter into planning obligations, either in agreement with local planning authorities or as unilateral undertakings, see ss.106, 106A and 106B of the Town and Country Planning Act 1990, as amended by the Planning and Compensation Act of 1991.
32 In *R.* v. *Plymouth City Council ex p Plymouth and South Devon Co-operative Society Ltd* [1993] *Journal of Planning and Environment Law* 1099, for these planning obligations to be valid they had to (i) serve a planning purpose, (ii) fairly and reasonably relate to the development permitted and (iii) not be *Wednesbury* unreasonable. More recently, the test was refined by the House of Lords in *Tesco Stores Ltd.* v. *Secretary of State for the Environment* [1995] 1 WLR 759 which held that determining whether a planning obligation is a material consideration, and thus a reason for accepting the application which might otherwise not proceed, the question was whether it had some connection with the proposed development which is not *de minimis*. If that connection is established, the planning obligation has to be taken into account by the local planning authority. In particular, Lord Hoffman held that a planning obligation could be valid even where it did not satisfy test (ii) in *Plymouth*. The weight attached to any obligation was held to be entirely a matter for the decision maker. The distinction is thus now between planning obligations *required* by local planning authorities and those *offered* by developers (Moore 1997: 302–303).
33 As in *Lopez Ostra* v. *Spain*, op. cit. note 8. For an analysis of how private interests might usefully prise open conceptions of the public good see McGillivray and Wightman 1997.
34 'Agency savaged over regulation of cement kilns', *ENDS Report* 266, March 1997: 30–32.
35 See, eg, *R.* v. *Her Majesty's Inspectorate of Pollution ex p Greenpeace* [1994] 4 All ER 329.
36 For example at Twyford Down, see Bryant et al. 1996, and *Twyford Parish Council* v. *Secretary of State for the Environment and Secretary of State for Transport* [1992/3] Env LR 37.

References

Austin, R. and Schill, M. (1994) 'Black, Brown, Red and Poisoned', in Bullard, R.D. (ed.) *Unequal Protection: Environmental Justice and Communities of Colour* (San Francisco: Sierra Club Books).
Baden, B. and Coursey, D. (1997) 'The Locality of Waste Sites Within the City of Chicago: A Demographic, Social and Economic Analysis', The Harris School Working Paper No. 97-2, Chicago.
Been, V. (1993) 'What's fairness got to do with it? Environmental Justice and the Siting of Locally Undesirable Land Uses', *Cornell Law Review* 78: 1001.
Bell, S. (1997) *Ball & Bell on Environmental Law*, 4th edn (London: Blackstone Press).
Binder, G. (1987) 'On Critical Legal Studies as Guerrilla Warfare', *Georgetown Law Journal* 76: 1.

BMJ (British Medical Journal) (1996) 'Editorial', *British Medical Journal* 312 (20 April): 999–1003.
Boerner, C. and Lambert, T. (1995) 'Environmental Justice can be achieved through Negotiated Compensation', in Petrikin (ed.) (1995).
Brown Weiss, E. (1992) *In Fairness to Future Generations* (Tokyo: United Nations University Press).
Bryant, B. et al. (1996) *Twyford Down: Roads, Campaigning and Environmental Law* (London: E. F. & N. Spon).
Bullard, R.D. (1997) 'Anatomy of Environmental Racism and the Environmental Justice Movement' in Revesz, R.L. (ed.) *Foundations of Environmental Law and Policy: Interdisciplinary Reader in Law* (Oxford: Oxford University Press).
Burnett-Hall, R. (1995) *Environmental Law* (London: Sweet & Maxwell).
Calabresi, G. and Bobbit, P. (1978) *Tragic Choices* (New York: Norton & Co.).
Crawford, C. (1996) 'Medical Monitoring and The Future of CERCLA', *Arizona State Law Journal* 28: 839.
Cutter, S. (1993) *Living with Risk* (London: Edward Arnold).
Department of the Environment (1995) *Guide to Risk Assessment and Risk Management for Environmental Protection* (London: HMSO).
Department of the Environment (1996) *The United Kingdom National Air Quality Strategy*, Consultation Draft (London: HMSO).
Engels, F. (1987) *The Condition of the Working Class in England* (London: Penguin Classics).
Environmental Analysis Co-operative (1996) *Released Substances and their Dispersion in the Environment* (London: HMSO).
EPA (Environmental Protection Agency) (1996) *EPA Draft Environmental Justice Strategy*, Washington DC, available from http://es.inel.gov/program/exec/eo–12898.html
Freeden, M. (1991) *Rights* (Milton Keynes: Open University Press).
Gunn, W.A. (1996) 'From the Landfill to the Other Side of the Tracks: Developing Empowerment Strategies to Alleviate Environmental Injustice', *Ohio Northwestern University Law Review* 23(4): 1227.
Hart, H.L.A. (1979) 'Between Utility and Rights', in A. Ryan (ed.) *The Idea of Freedom*, excerpted in M. Freeman (1994), *Lloyd's Introduction to Jurisprudence* (London: Sweet & Maxwell).
Hayward, T. (1998) 'Constitutional Environmental Rights and Democracy', Paper presented to the Political Studies Association Conference, University of Keele.
HM Treasury (1996) *The Setting of Safety Standards* (London: HMSO).
Health and Safety Executive (1988) *The Tolerability of Nuclear Power Stations* (London: HMSO).
HMIP (Her Majesty's Inspectorate of Pollution) (1994) *Environmental, Economic and BPEO Assessment Principles for Integrated Pollution Control: Discussion Document* (London: HMSO).
Hughes, D. (1996) *Environmental Law* 3rd edn (London: Butterworths).
Kunreuther, H. and Easterling, H. (1992) 'Gaining Acceptance for Noxious Facilities with Economic Incentives', in Bromley, D.W. and Segerson, K. (eds) *The*

Social Response to Environmental Risk Policy Formulation in an Age of Uncertainty (Boston: Kluwer).
McGillivray, D. and Wightman, J. (1997) 'Private rights, public interests and the environment' in Hayward, T. and O'Neill, J. (eds) *Justice, Property and the Environment* (Aldershot: Avebury).
Mason, J.K. (1992) 'Organ Donation and Transplantation', in Dyer, C. (ed.) *Doctors, Patients and the Law* (Oxford: Blackwell Scientific Publications).
Miller, D. (1976) *Social Justice* (Oxford: Clarendon Press).
Miller, D. (ed.) (1991) *The Blackwell Encyclopaedia of Political Thought* (Oxford: Blackwell Publishers).
Moore, V. (1997) *A Practical Approach to Planning Law* 6th edn (London: Blackstone Press).
Munzer, S.R. (1994) 'An Uneasy Case against Property Rights in Body Parts', in Paul, E.F. et al. (eds) *Property Rights* (Cambridge: Cambridge University Press).
Mylrea, K. (1994) 'Drawing the Dividing Line between Planning Control and Pollution Control', *Journal of Environmental Law*, 6 (1): 93–106.
Nozick, R. (1974) *Anarchy, State and Utopia* (Oxford: Basil Blackwell).
Petrikin, J.S. (ed.) (1995) *Environmental Justice* (San Diego: Greenhaven Press).
Piller, C. (1993) *The Failsafe Society: Community Defiance and the End of American Technological Optimism* (Berkeley: University of California Press).
Rabe, B.G. (1994) *Beyond NIMBY: Hazardous Waste Siting in Canada and the United States* (Washington: The Brookings Institution).
Rappaport, R.A. (1994) 'Human Environment and the Notion of Impact', in Johnson, B.R. (ed.) *Who Pays the Price?* (Washington DC: Island Press).
Rawls, J. (1972) *A Theory of Justice* (Oxford: Clarendon Press).
Raz, J. (1986) *The Morality of Freedom* (Oxford: Oxford University Press).
Sands, P. (1995) *Principles of International Environmental Law* (Manchester: Manchester University Press).
Schrader-Frechette, K. (1991) *Risk and Rationality: Philosophical Foundations for Populist Reforms* (Berkeley: University of California Press).
Skull Valley Goshute Tribe (1995) 'Native Americans Have the Right to Make their Own Land-Use Decisions', in Petrikin (ed.) (1995).
Sheate, W.R. (1996) 'The Search for a UK Nuclear Waste Disposal Facility: A Case Study of Disputed "Project" Definition under the EC Directive 85/337/EEC on EIA', *Environmental Policy and Practice* 6(2): 75–86.
Szasz, A. (1994) *Ecopopulism: Toxic Waste and the Movement for Environmental Justice* (Minneapolis: University of Minnesota Press).
Titmuss, R.M. (1970) *The Gift Relationship: From Human Blood to Social Policy* (London: Allen & Unwin).
Vlastos, G. (1984) 'Justice and Equality', in Waldron, J. (ed.) *Theories of Rights* (Oxford: Oxford University Press).
Wenz, P. (1995) 'Just Garbage' in Westra, L. and Wenz, P. (eds) *Faces of Environmental Racism* (Lanham: Rowman & Littlefield).

PART IV
LEGAL MECHANISMS AND SOCIAL PRACTICES

8 Save as you Spend: Consumer Protection of the Environment and Local Social Cohesion

Françoise Jarvis

Introduction

Our consumer society places enormous demands on the environment in terms of use of resources, production processes and distribution demands. It also devalues the local economy by concentrating wealth in a few super-corporations and removing it from circulation in the local regions. This chapter will assess how the consumer can select the less environmentally destructive products and re-establish the local identity by trading with alternatives to the conglomerates.

In order to confidently purchase the most environmentally acceptable goods, the consumer needs to be furnished with the relevant information so that an informed choice between products can be made. This chapter will critically examine the sources of information available to the consumer regarding products and the businesses that make them, and also the reliability and trustworthiness of that information as a basis for making purchasing decisions. On the information ladder the first rung is the information to be found on the product itself or its packaging. This will include environmental statements and logos. The middle rung on the ladder is the company's own environmental statement on its management policies and environmental performance. The final rung allows access to information relating to the environment *per se*. The first two sources of information have been actively placed in the public domain by the company itself and passively received by the consumer. The third source, a general right of access to environmental information, allows the consumer to actively seek out information, including that which the company may prefer not to have advertised. This sort of free access to information has been referred to as 'empower[ing] people' (UK Government 1997). These sources of information are subject to legal controls, primarily to ensure accuracy and protection for the consumer but which also generate a fair playing field for the manufacturers who are competing for a share in the market. The trend has been in favour of self-regulation of industry under the umbrella of government-approved codes of practice.

The 'Green Consumer' will be frequently referred to in the following discussion and I have taken 'green' to connote more than just environmental issues to include ethical dealings as well, expressing concern for the whole production and consumption process and all those involved in it. This wider perspective is deliberately chosen to show how environmental concerns are inherently connected to issues of equity and fairness of the workers involved in product production and local issues, such as maintaining community control over labour and the economics of trading. The environment is a global concern felt locally. Trade is traditionally viewed as an individual relationship between the consumer and producer, with little regard for the wider community in which transactions occur. However, green consumerism has developed an identity in which individuals are seen as related by their shared concerns and approaches to trade. The green community is merely a body of ad hoc individuals but its spirit and indeed identity has flourished. Individuals in the green community are regarded as active participants, where participation is seen as a development ethic to achieve personal fulfilment, as well as society benefiting through participation (Robinson 1993). It is claimed that the advertising industry manipulates a sense of belonging to a movement which the green community inspires (Holder 1991: 329–330), thus potentially detracting from that community's influence.

This chapter will begin on the bottom rung of the information ladder by assessing the legal mechanisms which could be employed to ensure that product labels claiming environmental virtues can be substantiated. Environmental management systems and audits will then be critically reviewed before the avenues of access to general environmental information are explored.

In addressing some of the environmental difficulties of huge multinational corporations capturing a great proportion of the consumer market, this chapter will close by reviewing some alternatives to conventional businesses which could provide the green consumer with an environmental and ethical means of trading; namely local co-operatives and Local Exchange Trading Schemes (LETS). Both schemes offer a more personalised trading relationship which focuses upon community needs and stresses the relevance of local initiatives. They require a commitment from the consumer to support the schemes for it is only through consistent loyalty to them that they can achieve their aims of fostering local economic strength and community spirit. First, however, the extent and nature of green consumerism is considered.

Green Consumerism?

In 1994, the Mintel market research group reported that UK consumers were increasingly concerned about the impacts the products they purchased were having upon the environment. They found consumers were demanding more information regarding the environmental credentials of the products and manufacturers of those products. In response, products carrying specific environmental claims filled the market. Consumers responded to the plethora of 'environmentally friendly' products with cynicism and confusion.

One of the central questions is whether consumerism can actually be 'green' and whether there is such a person as the 'green consumer'. All human activities affect the environment; consumerism is no different. Demand for consumer products increases production, which requires energy, produces waste and reduces the global supply of raw resources. Green consumerism demonstrates an awareness of these problems and a desire to fulfil consumer demands whilst reducing the toll production and consumption places on the environment. It is the demand for such products which is of paramount importance in the free market. Given that green products continue to have an adverse impact upon the environment the only realistic aim is to reduce that impact to as low as feasible. However, green consumerism could be a danger in itself. As Wilkinson observes, 'Green consumerism maintains damaging economic activities' (1997: 170). It encourages the purchasing of green products under the illusion that there is a *benefit* to the environment by the consumption of such goods:

> Consumption inherently conflicts with environmental protection. Consumption means the stripping down and often wasteful use of natural resources, as well as all the garbage remaining once we have consumed the benefits. The notion of the 'smart shopper' also does little good for the environment if purchasing is based merely on price, selection, or quality of workmanship. (Kye 1995: 34)

The costs to the environment of designing, producing, marketing, distributing, utilising and disposing of consumer goods is still not being adequately reflected in the prices paid for produce. Instead the converse is happening, whereby products which do not impact on the environment are those which cost the most. This is an anomalous situation when it is considered that green items are less wasteful and more efficiently produced and thus should be cheaper. The Organisation for Economic Co-operation and Development (1975) defines the 'polluter pays' principle as accepting that production and consumption lead to the deterioration of environmental resources and that the market is failing to reflect the scarcity of these resources by the inadequate account taken in the price system of this deterioration.

Even if green consumerism is partially possible, does the green market exist? There can be said to be two varieties of consumer. The first is the true green consumer who will actually cease to consume if the product range does not offer a green choice; they would rather adapt their lifestyle to avoid use of the product, for example, drivers abandoning their cars. The second variety is the potential green consumer who would prefer to purchase a green choice, but if none is offered will buy from the existing product range regardless. These consumers are continuing to opt for the greener product, despite the current tendency for these products to cost more. NOP Social and Political (1997) reported 95 per cent of domestic water customers would prefer to continue paying the same water bill and see more investment in the environment than have their water bills reduced. Over two-thirds of those surveyed said they would pay more on their current bills if the difference was used to clean rivers and coastal waters or ensure an adequate supply of water. A body of potential green consumers does exist, with ten per cent of the population having joined an environmental organisation, compared to four per cent who have joined a political party, according to a MORI poll (*The Guardian*/WWF-UK 1997).

The future for green consumerism lies with this body of purchasers. They make consumer choices founded on their environmental conscience and could be encouraged by the market to continue to do so. The range of alternatives to mainstream businesses and products has great potential if these consumers are alerted to their existence and practices.

The discussion, therefore, turns to what it is that differentiates the green product from the rest on the market. The production process will use better and cleaner technology; the raw materials should be sustainable;[1] the locality of the production should be such as to reduce transport pollution and the product and its packaging should be recyclable. This involves a life-cycle analysis of the product itself; the cradle-to-grave approach of a product's history. The packaging of the product has become an issue in its own right with three per cent of landfill in the United Kingdom coming from this source and sixty per cent of all tradeable goods in the European Single Market being packaged (Long 1997).[2] The packaging often fulfils its purpose in protecting the contents and thus reducing spoilage but then the majority of consumers reject the product, even if the contents have been unaffected, because the packaging is damaged. Either the packaging itself needs protecting or the unspoilt goods need to be transferred out of the damaged packaging, creating yet more waste.

Pearce et al. (1989: 153–156) demonstrate how the free market will 'green' itself if consumers freely choose less polluting products over more polluting ones as market forces will lead to a change in the pollution potential of the product. Pearce et al.'s definition of Green Consumerism depends upon an informed consumer who is in a position to evaluate the pollution potential of a variety of products: information about the product to be purchased and information about the company presenting it to the consumer. Information is thus the key concern when 'greening' our shopping habits. The White Paper on the environment, *This Common Inheritance* (Department of the Environment 1990: para. 17.27) sees the provision and public monitoring of environmental information as 'one of the most effective stimuli to improving the environment throughout Europe'. The provision of information is also a relatively cheap option for the government to promote. Rowan-Robinson et al. (1996) list one of the benefits of improved public access to environmental information registers as informing consumer choice, so that they can opt for the green product. This they term 'the personal responsibility role'. Purchasing less environmentally harmful products is one means of satisfying our personal responsibilities.

Green consumerism has so far concentrated on the product but I suggest the green consumer could look beyond the product itself to the business ethics of the companies behind the products. Green trade should be restricted to companies who only invest in ethical ventures and who demonstrate respect for workers' rights to decent conditions and remuneration. This takes us beyond the cradle and grave to include conception, parental responsibilities and education. It is not simply the raw materials and production process which satisfy 'green credentials'. There are businesses which are run on the principles of workers sharing the profits of the venture and which value labour as the most important resource available, which should be nurtured and developed. Two forms of such ethical business will be focused upon in this chapter: the co-operative and Local Exchange Trading Schemes. Before examining these alternative trading systems the current regulations dealing with environmental claims and information relating to conventional business need to be assessed.

Product Information

'Softer on the Environment'
                                Claim made about Nouvelle Toilet Roll.

The claims and logos which appear on a product or product's packaging are the most direct source of information available to the consumer. The National Consumer Council (Smallbone and Sutcliffe 1996), at the request of the Departments of Trade and Industry and the Environment, conducted extensive consumer questioning and surveys about green claims on products. They discovered a high level of environmental claims being made and consumer dissatisfaction with them. Some of them were nonsensical or made virtues out of mediocre performances such as, 'Container made from 25% recycled material' (Sparkle furniture spray) and many were incomprehensible and vague such as 'Faith in Nature' (Clear Spring dishwasher liquid) and 'Environmentally Friendly'.[3] Numerous aerosol dispensers misleadingly carried 'ozone friendly' or 'no CFCs' as a green marketing claim and paint cans claimed the product was 'lead-free'. It is illegal for domestic consumer products to contain CFCs (Johnson and Corcelle 1995: 170) and it is illegal for paint to contain lead. Arguably it is not helpful for producers to attempt to make a virtue out of satisfying a legal obligation and by doing so they are devaluing the benefits of true environmental statements and indeed the entire environmentalist's arguments supporting greater access to environmental information. It is probably possible for every consumer product to have some quality which lends itself to a degree of green credentials, such as supporting local economies and thus, the consumer's rights have been cheated and diverted from the truth. In relation to advertisements, Holder (1991) states words such as 'green' have been polluted by misuse.

It is accepted at government level that control over green claims is required as claims on products are outside of the remit of the Advertising Standards Authority, which partially explains why so many green claims have previously not been challenged. The response has taken two approaches: first, to rely on the existing command and control legislation and, second, the 'soft-law' approach of self-regulation via the development of a voluntary code of practice.

The existing legislation which ought to deter producers from making these factitious statements about their products is the Trade Descriptions Act 1968 which is the traditional remedy for demonstrably false or misleading descriptions of a product. Section 1(1) of the 1968 Act makes it an offence in the course of business or trade to apply a false trade description to any goods or to offer or supply any goods to which a false trade description is applied. A description which is misleading, although not false, is also covered by this legislation. The Act does not specifically list environmental claims in section 2 as being covered by the remit of the Act, so there has been some uncertainty amongst the local trading standards departments, who have the power to bring prosecutions, as to whether the Act covered these situations. However, the Department of Trade and Industry is satisfied that it can be used to prosecute for factually false and misleading green claims. The main difficulty with this criminal law is that it is often impossible to prove a vague green claim is actually false. A statement, 'Made from 100% recycled material' can be easily verified, but 'Easy on the Environment' is so broad and meaningless as to be impossible to quantify. Thus the Trade Descriptions Act is limited in its application in relation to environmentally related claims. So far there have been just four successful prosecutions[4] and five unsuccessful prosecutions (Smallbone and Sutcliffe 1996). A private member's bill was introduced in 1994 to amend the Act so that it clearly covered environmental claims and to make sure manufacturers would be obliged to substantiate any claims they made, but lack of Parliamentary time meant the amendments fell.

The second response to the problem is to formulate a code of practice. The last administration supported a voluntary code, but the current government appears to be more open to the possibility of a code with statutory backing, again by amending the Trade Descriptions Act.[5] To coincide with the publication of the National Consumer Council's report the previous administration produced a strategy paper on environmental information about consumer products (DoE 1996). The strategy did not aim to control such information but to influence it and promote the action of the market. One result of the strategy was the publication of a consultation paper in early 1997 advocating the voluntary code of practice approach (DoE and DTI 1997). This strategy is not only to ensure the market operates more openly and fairly but also to encourage sustainable development on the hypothesis that the environmental impacts of production methods will be reduced in the newly open and efficient marketplace. In 1998 a new government code on green claims was launched with the aim of helping businesses avoid misleading claims and demonstrating how they can give positive environmental information to the consumer (DETR 1998). It is thought the code will operate along similar lines as the Advertising Standards Authority which oversees print advertising (ENDS 1997). This follows on from the principles enunciated in the *Guidelines for Non-advertising Green Claims* (DTI 1994), which suggests a high degree of integrity in activities involving green claims and ensuring the claims are substantiated. However, the success of the guidelines has been muted with certain sectors even accusing the DTI of breaching them (ENDS 1996b). The new code of practice is closely modelled on the draft International Standard on Environmental Labelling, ISO 14021 (ENDS 1998c), which is due to be approved in 1999. As Elworthy and Holder (1997) observe, businesses have had considerable success in persuading government they should be left to organise their own green corporate culture. This is not surprising when the last government's support for deregulation and self-regulation is considered. Teubner and Farmer (1994) discuss the utility of using external legislative intervention to control companies, when internal self-organisation can be seen to sensitise the company to environmental demands. They claim that external 'command and control' has reached its limits due to its inflexibility and ability to respond to the demands of business. Under certain conditions they assert that self-organisation can make an enterprise more responsive to ecological issues than legislation.

If the present government decides to give the code of practice a statutory backing, Parliamentary time will need to be found to amend the Trade Descriptions Act, possibly to incorporate the ISO standards. Until that happens, consumer cynicism may not be adequately addressed.

The Eco-label

There is an environmental logo in the marketplace which aims to guarantee accuracy, and which consumers are encouraged to trust: the eco-label. The eco-label is an EC concept and is provided for in Regulation 880/92/EEC,[6] which operates by identifying a product group which has a similar purpose and which competes in the market. Ecological criteria relating to the life-cycle of the product group are then identified such as its use of raw materials, the production process, its distribution and finally, its utilisation and disposal. Severe delays in launching the scheme and establishing the product group criteria have resulted in there being few product groups that are capable of joining the scheme and being awarded the label.

Manufacturers are free to submit their product to be assessed by the set criteria. The UK Eco-labelling Board administers the award, using its discretion to refuse an award, even if the product satisfies the criteria, which at present is set to allow only 20 per cent of products on the market to qualify (ENDS 1996c), on the basis that it may still be disadvantageous to the environment, for example, a chemical-based pesticide. The label, a distinctive blue and green 'flower', is valid for three years, although it can be withdrawn earlier, and is used in the advertising and packaging of the product. Originally it was envisaged that the eco-label would replace any existing national labelling schemes, of which the German Blue Angel is one of the most successful; current proposals focus upon better co-ordination between any national scheme and the European scheme with the national scheme being phased out within five years for product groups to which the eco-label has been extended (UK Eco-labelling Board: 1997a, 1997b). Once the criteria have been established for more product groups and the award begins appearing with more frequency, it is hoped that the consumer will be able to readily identify it and purchase in the confidence that the product has been rigorously examined for its impact upon the environment at every stage in its production. The eco-label does not prevent producers from using their own green logos or claims, so the potential of the eco-label lies in consumer awareness and preference for products displaying the EC standard. The American Forest and Paper Association challenged the label, taking the view that it is a trade barrier, for products failing to carry the label will be overlooked in favour of those carrying it, thus creating a market disadvantage (ENDS 1996a). The concern of the AFPA demonstrates the potential of the label to achieve its purpose and make the market less favourable for non-participating products.

The lengthy delay in seeing the eco-label in the market has led to re-evaluations at the European and national levels. In early 1996 the European Commission proposed substantial amendments to Regulation 880/92, in order to increase the efficiency and effect of the label. These include establishing an independent Eco-Label Organisation at the European level to develop the product criteria. A graduated label is introduced under the amendments which would allow more information to be communicated to the consumer by the award of one to three 'flowers' depending on performance at specific criteria and the application fee is reduced to encourage smaller firms to join. Nationally, the Department of the Environment, Transport and the Regions is debating the introduction of a UK labelling scheme, which would give greater control to industry in the setting of the criteria. Following the Canadian example, it may be possible for a company to preempt the criteria by submitting their product and stating why they believe it is 'green' enough to be awarded an eco-label (ENDS 1998b). The possibility of a private company operating the scheme is also under discussion. This would be another move away from regulatory control and further embrace the freedom of businesses to self-organisation.

Product labels and statements mark the front line in product–consumer relations. Labels that shoppers are urged to trust, such as the eco-label, lose their full potential and credibility if they are lost amidst numerous other logos.

The Energy Label

The Energy Label is another European Community initiative,[7] which will provide certain ecological information about the product. This label is of a compulsory nature, unlike the voluntary participation in the eco-label, and applies to traditional 'white goods' such as refrigerators, freezers, washing machines and tumble-dryers. The label will give an indication of the energy consumption of the machine and also other resources such as water (relevant to dishwashers and washing machines). The energy efficiency of the appliance is rated on a sliding scale which must be shown on the label. The virtue of this label is that it must feature on the machines themselves and in product brochures and mail-order catalogues. The information acts in a dual capacity: the customer can purchase the more efficient appliance and thus help to protect the world's resources and simultaneously reduce their energy bills. A potential source of concern is that the information is provided by the manufacturers themselves so safeguards as to accuracy need to be guaranteed. It is presumed that competition within the market will mean that claims will be keenly scrutinised and the Trade Descriptions Act will cover false information.

Information Relating to the Organisation

'Green Business is Good Business' –
John Gummer, Secretary of State for the Environment.[8]

Businesses today have a multitude of environmental legislation to comply with. This could create problems if not managed correctly, with a company falling foul of regulations through ignorance or incompetence. By installing an environmental management policy, businesses can ensure an internal review picks out any potential violations and hazards before they become the concern of the regulatory authorities. An environmental audit should lead to operational and managerial improvements and thus efficiency for the firm (Knights 1991). Companies are seeing the marketing potential of environmental audits, reports and management systems and are turning them to their advantage. Rose (1996) sees environmental reporting raising the profile and image of the company as well as ensuring the primary aim of legislative compliance and increased efficiency. Although Ost (1994) queries whether businesses react to environmental management schemes in quite the right spirit, viewing them as opportunities to 'seduce' rather than inform, environmental reports are beginning to improve in quality, moving away from a 'glossy' green statement to a more accurate statement which includes the bad news as well as the good.[9]

Environmental Audits, Management Systems and Reports

Environmental audits and environmental management systems allow businesses the freedom of self-regulation whilst simultaneously ensuring they comply with statutory provisions. The audit and management systems operate in parallel creating a corporate image which may appeal to the green consumer who will be the ultimate watchdog over their activities.

The European Community introduced an environmental management and audit scheme, known as EMAS, in 1993.[10] The scheme began operating in 1995 and offered Europe-wide recognition to firms which managed their environmental impact and gave commitments to improvements. EMAS is a management tool which companies are encouraged, although not obliged, to participate in (ENDS 1992a, 1992b). Thus the external regulation is available to the organisation for internal self-review. The environmental audit will primarily serve to ensure the site is in full compliance with all relevant pollution legislation whilst there must be an environmental policy to include a programme of environmental performance improvements.

A written statement, verified by an external independent assessor, outlining the management policy must be made available to the public. This obviously increases the information available to the consumer who can now make purchasing decisions influenced by company as well as product information. However, controversy arises when the company uses the information as a form of green advertising. Hunter (1994) claims this disclosure should induce the company to go beyond mere compliance with current legislation. The problem is that some companies claim positive environmental efforts have been achieved when all they have done is comply with the relevant legislation and protect themselves from future liabilities, something Cahill (1996: 13, 22) claims is the primary purpose of the audit, with 'increasing environmental awareness' merely a side-effect.

The company's enhanced green credentials are the incentive to participation. Another incentive is that a green business is a less wasteful business, an efficient business and thus a more profitable one (Fairley 1995). Hajer (1995) discusses ecological modernisation in his work *The Politics of Environmental Discourse* and examines the fragmented approach to environmental issues currently adopted by environmentalists, arguing that a collective coherent approach between all the disciplines, including economics and political science is the path forward. Business competitiveness is positively affected and access to new markets can be established. Hatchwell (1992), for example, believes public and local authority confidence in the company will be so enhanced that planning permissions, development initiatives and applications for state grants will be viewed more favourably.

Those who meet the EMAS requirements will be entitled to display a letterhead, indicating the extent of their participation in the scheme, on their business correspondence. The audit therefore plays a role in the company's business transactions, with companies showing a preference to deal with other companies committed to the scheme. Kiss and Shelton (1997) believe the audit also provides guarantees to potential buyers of the business who will be aware of any environmental liabilities which could arise.[11]

Environmental Information

> '... to encourage individual people to do what they can to improve the environment themselves by giving them better information'.
> This Common Inheritance, Cm 1200, 1990, para 2.14.

Lewis and Wyles (1990: 104) state that 'Experience has shown that increased public awareness leads inevitably to higher standards in waste and emission control'; however, many companies have not implemented an environmental management policy or undertaken an environmental audit which would improve efficiency and lead to greater transparency in their dealings. Indeed just a handful of UK companies have been registered on the EMAS scheme. This does not mean the non-participating companies are able to operate behind closed doors without any external public scrutiny. Consumers have two general means of accessing environmental information relating to particular companies.

First, the Environment Agency is responsible for maintaining a series of public registers under various enactments. The principal Public Registers[12] are the Register of Industrial Works, Radioactive Substances Register, Water Quality and Water Abstraction Registers, the Waste Management Licence Register and, most usefully, the Integrated Pollution Control Register, which holds information on certain industrial processes.[13] The government places much faith in the registers system, promoting them as an administratively practical way to communicate information in a clear and transparent manner to the public (Bakkenist 1994), but as Rowan-Robinson et al. (1996) discovered the registers are under-utilised and Pearce et al. (1989) state the green consumer is generally uninformed about the industrial processes involved and are unable to affect the choice of process adopted by manufacturers.

The second avenue of access to general environmental information arose from the European Council Directive on the Freedom of Access to Information on the Environment which was adopted in 1990 and implemented into UK legislation by the Environmental Information Regulations 1992.[14] The presumption within the Regulations is that there will be unrestricted access for the public to information held by public bodies, including local authorities, Crown Ministers and others who have public responsibilities for the environment.[15] A review, undertaken of the Directive and the transposing Regulations, concluded that there has been an improvement in access and a stimulation of the public's interest in environmental matters (House of Lords Select Committee on the European Communities 1997; Jewell 1997), although Charlesworth (1995) believes the Regulations have 'had very little impact'. The improvements which can be made are divided into the practical and the legal. Rowan-Robinson et al. (1996) and Burton (1989) examine the practical issues such as geographical access and public awareness of the right to request information, whereas the legal reforms would focus on aspects of the regulations, such as the definition of 'information on the environment'. Also some bodies have regarded themselves as falling outside the remit of the regulations, and the Department of the Environment has allowed this self-selection for opting out to continue. It is for the national courts, applying European Community law, to decide if a body is an emanation of the State and so covered by EC obligations such as these (Bell 1997: 66). Sands (1994: 4) lists British Nuclear Fuels plc, the Radioactive Waste Management Advisory Committee and the now privatised water utilities as regarding themselves as outside of the legislation, despite the recent High Court ruling in *Griffin* v. *South West Water Services Ltd*.[16] In *Griffin*, in the context of employment law, the court held South West Water Services, a wholly owned subsidiary of South West Water plc, the successor of the South West Water Authority, to be a State Authority for the purposes of EC legislation. Other improvements which need to be made to the Regulations include a review of the exceptions to access to information, the charging scheme which varies between authorities and the appeal process to deal with refused requests for information.[17]

These current arrangements for controlling environmental product claims and providing information to the consumer can be said to be inadequate as misleading claims still occur and the registers and the general access to information route is not being utilised by the public. If conventional business cannot provide the potential green consumer with the required trading options, perhaps alternative forms of business can fill the gap.

Alternative Trade Arrangements

> '... the idea [is] that members of an organisation, nation or planet should feel they have a stake in it, are responsible for it and have the power to exert influence'.
>
> Harper (1995: 34)

Ethical business and investment services are a growth industry (Ethical Investment Co-operative 1997) with even mainstream businesses recognising the consumer demand for green credentials for the products they buy and companies that they purchase from. Some businesses have always based their existence on an ethical stance and indeed exist as an alternative to mainstream businesses. These organisations are not necessarily run in terms of profit generation but exist to fill community needs beyond mere consumption. They recognise that humans are interactive beings and that trade facilitates the creation of new relationships within the community and even establishes local social cohesion.

Ethical Trade

Environmental concerns are not limited to pollution emissions and recyclability but also cover the environment of the production workers and the environment of the region from which the raw materials are harvested. Numerous organisations offer consumer products with guarantees that those products have been brought to the consumer by ethical means as regards the environment and also the workers involved in their production, particularly those from the developing world. Oxfam, Christian Aid and Traidcraft are just some of those organisations who have co-operated together and use the Fairtrade Mark under the approval of the Fairtrade Foundation. The government is becoming increasingly active in this field and encouraging fairer trading practices. The Secretary of State for International Development recently declared a commitment to promoting fair trade products with a financial grant of £500,000 to support ethical shopping.[18]

The Fairtrade Mark is an independent label informing the consumer that Third World workers received a better deal in the production of that product than they would otherwise have received at the hands of conventional, non-ethical business ventures. The Fairtrade criteria include the workers' wages and working conditions but also assess the environmental standards employed (Fairtrade Foundation 1996). The Fairtrade Foundation (1998) apply the following principles to their trading practices:

> In order to maximise the benefits to producers the price paid should be clearly related to the final price of the merchandise; produce should come from groups who operate for the benefit of their members and the community and/or where conditions and wages are above average and products should not interfere with the rights and resources necessary for the local community.

The tension between fair trade, especially in developing countries and environmental trade now becomes more apparent. The virtues of *local* trading are enhanced community identity and the local economy and reduced distribution costs and transport pollution. However, trade with developing states is not to be fully discouraged as it can form the foundation of ethical trading relationships. Developing states can be encouraged to instigate their trading practices in sustainable fashions, respecting the surrounding local environment and the conditions in which workers operate. Trade with such communities enhances their local identity and provides cultural diversity in ours. Thus, trade outside the near locality is not to be shunned but the inequality of international trading relationships should be reconsidered. The Fairtrade Mark is an indication that these inequalities are being addressed.

The financial sector has a limited historical involvement in ethical trade, but recently it has embraced ethical investments, screening financial products such as pensions and personal equity plans (PEPs) so that investors' money is not used to inadvertently support political parties of any persuasion or corporations which do not regard sustainability, pollution control or labour relations (Ethical Investment Co-operative 1997). Schmidheiny et al. (1996: xxii) state:

> Mainstream investors in equities (stocks and shares) largely dismiss environmental concerns because they are seen as moral issues outside their realm. Those in the financial community who are contracted to manage funds for others point to their legal duty to maximise returns on investments without reference to the morality of environmental damage or social justice.

They go on to question the short-termist, profit-only, mentality of the financial sector but believe that the financial market reflects human concerns and so must in time come to reflect concerns over environmental degradation. It is satisfying to note the rise in popularity of ethical investment businesses, perhaps demonstrating that those human concerns are now being reflected in the market.

Co-operatives

The nature of the conventional capitalist market encourages the short-term and environmentally short-sighted position which Schmidheiny et al. describe. Mainstream organisations are owned by external shareholders and so operate with the primary aim of increasing the shareholders' wealth, whereas a co-operative is a business organisation which is owned and controlled by its members and so it reinvests its profits in the company or distributes them to its members. The Wales Co-operative Centre (1997) web-site information observes:

> The principle of 'labour hires capital: capital does not hire labour' applies in a co-operative. In a conventional share company the shareholders put up the capital, hire labour at the market rate and profit is distributed to the shareholders in proportion to their share holding. In a co-operative labour will employ capital, paying its market cost in terms of interest and any profit belongs to labour. Membership, not money, is in control.

Co-operatives have existed since the early nineteenth century when organisations based on the ideals of Robert Owen began operating. The earliest forerunner of the consumer-owned co-operation movement was the Rochdale Friendly Co-operative Society founded in 1830 by a group of flannel workers (Bonner 1970; Webb and Webb 1921). According to Young and Rigge 'co-operatives have always been seen as an alternative to private ownership' (1983: 22). People who are involved in a co-operative are its workers, its owners and its management. Their personal progress is inherently linked with the well-being of the co-operative and thus the other participants. Most co-operatives are run on a set of six governing principles:

- Membership is voluntary and open to all those who are willing to take responsibility for ownership.
- There is democratic control in the form of one member one vote regardless of economic input.
- There is a limited return on investment.
- Profit surplus is distributed equally among members or reinvested.
- Provision is made for the education of members and the education of the general public in the business principles and ethics of co-operation.
- Co-operation amongst co-operatives at local, national and international levels is supported. (Young and Rigge 1983: 42; Consumer Co-operative 1997.)

Following these principles the investors in the company are the workers themselves. Inevitably, there will be a tension between wanting to progress as an individual, for example by awarding higher salaries, but also a desire to further the business' success by returning profits to the company. There are a number of different forms of co-operative including the workers' co-operative and credit unions. A consumer co-operative or workers' co-operative which wishes to trade as a business will need either to register as a society with the Registrar of Friendly Societies or form a company incorporated under the Companies Act 1985, just as conventional businesses need to (Jenkins 1958; Wales Co-operative Centre 1997). The co-operatives' social objectives are traditionally locally based: they provide jobs locally and keep capital in circulation locally, but these ideals have developed to demonstrate not only care for the local community but also the global community by taking on board environmental concerns. It is this caring approach to business which creates the true value of the co-operative movement.

The co-operative principles are more far-reaching than consumer co-operatives. The principles can be used as a basis for community living as demonstrated by the founders of the Centre for Alternative Technology, Machynlleth, who established a community in which all members were equal and all owned, worked and managed the community. All full-time members of the Centre receive the same wage, which is currently below that of the average wage in the surrounding area. Some members see this as an anti-consumerist statement, whilst others view it as an example of a marginal society unable to take good care of itself (Harper 1995: 37). This initiative is a relatively small-scale project, primarily designed as an exhibition; however, the workers live on the site (and within the exhibitions), and have established a viable community.

Co-operatives offer an alternative to conventional businesses, whereby consumers know profit is not the main incentive behind the venture, but the principles of care are. Dealing with a co-operative is exactly the same as with mainstream companies and does not require a radical change in lifestyle by the consumer. This is probably one of the reasons for their success – they make ethical shopping undemanding.

LETS

Current society depends upon money being in circulation in order to purchase services and goods but Local Exchange Trading Systems (LETS) remove this requirement thus enabling cash-poor people to effectively take part in a trading relationship. Traditional cash-based transactions fail when the person who requires the service or good (the consumer) has a need and the provider is willing and able to work but the consumer is unable to commission the work due to lack of funds (Williams 1996). In theory, money ought to be a facilitator of trade but the theory collapses when surplus cash is invested in order to make more money rather than being made available for trade, and interest is charged on loans, thus again taking money out of circulation (Lang 1994). LETS offer a greater departure from conventional business. Compared to co-operatives, LETS has a much more recent history. LETS, an import from Canada, began to be established in the mid-1980s and the phrase LETS was coined in 1983 (Lang 1994). LETS create a parallel market within the local community. It does not seek to replace the national currency and occasionally trading will consist of a combination of local currency for the labour and national currency for the materials. LETS are organisations which have no formal legal status. They can be formed by anyone, at any time and in any place. They do not need to be registered and the establishment of a LETS is not burdened by formal legal procedure. The objectives of LETS are economic empowerment, community-building and reducing social inequality (Williams 1996; Thorne 1996; Purdue et al. 1997). In essence they are local, community-enhancing schemes which involve an exchange of services and trades without traditional forms of money (the national currency) ever changing hands.

LETS could be viewed as a sophisticated form of barter, but rather than a bag of apples being exchanged for a haircut, the apples are acquired in exchange for a cheque representing an amount of LETS units, which is recorded by an administrator. The LETS 'currency' or unit is a local concept, for example, bobbins are used in Manchester and beacons in Malvern. The unit may closely reflect the value of real money, that is, one bobbin being equal to one pound, thus making the pricing of each service realistic, or it may equate to an hour of work, thus the lawyer requires one LETS unit per hour of work just as the plumber does. The apple seller now has a number of LETS units to her credit which she may wish to trade with other LETS participants for a haircut and then a massage, thus the 'barter' can involve any number of people. All members of the LETS are provided with a directory listing the other members, which services or goods they can offer and also what they require. Periodically all members receive a statement showing any units of credit they have or any minus units. Minus units are to be encouraged as they are not seen as debts but rather illustrate a commitment to provide work for the other members of the scheme at a future point in time. A member does not need to be in credit before she can begin trading and no interest is charged on a minus account. Thus a community is established between the members with the economic activity remaining within, and benefiting, that community. Unlike the global market, currency generated in one area is not removed for the benefit of another region but continues to circulate within the local economy.

LETS are truly local schemes often with a defined catchment area. It is important to the members of a LETS that they work locally and see the scheme enhancing the lives of the local community. Some LETS members join the scheme out of little economic incentive but specifically to meet other local people and to establish themselves in the community. The transient society of today offers little time to some people to establish relationships with their neighbours. Lang (1994: 28–34) emphasises the increased safety to women and the elderly of 'employing' LETS workers, as well as the *feeling* of security and belonging which the scheme provides. The Edmonton LETS (1998) state that one of their primary purposes is to encourage members to recognise that they have a skill to offer the others and that they are a valuable resource to the community. The emphasis on 'local' is also recognition of the high environmental cost of transporting goods over the global commons. Also, when equipment breaks down it can often be repaired and yet it is not, because it may be too much trouble to get it fixed or it may be cheaper to simply replace it. Repairers should normally be in demand in a LETS scheme and thus broken goods can be fixed for LETS units rather than discarded as yet more waste and a new product purchased (Lang 1994).

As LETS are non-profit-making, with a private membership (although all are welcome to join), for legal purposes they are regarded as unincorporated societies. The law plays a particularly unobtrusive role as far as LETS are concerned, so far only becoming interested in their activities when the issue of taxing LETS earnings arises. As a LETS unit is not always equivalent to the national currency, the prospect of being taxed for any LETS credits needs to be considered. As far as the Inland Revenue is concerned if the transaction is akin to doing a favour then it is not subject to tax, but if the exchange is a regular occurrence this may make it a business in its own right and thus liable to tax (Lang 1994; Williams 1996). The social equality objective of LETS is undermined by the Department of Social Security's attitude to work undertaken via a LETS exchange. The Department regards a LETS income as constituting an earning and thus the unemployed are discouraged from participating effectively in the scheme.

Of what interest is a LETS scheme to the green consumer? Purdue et al. (1997) studied the type of person enrolling in the schemes and found much sympathy between such members and those of other 'alternative' or 'green' lifestyles, such as festival attendees or participants in organic vegetable box schemes. An organic box scheme depends upon a member of the local community acting as a drop-off point for the produce and this can be one of the services offered by a LETS member. LETS frequently offer organic produce for sale in return for the local currency. The organic food market in the UK doubled from 1990 to 1995, with many people expressing concern at intensive farming practices, fears enhanced by the BSE crisis. An interviewee questioned by Thorne said of LETS 'It attracts people who are oriented to change anyway, change and evolution to a different style of living ...' (1996: 1365). Although the primary purpose for joining the LETS is usually economic, with many low-income households participating (Williams 1996), the members are conscious that what they are doing is also about building community ties and creating a social network. The potential problem of members running up a large commitment, by spending but not working in return, and then absconding has not apparently been realised. Lang (1994: 83) puts this down to the nature of those joining the scheme and Thorne (1996: 1368) stresses the reliance on trust placed upon each member. By placing credit with a LETS rather than sterling in a bank the green consumer is assured that their wealth is not being used by the financial institution to finance companies and practices, even political parties, which endanger the environment. Many of the LETS members are also consumers and growers of organic produce, which they sell in exchange for LETS currency (Purdue et al. 1997: 648), demonstrating their awareness and commitment to less industrialised production techniques. Local authorities should be encouraging LETS as one way to achieve their Local Agenda 21 commitments.

Conclusions

There are two levels to green consumerism. First, and of most importance to the potential green consumer, is the ability to choose between rival products and to select the least environmentally harmful. This can be effectively facilitated by accurate product information. This should lead to an illustration of the classic free market economy in operation, but the market has become saturated by firms anxious to advertise their green credentials to the consumer. Diametrically opposing views arise on the issue of whether greater external pressure in the form of legislation is required to suppress further proliferation of unsubstantiated environmental claims about products and companies, or whether in a spirit of modernisation, businesses should be left to evolve their own ecologically sound practices which will respond and adapt to pressures from the environment, society and the economics of the market. This second view needs to be tempered by the public's concern to receive accurate information relating to environmental credentials and not merely the results of audits initiated by a company as a public relations exercise which is little more than evidence of compliance with existing legislation.

The second level of green consumerism looks beyond the product and company and their immediate impact on the environment and embraces an all-encompassing perspective of the environment which is rooted in community cohesion. Equity and fairness become the benchmarks of a green organisation. The alternatives to mainstream companies, such as LETS and co-operatives, not only facilitate economic trade but also foster community identity, focusing on the development of the locality. Joining a LETS or showing a preference for co-operative firms demonstrates a commitment to a fairer system of business; a system of business which respects and values workers and the environment and takes these concerns to the centre of their management. There is a limit to how much individual consumer behaviour can achieve, which is why the body and spirit of alternative trading systems is so enticing. Consumerism will continue to affect the environment, but careful purchasing can aid the protection of the environment and create a personal stake in it by expressing the value of our fellow workers' skills and commitment.

Notes

1 The UN World Commission on Environment and Development (1987) defined sustainable development as 'development that meets the needs of the present without compromising the ability of future generations to meet their own needs'. In the production process this would involve using renewable energy resources over finite sources and using materials which do not deplete global supplies.

2   The EC Packaging Waste Directive (94/62/EC) OJ L 365/10, 31.12.94, seeks to furnish information on whether the packaging is recyclable.
3   The Co-op Stores have banned the meaningless phrase 'Environmentally Friendly' as a slogan and Sainsbury's have removed the term 'environmentally friendlier' from their own brand packaging (ENDS: 1998a).
4   *Surrey County Council* v. *ARM Marting*, 8.5.89, claim that the product was biodegradable when it actually could not degrade without additional emulsifier; *LB Merton* v. *Addis Ltd*, 3.10.90, claim to be ozone friendly when in fact the product contained halon 1211, an ozone depleting gas; *Warwickshire CC* v. *Asda*, 14.3.91: wrongful claim that production was without CFCs; *Norfolk County Council* v. *Halfords*, 18.4.91: claim that the product was ozone friendly but contained 11-trichloroethane, an ozone depleting gas (Smallbone and Sutcliffe 1996). None of the four cases has been reported.
5   Personal communication, Department of Trade and Industry 1997.
6   Council Regulation 880/92/EEC, OJ L 99/1, 11.4.92 on a Community eco-label scheme.
7   Council Directive 92/75/EEC OJ L 297/16 of 22 September 1992 on the indication by labelling and standard product information of the consumption of energy and other resources by household appliances, OJ L 168/1, 10.7.93.
8   Department of the Environment Press Release, 13.6.96.
9   *The Financial Times*, 14.9.95.
10 Council Regulation 1836/93/EEC allowing voluntary participation by companies in the industrial sector in a Community eco-management and audit scheme, OJ L 168/1, 10.7.93.
11 The environmental audit has been established in the US for many decades now, so the European system incorporates compatibility with the other international audit schemes such as ISO 10011. In the UK, BS 7750 has also played a role providing details to the operation of a management system.
12 Other registers maintained by the Environment Agency include the Maps of Waterworks, Maps of Main Rivers, Carriers and Brokers of Controlled Waste Register, Works Discharge Register, Chemical Release Inventory and Genetically Modified Organisms Register.
13 Under the Environmental Protection Act 1990, Part 1 and Environmental Protection (Prescribed Processes and Substances) Regulations 1991, SI 1991/472, as amended, companies must obtain an authorisation from the Environment Agency in order to operate their most complex and polluting industrial processes. Details of these processes, authorisations and even applications for an authorisation must feature in the public registers as well as any violations of the conditions or variations of the authorisations.
14 Council Directive 90/313/EEC on Freedom of Access to Information on the Environment, OJ L 158/56, 23.6.90. Implemented in the United Kingdom by the Environmental Information Regulations 1992, SI 1992/3240.
15 Principle 10 of the United Nations Conference Declaration on Environment and Development, Rio De Janeiro, 13 June 1992, UN Doc A/CONF.151/5/Rev.1, states:
   'Environmental issues are best handled with the participation of all concerned citizens, at the relevant level. At the national level, each individual shall have the appropriate access to information concerning the environment that is held by public authorities ... States shall facilitate and encourage public awareness and participation by making information widely available ...'
16 [1995] Industrial Relations Law Reports 15.
17 A White Paper has been introduced proposing a general statute on freedom of access to information held by public authorities (UK Government 1997). The review and appeals

procedure for any denied requests for information will be referred directly to a new Independent Information Commissioner whose decisions will be judicially reviewable.
18 Claire Short, reported in *The Guardian*, 3 January 1998.

References

Bakkenist, G. (1994) *Environmental Information – Law, Policy and Experience* (London: Cameron May).
Bell, S. (1997) *Ball and Bell on Environmental Law*, 4th edn (London: Blackstone Press Ltd).
Birtles, W. (1993) 'A Right to Know: The Environmental Information Regulations 1992', *Journal of Planning and Environmental Law*, July: 615–626.
Bonner, A. (1970) *British Co-operation* (Manchester: Co-operative Union Ltd).
Burton, T.P. (1989) 'Access to Environmental Information: The UK Experience of Water Registers', *Journal of Environmental Law*, 1 (2): 192–208.
Cahill, L. (1996), *Environmental Audits* (Maryland: Government Institutes, Inc.).
Charlesworth, A. (1995) 'Examining the Applicability of the Environmental Information Regulations 1992: A Strange Case', *Journal of Environmental Law*, 7: 297–303.
Consumer Co-operative (1997) http://www.bath.ac.uk/Centres/Ethical/OOTW/whatisac.htm
DETR (Department of the Environment, Transport and the Regions) (1998) *Green Claims Code* (London: Department of the Environment, Transport and Regions).
DoE/DTI (Department of the Environment and Department of Trade and Industry) (1997) *Green Claims – Code of Practice – A Consultation Paper* (London: Department of the Environment).
DoE (Department of the Environment) (1996) *A Strategy on Environmental Information about Products for Consumers in the UK* (London: Department of the Environment).
DoE (Department of the Environment) (1990) *This Common Inheritance – Britain's Environmental Strategy*, Cm 1200 (London: HMSO).
DTI (Department of Trade and Industry) (1994) *Guidelines for Non-Advertising Green Claims* (London: Department of Trade and Industry).
Elworthy, S. and Holder, J. (1997) *Environmental Protection* (London: Butterworths).
Edmonton LETS, (1998) http://www.freenet.edmonton.ab.ca/lets/
ENDS (1992a) Report 205 February, 'Voluntary environmental agreements: Sectoral covenants in the Netherlands', pp. 18–20.
ENDS (1992b) Report 206 March, 'EC eco-audit scheme: An opportunity for voluntary industry action', pp. 18–20.
ENDS (1996a) Report 252 January, 'US paper industry attacks EC eco-labelling scheme', p. 26.
ENDS (1996b) Report 254 March, 'New code, but no legislation, to control green claims', p. 29.
ENDS (1996c) Report 263 December, 'Commission woos industry with eco-labelling revamp', pp. 19–20.

ENDS (1997) Report 265 February, 'Government sticks to voluntary approach on green claims', p. 26.
ENDS (1998a) Report 276 January, 'Company News', p. 4.
ENDS (1998b) Report 276 January, 'Industry supports UK national eco-labelling scheme', p. 27.
ENDS (1998c) Report 277 February, 'Voluntary code on green claims given a year to suceed', pp. 29–30.
Ethical Investment Co-operative (1997) *Your investments needn't cost the earth ...* (Cheshire: The Ethical Investment Centre).
Fairtrade Foundation (1996) *Shop for a Fairer World* (London: Fairtrade).
Fairtrade Foundation (1998) http://www.bath.ac.uk/Centres/Ethical/OOTW/Fairtrade.htm
Fairley, R. (1995) 'Environmental Policy and Audit – What's in it for us?', *Environmental Law and Management*, 7: 31–35.
The Guardian/WWF-UK (World Wide Fund for Nature – UK) (1997) *One Thousand Days* (London: *The Guardian*).
Hajer, M. (1995) *The Politics of Environmental Discourse – Ecological Modernisation and the Policy Process* (Oxford: Clarendon Press).
Harper, P. (1995) *The C.A.T. Story* (Machynlleth, Powys, Wales: The Centre for Alternative Technology Publications).
Hatchwell, P. (1992) 'Eco-auditing – the new EC proposals', *Environmental Information Bulletin*, 7: 9–13.
Holder, J. (1991) 'Regulating Green Advertising in the Motor Car Industry', *Journal of Law and Society* 18 (3): 323–346.
House of Lords Select Committee on the European Communities (1997) First Report, *Freedom of Access to Information on the Environment*, Session 1996–97, First Report, HL Paper 9.
Hunter, R. (1994) 'EU Eco-Management and Auditing Regulation', *International Environment Reporter*, pp. 142–149.
Jewell, T. (1997) 'Freedom of Access to Information on the Environment', *Environmental Law and Management*, 9: 25–27.
Johnson, S. and Corcelle, G. (1995) *The Environmental Policy of the European Communities* (London: Kluwer Law International).
Jenkins, D. (1958) *Law for Co-operatives* (Oxford: Basil Blackwell).
Kiss, A. and Shelton, D. (1997) *Manual of European Environmental Law* 2nd edn (Cambridge: Grotius).
Knights, B. (1991) 'Environmental Management', *Utilities Law Review*, 2: 179–183.
Kye, C. (1995) 'Environmental Law and the Consumer in the European Union', *Journal of Environmental Law*, 7 (1): 31–54.
Lang, P. (1994) *LETS Work – Rebuilding the Local Economy* (Bristol: Grover Books).
Lewis, R. and Wyles, K. (1990) 'Public Access to Environmental Information', *Utilities Law Review*, 1(2): 102–104.
Long, A. (1997), 'The Single Market and the Environment: The European Union's

Dilemma: The Example of the Packaging Directive', *European Environmental Law Review*, 6 (7): 214–219.

Mintel (1994) *The Green Consumer*, Vols I & II (London: Mintel).

NOP Social & Political for the Environment Agency (1997) *Environment Expenditure* (London: Environment Agency).

Organisation for Economic Co-operation and Development (1975) *The Polluter Pays Principle: Definition, Analysis, Implementation* (Paris: OECD).

Ost, F. (1994) 'A Game without Rules? The Ecological Self-Organization of Firms' in Teubner et al. (eds) (1994).

Pearce, D., Markandya, A. and Barbier, E. (1989) *Blueprint for a Green Economy* (London: Earthscan Publications Ltd).

Purdue, D., Dürrschmidt, J., Jowers, P. and O'Doherty, R. (1997) 'DIY Culture and Extended Milieux: LETS, Veggie Boxes and Festivals', *Sociological Review*, 4: 645–667.

Robinson, D. (1993) 'Public Participation in Environmental Decision-Making', *Environmental and Planning Law Journal*, October 1993, pp. 320–340.

Rose, I. (1996) 'Industry and Access to Information on the Environment' in Somsen, H. (ed.) *Protecting the European Environment* (London: Blackstone Press Ltd).

Rowan-Robinson, J., Ross, A., Walton, W. and Rothnie, J. (1996) 'Public Access to Environmental Information: A Means to What End?' *Journal of Environmental Law*, 8 (1): 19–42.

Sands, P. (1994) 'Access to Information', *Environmental Judicial Review Bulletin*, 1 (1): 3–5.

Schmidheiny, S., Zorraquin, F. and World Business Council for Sustainable Development (1996) *Financing Change. The Financial Community, Eco-efficiency and Sustainable Development* (Cambridge, MA: MIT Press).

Smallbone, T. and Sutcliffe, M. (1996), *Green Claims – an investigation into marketing claims about the environment* (London: National Consumer Council).

Teubner, G. and Farmer, L. (1994), 'Ecological Self-Organization' in Teubner et al. (eds) (1994).

Teubner, G., Farmer, L. and Murphy, D. (eds) (1994) *Environmental Law and Ecological Responsibility* (Chichester: Wiley).

Thorne, L. (1996) 'Local Exchange Trading Schemes in the United Kingdom: A Case of Re-embedding?', *Environment and Planning A*, 28: 1361–1376.

UK Ecolabelling Board (1997a) Newsletter.

UK Ecolabelling Board (1997b) *The EU Ecolabelling Scheme*.

UK Government (1997) *Your Right to Know – The Government's Proposals for a Freedom of Information Act*, Cm 3818 (London: The Stationery Office Limited).

United Nations World Commission on Environment and Development (1987) *Our Common Future* (Oxford: Oxford University Press).

Wales Co-operative Centre (1997) http://info.cf.ac.uk/ccin/main/socecon/co-op/wcop1.htm

Webb, S. and Webb, B. (1921) *The Consumers' Co-operative Movement* (London: Longmans, Green and Co.).

Wilkinson, D. (1997) 'An Idiomatic Discussion of Environmental Legislation' in

Ireland, P. and Laleng, P., *The Critical Lawyers' Handbook 2* (London: Pluto Press).

Williams, C. (1996) 'The New Barter Economy: An Appraisal of Local Exchange and Trading Systems', *Journal of Public Policy*, 16 (1): 85–101.

Young, M. and Rigge, M. (1983) *Revolution from Within – Co-operatives and Co-operation in British Industry* (London: Weidenfeld & Nicholson).

9 Common Property and Private Trusts

Paul Kohler

Introduction

> *'Well, men, what shall we do with the Common?'*
> Yanka Bryl, 'The Common' in *An Anthology of Soviet Short Stories*
> (1976: Vol. 2, pp. 129, 132)

The Common (like the question) has a fine pedigree. The Romans had a total of four categories of non-private property ranging from things common to all men (*res communes*) to things belonging to no man (*res nullius*) and including along the way public things vested in either the state (*res publicae*) or public bodies (*res universitatis*) (Borkowski 1997: 153–155). Likewise the Common Law has, by definition,[1] always recognised a range of common rights over property,[2] now supplemented by a number of statutory provisions such as those relating to public rights of way[3] and, perhaps, a public right to roam.[4]

As for 'what shall we do with the Common?', this is a problem that has divided philosophers from the disagreements of Plato and Aristotle onwards. 'Plato's communism' wrote Russell 'annoys Aristotle' who thought that '[p]roperty should be private, but people should be so trained in benevolence as to allow the use of it to be largely common' (Russell 1961: 199). Thus whilst Plato conceived of widespread ownership, Aristotle concentrated on the common rights that might exist in respect of privately owned things. As I hope to show, this is less a matter of substance than of degree.

In recent years battle has been joined by the jurists. Harris recently declared that '[c]*ommon property* means no property' (Harris 1995: 438). In contrast Waldron has stated that '[i]n a system of common property, rules governing access to and control of material resources are organised on the basis that *each* resource is in principle available for the use of *every* member alike' (Waldron 1988: 41). Thus, whilst Harris views a common property system as a contradiction in terms because no system can be said to exist where there is no mechanism to prevent individuals taking what is part of the common for themselves, Waldron refers to common property as necessarily involving 'rules governing access' which are necessary 'when allocative decisions are made'.

We will return to these points later, but at this stage a word of warning is probably required. Not everything is as it seems. Gray, for example, would appear to be siding with Harris when he states that '[u]npropertised resources remain in the commons, available for use and exploitation by all'[5] but he continues by insisting that 'it is not inconsistent' with this view 'that some parts of the *commons* may be subject to varying degrees of public (as distinct from private) regulation' (Gray 1991: 252, 268). Thus when Gray speaks of 'unpropertised resources' he does not preclude the possibility of the allocative control of such resources which I will later argue is the hallmark of a common property system.

As is perhaps already becoming apparent, much of the debate suffers from a failure to articulate exactly what it is that is being considered. Consequently one of my first tasks will simply be to explain what I mean when I speak of the Commons (and likewise common property). Before doing so, however, I should indicate what else I am hoping to achieve in this chapter.

In contrast to the lofty aims of those cited above, my purpose is essentially a simple one. After defining my terms in Part I my argument will involve three relatively modest further steps. In Part II I will endeavour to explain why notions of common property are fundamental to any conception of society; in Part III I will consider the role those notions play in our particular society; and, finally, in Part IV I will explain how, somewhat paradoxically, the mechanism of the private trust can be used to give renewed impetus to the concept of common property in a form which can be consciously adopted by communities within our society, even in the absence of society's approval (cf. the position of charitable trusts). As will be seen from this outline, my analysis is primarily not normative but descriptive. Even in Part IV where I consider the role I envisage the private trust playing in this area, I am describing a form that already exists although its potential has not been fully realised.

In adopting a descriptive rather than normative approach I am consciously seeking to distance myself from the writings of jurists such as Reich, Macpherson and Gray who have all traversed superficially similar ground but with the aim of broadening (rather than describing) the ambit of property. In 'The New Property', Reich (1964) argued that the new forms of wealth (such as welfare benefits) which had arisen in the wake of the increased role of government demand the same legal protection as that accorded to private property. For a critical analysis see Sackville (1978: 246). The reason for adopting such a strategy was, basically, twofold. Tactically Reich appeared to be trying to entrench welfare payments by bringing them within the ambit of the constitutional safeguard preventing the deprivation of 'property without due process of law'. Whilst as a polemic the article was attempting to utilise the rhetorical power of private property.[6] Macpherson (1975), who offered interesting insights concerning the nature of property, also sought, at a more fundamental level, to redefine the 'concept and institution of property' so that individuals would not be excluded from the 'accumulated productive resources of the whole society'. More recently Gray has sought to 'reconceive the law of property' as part of a process 'creating a new commonwealth of dignity and equality' (Gray 1994).

One final disclaimer is in order before I begin. Although my approach is essentially descriptive this does not mean my notion of property is static. On the contrary what I am attempting to describe is its essentially fluid quality. Both private and common property are in a constant state of flux and thus my description is based upon a notion of property as a dynamic concept (Gray 1991: 273–274). It is this dynamism which lies at the heart of my analysis and to which I will now turn.

Part I: The Nebulous Concepts of Property and Ownership

Intuitively property seems to be concerned with a person's relationship to a thing. On a non-legal, almost atavistic, level, there is much truth in Hegel's observation that 'by appropriating, owning and controlling objects, a person can establish his will as an objective feature of the world and transcend the stage in which it is simply an aspect of his inner and subjective life' (Hegel 1952: s.46). However as a matter of cold logic talk of property *rights* must entail something more.

As Kelsen noted: 'Since the law as a social order regulates the behaviour of individuals in their direct or indirect relations to other individuals, property too, can legally consist only in a certain relation between one individual and other individuals' (Kelsen 1970: 131). Consequently, despite intuitive assumptions to the contrary, property is concerned not with relationships to a thing (which is after all simply a fetish), but with relationships between people. For, as Hohfeld (1978) famously articulated, one cannot have rights unless others are under a correlative duty in respect of those rights.[7] Yet not all relationships between people come within the ambit of property. As Ackerman made clear, 'property law discusses the relationships that arise between people *with respect to things*' (1977: 26, emphasis changed). But even this definition fails to explain exactly what is meant by a property right. Contractual rights, for example, also often deal with exactly such a relationship. To hone the definition further we consequently need to distinguish rights *in rem*[8] from rights *in personam*[9]. It was Austin who noted that '[t]he phrase *in rem* denotes the compass, and not the subject of the right ... that the right in question avails against persons generally' (1885: Vol. I, 369–370).[10] In contrast '[t]he phrase *in personam* ... denotes that the right avails exclusively against a determinate person, or against determinate persons'. As a species of right *in rem*[11] property rights thus deal with the relationship in respect of things that exists between the individual and the society of which he is part. And that, finally, leaves us with the things themselves. For not every thing (*sic*) is the subject of property.

In the film *Total Recall*, Arnold Schwartzenegger inhabits a planet on which there is a shortage of oxygen and where, as a consequence, property in air is a valuable and alienable commodity. As Cohen pointed out, property is a function of privation. If there is a superabundance of something, there is no need for property rights to exist in it for there is more than enough to go round and hence no need to separate yours from mine (or for that matter ours from theirs) (see also Chapter 7). No doubt the inspiration behind *Total Recall*, the example Cohen used was air:

C: Would you agree that air is extremely valuable to all of us?
E: Yes, of course.
C: Why then is there no property in air?
E: I suppose because there is no scarcity.
C: Suppose there was no scarcity of any material object.
E: I suppose then there would be no property in material objects. (Cohen 1954: 364)

There is thus no need for property in things of which there is a plentiful (and inexhaustible) supply and, it should be noted, even where privation exists there may be ethical or policy considerations that prevent certain things becoming the subject of property.[12] Consequently when I speak of property in things I am, in common with many commentators, referring to *resources*: by which I mean things which are finite (but not necessarily tangible, of course) and to which there are no ethical or policy objections in making the subject of property (see Waldron 1988; Eleftheriadis 1996; Ackerman 1977).

The extract from Cohen is based upon lectures given more than half a century ago and his use of air as an example of a thing to which notions of scarcity do not apply has, arguably, not survived environmental developments. This caveat, however, underlines the point made in the introduction.

Property is a dynamic concept. As society changes, the notion of what is and is not a useable resource capable of being the subject of property also changes. A few examples will underline the point. Up until the sixteenth century there is little evidence of the term 'property' being applied to land under the English Common Law (Seipp 1994). Whilst in 1828 when C.J. Swan, the Secretary to the Royal Property Commissioners, invited Bentham to help the Commission in its deliberations, one of his first tasks was to list those things which were not regarded as property and which had not been included in Blackstone's work on the subject (such as company shares and copyright) (Sokol 1994).

Despite appearances there is much more to this than simply a semantic point concerning Chancery lawyers' categories. A series of cases culminating in *Tulk* v. *Moxhay*[13] in 1848 established the restrictive covenant as a species of property right. Prior to this the law provided no mechanism whereby it was possible to sell a portion of land safe in the knowledge that subsequent owners of the plot sold would not do something that would spoil the enjoyment of the plot retained. In an agrarian and static society where there was a technological limit on what you could do with your land so as to affect your neighbour (and little if any demographic pressure), this did no great harm and there was consequently no need (and thus no pressure) to recognise such a species of property right. But come the Industrial Revolution and with it demographic upheaval and the technology to blight neighbouring land, one can see why the law, after a suitable period, was compelled to respond. The ability to build 'dark satanic mills ... in England's green and pleasant land' (W. Blake, *Jerusalem*), particularly the green and pleasant land bordering your own, had the potential to inhibit the alienation of land for there was now a very real disincentive in selling a portion of your land. Whilst a vendor could impose contractual terms limiting what the purchaser did with the land bought, such a term was of no avail once a subsequent title holder, who was not a party to the original contract, entered the frame. The vendor thus had no means of protecting the land he retained from being affected by such developments on the land parted with and every incentive to retain rather than sell any portion of his land. The recognition of the proprietorial status of restrictive covenants thus became an economic imperative freeing up the market in land. Similar points could likewise be made in respect of other rights which have crossed the contract/property divide such as leases and easements (see Simpson 1986).

This is, of course, a continuing process. Property is dynamic because society is dynamic. Returning to Cohen's example there are now EC directives on air quality the effect of which,[14] arguably, is to give individual citizens property rights in air (Cohen 1954: 205–206). Similarly, in the wake of developments such as the Kyoto Summit on global warming, a market in pollution permits has been established on the Chicago Board of Trade, the effect of which is to turn air quality into a tradable resource.[15] Looking to the future we can but speculate but in both cyber space and outer space the pressure to recognise new property rights is growing. The World Wide Web has the potential to stretch the current boundaries of intellectual property to breaking point. In the face of the contemptuous disregard of the rules of copyright (and the inability to effectively counter such infringements) it is at least arguable that this will have profound long-term implications for the development of intellectual property rights in both virtual and perhaps even non-virtual reality.[16] In the realm of outer space, speculation concerning water deposits on the moon has renewed interest in the once purely academic question of ownership rights in space.[17] There is, it is true, two international treaties on the subject, namely the Outer Space Treaty and the Moon Treaty, the latter of which outlaws property rights in celestial bodies. However it is surely indicative that in the light of technological advance the Moon Treaty has been signed by fewer than ten countries of which only one has any pretensions in respect of space exploration (that signatory being Australia, which it would be fair to assume is not at the cutting edge of space research).

Thus far I have described the term property without examining the rights to which the notion of property is attached. I have described it as a relationship between people in respect of things and *en route* indicated the nature of the relationship and the type of things that might be made subject to it. I must now consider the substance of the relationship and in so doing attempt to distinguish private from common property.[18]

The right to exclude is normally regarded as the essence of property (see, for example, Bentham 1970: 177), but that is because of our habit of conceiving of property in terms of private ownership. There are at least two problems with such an approach. Most fundamentally it ignores common ownership whilst more obliquely it confuses the concept of property with the notion of ownership. Dealing with the first problem, Macpherson made the following observation:

> From the earliest ideas of property, say from Aristotle down to the seventeenth century, property was seen to include both of two kinds of individual rights: both an individual right to exclude others from some use or enjoyment of some thing, and an individual right not to be excluded from the use or enjoyment of things the society had declared to be for common use – common lands, parks, roads, waters. (Macpherson 1977: 73)[19]

Property only includes the right to exclude in so far as there are non-rights holders who can be excluded. With private property there will always be such persons but, in so far as common property means common to all in society, the opposite is true. (That is not to say however that access cannot be limited.) Thus when I speak of the Commons (or common property) I am referring to resources in respect of which the fundamental property right held by individuals is the right not to be excluded from the resource. As I hope to show in Part II this is a category of property as important as its private law counterpart although it is often simply overlooked by judges, academics and practitioners.

Dealing with the second problem, the confusing of the concept of property with the notion of ownership requires a short digression regarding the nebulous concept of ownership. The term 'owner' is a difficult one (see, for example, the problems it poses for Honore (1961: 124–128)). Whilst property lawyers are all too ready to disabuse novices concerning their notions of property the same rigour is not applied to ownership (see Ackerman 1977: 26–27). However strictures regarding the fallacy of talking about 'property as things' is equally applicable to our habit of referring to the 'thing's owner'. Bentham's observation provides an explanation of how this arises:

> ... in common speech in the phrase *the object of a man's property*, the words *the object of* are commonly left out; and by an ellipsis, which, violent as it is, now become more familiar than the phrase at length, they have made that part of it which consists of the words *a man's property* perform the office of the whole. (Bentham 1948: 337)

By conflating the 'object' with the 'property that exists in the object', ownership of property has come to be seen as simply 'ownership of the object' rather than 'ownership of property in the object'. But as the essence of property is rights in respect of things so ownership of property must be concerned with ownership of rights in respect of things. Thus when we speak of the owner of a thing the phrase is meaningless unless we mean by that the owner of rights in the thing. It follows from this that there may well be more than one owner of rights in a thing, none of whom own the thing itself.

It is noteworthy that in his seminal essay on Ownership, Honore (1961) is much troubled by the means by which we identify the owner of a thing and offers a number of tests which by his own admission fail to offer a satisfactory explanation. In the course of his discourse he contrasts the position of the owner of land (by which he means the lessor) with the lessee. But this example lays the fallacy bare. Within the leasehold relationship there is not one owner but two. The lessor is the owner of the reversion whilst the lessee is the owner of the lease. Both own property in the land but neither own the land itself because to speak of owning a thing is meaningless without identifying with what rights the ownership is concerned.[20] Consequently the right to exclude is simply one of the rights that might be owned in respect of a thing. It is a particular incident of property but by no means its hallmark.[21]

Thus when we speak of ownership all we are doing is identifying where certain property rights reside. In so doing we have contrasted private property, which is property rights owned by individuals, with common property, which is property rights owned by all. However we now need to introduce the idea of communal ownership and to contrast it with co-ownership. In contrast to communal ownership, co-ownership is simply an example of private property where property rights are vested in a group of individuals each of whom has a vested interest which he or she may alienate if they so choose.[22] Communal ownership, on the other hand, is a species of common property, although here the property rights do not belong to society in general but in a sub-set of society, namely a community of some description. The difference between communal ownership and co-ownership is a crucial one. Admittedly the categories are superficially similar. As regards their fellows both co-owners and communal owners have a right not to be excluded and, against the rest of the world, a right to exclude. But whilst co-owners each have a right vested in them as individuals no such vesting occurs in communal ownership. For in communal ownership the rights that exist arose not from vesting but from status as a member of the community and, in consequence, an individual member possesses no vested interest capable of being alienated or otherwise dealt with outside of the community.

It is perhaps time for us to consider what roles these concepts and notions play in practice.

Part II: The Central Importance of Common Property

The idea of society is inextricably bound up with the concept of both private and common property. The mutual interdependence of individuals which is the hallmark of any society requires there to be both common property to afford a stage for such interdependence and private property to give voice to that individuality (see Rawls 1971). In any particular society the exact mixture of private and common property rights will differ as the result of the historical, economic, ideological and sociological pressures that have arisen within that particular community (Rose 1986). In the context of land-holding regimes, in the real world this is a process 'far more subtle than the mind of any single individual' (Ellickson 1993: 1400), but a couple of simplistic examples will help illustrate the point.

Take an ultra-communist society which supposedly rejects all notions of private property. In such a place there will still have to be rights which accord with such an institution in respect of certain resources. For example, the food on my plate or, at least, in my mouth must, in such a society, be capable of moving from the common to the private for otherwise anarchy will prevail. The same is surely true for many other resources such as clothes and accommodation. Likewise, in an ultra-free market society where all resources are privately owned, there will still need to be rights akin to common property rights to enable that society to function. For example, it would be quite possible for certain property rights in respect of the roads in a community to be privately owned. However there would have to be rules governing access to this resource preventing the private owner from unreasonably refusing use of the road to members of that society. In short, any system under which others could pluck food from my mouth or in which the private rights holder in the highway could force me to starve, imprisoned in my house without access to the road, would lack the necessary ingredients of order and interdependence to qualify as a society.

In Part I I attempted to disentangle the notions of ownership and property. Property is the rights in relation to the thing whilst ownership identifies where those particular rights reside. Whilst the term 'common property' is applied to those rights which can be held by individuals collectively as members of society (or some sub-set of society) and the term 'private property' is applied to those rights which can be held by individuals as individuals (either alone or in groups each with a vested interest) the above examples make clear that the two categories are not mutually exclusive. In other words the same thing might be the subject of both private and common property rights. This underlines why it is a mistake to talk about the owner of a thing for often the same thing will have a number of owners of different types of right, some of which might be private property rights and some of which might be common property rights. In the ultra-free market society considered above, private property rights exist in the roads but there is also a common property right whereby members of society are given a right not to be unreasonably excluded from the resource. Likewise in the ultra-communist society, food is owned in common but to prevent anarchy there are rules akin to private property rights (although not necessarily classified as such) giving individuals the right to exclude interference with the resource at some point (be that the placing of the food on one's plate, in one's mouth or at some other suitable juncture).

As indicated in the introduction, such talk of common property is contentious. Some doubt whether the category has any meaning whatsoever (Harris 1995: 438) and thus a defence is now due. Harris, in claiming that 'common property means no property', cited the example of *Bradford Corporation* v. *Pickles*.[23] In that case the House of Lords held that no matter what the motive, it was lawful to sink a well and extract subjacent percolating water. According to Harris:

> ... the label *common property* could have been applied, in English Law, to subjacent percolating water. Anyone who can lawfully sink a well commits no wrong, in any circumstances, by the further act of drawing off percolating water from under his neighbour's ground. To describe underground percolating water as *common property* would signify no more than the trespassory rules conferring ownership interests could have been, but have not been, extended to that resource. In fact the term is not applied to it by the courts because all that need be said has been said in terms of articulating the absence of ownership interests. (Harris 1995: 437)

This is a variation on the theme of Garrett Hardin's infamous 'The Tragedy of the Commons' (1968) which sought to argue, in the context of a common used by herdsmen, that common property was unsustainable because, as the costs of overuse were borne collectively but the benefits enjoyed individually, it necessarily led to the over-utilisation of the resource and to its eventual exhaustion. Despite being regarded by some as 'a first principle – an article of faith in resource economics' (Reisner 1991: 422) there are severe weaknesses in the argument. The theory posits economically rational herdsmen without the foresight to see that, as economically rational herdsmen they will all be tempted to over-exploit which will remove the benefit, and thus the temptation, to do so. More fundamentally, the theory does not prove what it sets out to prove. It is not, after all, common property which causes the problem (if problem there really is) but the interface between private and common property that is problematic. It is because the common is collectively owned whilst each herd is privately owned that individual herdsmen are supposedly tempted to increase their herd to the point where the common is exhausted.[24] The argument could equally have been employed in an attempt to argue that private property is flawed because of the selfish excess created by individual ownership of rights in each herd. Most tellingly of all, Hardin's thesis is disproved by experience. Despite his pessimism, common property has played a significant role in societies throughout the ages. In the context of land tenure, for example, common land was the mainstay of farming in northern Europe throughout the Middle Ages[25] and in the Swiss Alpine meadows it is still the norm.[26] Furthermore, as we shall see, common property continues to prosper in a multitude of forms and in a multitude of societies in the face of Hardin's premature obituary (see Field 1990).

The fundamental flaw in both Hardin's and Harris's attack on common property is their failure to appreciate exactly what is meant by common property. In their view all it entails is a finite resource to which open access is permitted and where nothing stands in the way of over-exploitation. However this is not common property but unowned property. As with all finite resources the open access that necessarily results from the absence of a property regime risks the danger of over-exploitation. Thus the percolating water in *Bradford Corporation* v. *Pickles* and Hardin's common are unowned resources which, absent a property regime, are constrained by no jurisdictional means of limiting access. In contrast, a common property system must, to be a property system at all, have some means of limiting access. Whether those limitations are as a result of self-regulation, custom or law is not significant provided that those who are part of the community to which these rights belong recognise that they do not have unlimited access to the resource. The point can be seen if one looks for a moment at 'the oceans of the world' which Hardin believes 'continue to suffer from the survival of the philosophy of the commons' (1968: 1244). Whilst this was once true, it is no longer so. Prior to international treaties regulating access to fishing outside of territorial waters this was an unowned resource susceptible to over-exploitation. However, in response to over-fishing, international treaties were signed limiting access to this resource and thus introducing a common property regime in this area. In short, before the harpoon achieved its purpose Moby Dick was unowned property, but his offspring swimming free are now common property subject to an extremely onerous restricted access regime.[27]

Put simply, restricted access is a prerequisite for the operation of any common property system. This is perhaps easier to appreciate with some forms of resource than with others. Our quibbles aside, if there is a problem of over-exploitation, in Hardin's common, a custom or law limiting the size of each herd would necessarily deal with the problem as custom has dealt for a millennium with the danger of over-grazing in the Swiss Alpine meadows and the international treaties have, to a large extent, dealt with the problems of over-fishing in international waters. But the same limitations exist with quite different forms of common property. Consider an open space such as Regents Park in Central London which is normally never closed to the public. Whilst one would expect such a resource to come within any definition of common property there appears to be a difficulty for at first glance it seems to be open access. Yet such a park is no more open access than the Swiss Alpine meadows. It is just that the limitations that restrict access to the resource are so well accepted that it is hard to conceive of them as separate from the resource itself. There are, of course, a host of laws and by-laws stating what can and cannot be done in the Park which are the means by which access is limited. One would need to do no more than pitch a tent in the centre and await the arrival of the Parks Constabulary to see just how restricted access to this particular resource really is. The same is true of the public highway which is another form of common property although rarely conceived of in such terms (but see Demsetz 1967). Again it would at first appear to be open access but, on further consideration, it likewise becomes obvious that one's use of it is even more severely limited. The Euston Road, for example, can be used for traversing but not loitering. If you decide to rest there you can in theory be charged with its obstruction, as you can if you decide to sell your wares from it (without the necessary licence) or, unwisely, move your tent there at the behest of the good officers of the Parks Constabulary.[28] Just like the Swiss Alpine meadows and Regents Park, the Euston Road is an example of a finite resource which is subject to a limited access regime.

From these examples it can be appreciated that common property, like private property, is a limited access regime. It is not a synonym for open access but another solution, along with private property, to the problems of open access (see Stevenson 1991). The examples used have been picked for their parochial quality to underline that in this society, like every other, common property is ever present. It is now time to consider how far the English Common Law has recognised this essential truth.

Part III: Common Property and the Common Law

So to what extent does the English Common Law recognise common property rights? If one is to believe Blackstone the answer is not at all. Yet, despite the seeming confidence of his assertion, there is little truth in the famed pronouncement that 'the right of property is that sole and despotic dominion which one man claims and exercises over the external things in the world, in total exclusion of the right of any other individual in the universe' (Blackstone 1787: 2, 15)[29]. For as the jurist von Jhering noted, admittedly outside of the Common Law context but pertinent to it none the less, 'There is no absolute property, ie property that is freed from taking into consideration the interest of the community, and history has taken care to inculcate this truth into *all peoples*' (Jhering 1878: 7, emphasis added). So, to a limited extent at least, all property is common property in so far as the community has rights in respect of it (see Powell 1968; Large 1973). In many instants this will be the essentially negative right *not to be excluded from protection from the misuse of the thing* as was recognised by the American Supreme Court over half a century ago in *Nebbia* v. *New York* where they stated that 'neither property rights nor contract rights are absolute ... [for] [e]qually fundamental with the private right is that of the public to regulate it in the common interest'.[30] Thus in driving your car (or someone else's for that matter) you owe a duty of care to the rest of society not to do so negligently, the effect of which is to give any member of society injured by you failing to do so a cause of action against you. As these are restrictions that apply to users of a thing irrespective of ownership,[31] such limitations on private property are commonly not regarded as proprietory but rather part of the law of obligations, public law or the criminal law and we will not consider them further here.[32]

Not only is it possible to argue that all property is (to a limited extent) common property in our (and every) society but alternatively that the realm of common property is of a much wider compass than its private law counterpart. If the Commons refers to resources from which individuals have a right not to be excluded, this has the potential to bring much, not normally regarded as property, within its ambit. For centuries, for example, the Common Law recognised that those involved in certain trades owed a duty, enforceable in tort, to serve all-comers at a reasonable price without discrimination.[33] The law of common callings, so called (see Craig 1991), applied to persons or corporations engaged in fields such as innkeeping, common carriers and ferrymen and recognised the importance of these trades as public utilities providing an essential service often within the context of a local monopoly.[34] Likewise it is possible to regard recent developments in anti-discrimination legislation as a similar manifestation of such common property. The tentative aims of the Race Relations Act 1965, in making racial discrimination in places of public resort an offence, similarly embraced an ideal of non-exclusion from a limited category of resources, the scale of which was much expanded three years later when the second Race Relations Act brought within the ambit of unlawful racial discrimination areas such as housing and employment (see Lester and Bindman 1972). As with the restrictions considered in the previous paragraph, these are areas normally not regarded as proprietary but rather as part of the law of obligations, public law or the criminal law and they will likewise not be considered further.[35]

Thus far we have considered examples at the extremes and many would consider fanciful the arguments that, because there is no such thing as absolute ownership, all property is common property, or that the definition of resources can be drawn so widely that the concept of common property can be expanded to include things not normally regarded as things. It is perhaps time to consider less contentious examples of common property recognised by the Common Law. And one does not need to roam far to find the quintessential example of common property, the Commons themselves, which are rights of common, protected either by the Common Law or custom (see Gadsden 1988). Rights of common can, according to Halsbury, be traced back to the Anglo-Saxon times where 'the majority of this country were organised into self-supporting agricultural village communities'. Such rights consisted of a limited-access regime in which individual members of a village community had the right not to be excluded from using the common lands for certain activities such as the grazing of animals, the cultivating of crops and other diverse activities. Although, in extent, much reduced by the move towards enclosures (see Cole and Postgate 1971: 121–123), common lands survive to this day, although now subject to a registration requirement (Commons Registration Act 1965).

In *New Windsor Corporation* v. *Mellor*,[36] for example, the Court of Appeal held that the inhabitants of the borough of New Windsor had a customary right to indulge in sports and pastimes on a piece of land known as Bachelors' Acre. Thus, although the fee simple was vested in the borough, the community had a right not to be excluded from taking part in such activities the effect of which was to give every member of the community *locus standi* to make application to the court to prevent the land from being used in a way that was inconsistent with the exercise of such a customary right. The fee simple owner was consequently prevented from continuing to use the land as a car park and a school playing field by reason of rights belonging to the community which could not be sold, gifted or otherwise disposed of and which even a century of disuse did not diminish.[37]

Rights of common are by no means the only form of common property unquestionably recognised under English Law. For example, rights that arise by prescription or more usually presumed dedication such as public rights of way over land offer a further glimpse of common property rights. Such a right, being only a right of passage, does not vest title to the highway in the public, for the owner of the fee simple retains his title at Common Law, subject only to this restriction upon his ownership interest. However, it is still an example of common property whereby the public in general have a positive right not to be excluded from the resource to the limited extent necessary to traverse it.

What is emerging at this point in the argument is that common property rights under English Law tend to be limited to particular use rights. Rights of common are particular rights carved out of the estate originally vested in the lord of the manor.[38] As was stated in *Doe d. Lowes* v. *Davidson* the estate owner has 'the entire dominion over the soil subject to the tenants' rights of common'[39] for, as noted in *Arlett* v. *Ellis*, 'all that the lord has not granted remains in him.' This is equally true when it would at first sight appear that the owner has granted away his entire interest under a sole right of vesture, herbage and pasture (Gadsden 1988: par 7.30). Thus in *Hopkins* v. *Robinson* where the entire benefit of grazing pastures was held in common, 'the soil', according to Chief Justice Hale, was still 'the lord's and he has the mines, trees, bushes etc and he may dig for turfs'.[40] One saw the same picture emerge in respect of the rights derived from custom in *New Windsor Corpo-*

ration v. *Mellor* and the same is, of course, true in respect of public rights of way. Thus whilst common property rights are recognised under English Law they are a closed category of use rights quite different to the open-textured nature of rights derived from the ownership of estates in land.

The reason why the greater interests derived from ownership of an estate in land is not subject to the same form of communal ownership as the common property rights considered above is because under the private law a legal estate in land (and likewise title in personality) can only be owned by someone or something invested with legal personality. A community (unless incorporated) does not have a legal personality of its own and thus no means by which title can vest. It is, at this point, instructive to consider for a moment the etymology of the term *person*. Initially the word was used to describe the mask that Greek and Roman actors wore on the stage. Gradually it became employed to designate an individual's role within the legal system and in Roman Law was applied to describe a private individual as opposed to one still submerged within his clan. With the introduction of a new procedure, the *legis actiones*, such individuals were provided with a means to assert their rights independent of the clan and, almost paradoxically, a term used to identify the rights of individuals emerging from the shadow of the clan became the very reason why clans could no longer assert rights themselves (see Thomas 1976). Even in the context of rights of common a diluted form of the Common Law's obsession with legal personality can be witnessed in the recent judgment of Mr Justice Harman in *Ministry of Defence* v. *Wiltshire County Council* where he agreed with counsel's submission that:

> ... it was impossible for a village green to be created by the exercise of rights save on behalf of some recognisable unit of this country – and when I say recognisable I mean recognisable by the law. Such units have in the past been occasionally boroughs, frequently parishes, both ecclesiastical and civil, and occasionally manors, all of which are entities known to the law, and where there is a defined body of persons capable of exercising the rights ... [41]

But scepticism on my part prompts the rejoinder that such limitations must necessarily exist for how else can such rights be exercised. In the context of the private law there must be someone who can assert ownership, and, to a limited extent the same is true in respect of rights of common. From such a perspective, quibbles to the contrary simply ignore the practical difficulties of enforcing rights that belong to something that the law itself can neither define nor control.[42] To respond further requires a brief examination of the private trust and it is that to which I will now turn.

Part IV: A Role for the Private Trust?

As has been indicated on a number of occasions in this chapter the same thing can have a number of owners in respect of differing rights in the resource. The landlord owns the reversion in respect of a piece of land whilst the tenant owns the lease. The lord of the manor (or the modern-day equivalent the local authority)[43] owns the estate in the land whilst the commoners own the rights of common. Even with chattels, the person in possession has a possessory title which exists quite independent of ownership rights in the thing.[44]

In addition to the different rights that can exist and be owned by different parties in the same thing, it is also possible under English Law to split those particular interests themselves between different persons. This is the essence of a trust. Up until now we have dealt with the horizontal division of rights in a thing so that, for example, the landlord has rights in respect of his reversion whilst the tenant has rights derived from the lease. In a trust, however, the rights stemming from ownership of any particular interest are split vertically so that differing incidents of ownership of the same right can be held separately. The basis of this division is the distinction between management and use whereby control of the resource is separated from its enjoyment. Under a trust the right to manage the property held on trust is given to a trustee who holds the legal title on behalf of a beneficiary who has the right to use and enjoy the resource in which he holds the equitable title.

The trust form is based upon the division of ownership between trustee and beneficiary and it is by means of this mechanism that we might give renewed impetus to the ownership aspirations of communities. Such observations are not new. Across the Atlantic, as Gray (1994) has so eloquently illustrated, the rhetorical and conceptual power of the trust has long been utilised to this end. International lawyers, for example, have invoked trust rhetoric in conceiving of an 'intergenerational equity' whereby each generation, as trustees, is burdened by obligations owed to future generations, as beneficiaries (Weiss 1983–4). On a more substantive level the historic public trust doctrine, which initially confirmed state ownership (in the absence of Crown title) of navigable waters and tidelands on behalf of all citizens, seems to be in the process of extending beyond such narrow confines to include more general environmental resources such as the countryside[45] and wildlife.[46] Such developments have been at the behest of academics who have long seen the potential for such advances in both the width (Sax 1969–70) and the jurisdictional ambit (Ausness 1986) and have contributed to a general change in the tone of the debate concerning environmental issues. In his seminal article 'Should Trees have Standing? – Towards Legal

Rights for Natural Objects', for example, Christopher Stone argued that natural objects might be represented or defended by a friend with legal personality (1972); this was echoed within days in the dissenting opinion of Justice William O. Douglas in the United States Supreme Court case of *Sierra Club* v. *Morton*.[47]

Interesting as these examples are they are of little significance to the development of English trust law. In so far as the American public trust doctrine involves notions of trust it is a specialised mechanism whose origin can be traced to the peculiar circumstances of the American Revolution and the displacing of Crown sovereignty by that of the people (see McCay 1995: 85–87). In this jurisdiction the public trust is limited to its charitable incarnation whereby trusts that fulfil certain requirements bestowing charitable status are exempt from some of the rules applicable to private trusts such as the rule against perpetual trusts and the beneficiary principle (see below). These conditions are not easy to fulfil and require the trust, *in a way that the law recognises*, to promote the public benefit by relieving poverty, advancing religion or education or otherwise benefiting the community. Whilst charitable trusts clearly have a role to play in the context of environmentalism and the aspirations of communities, they do not provide a complete answer.[48] The law of charities develops incrementally on a case-by-case basis which means that it tends to lag behind developments in society in general. Thus in *Re Grove-Grady*,[49] a gift to set up an animal refuge where the animals would be free from molestation by man was, from today's perspective at least, somewhat surprisingly deemed not to be charitable because no public benefit was deemed to arise. One suspects this is a precedent that would not survive a renewed outing in the Court of Appeal but it underlines the essential conservatism of the law of charities made all the worse by a conception of the public good which requires judges to adopt an approach that necessarily favours the status quo.[50]

It is thus to the law of private trusts that we must turn for a mechanism that will provide communities and others with an ownership vehicle which will function irrespective of whether or not their aspirations are deemed to be of benefit to the public. Again such an approach is not new. The case for stewardship is often articulated by reference to the trust/beneficiary relationship (for example, Lucy and Mitchell 1996: 584), but this is usually as a simile with little substantive content (see Gray 1994: 206). Yet the private trust, with its provision of a trustee in whom the legal title vests, does seem to offer communities without legal personality a substantive mechanism whereby they can enjoy open-textured interests such as estates in land.

The reason why the private trust is normally not thought up to the job of providing such a mechanism is because of what is known as the beneficiary principle (see Hayton and Marshall 1996: 190–219). This is a notion of some two centuries vintage based on dicta of Sir William Grant MR in *Morice* v. *Bishop of Durham* where he stated 'There must be somebody in whose favour the court can decree performance'.[51] The principle has had a mixed reception in the intervening period and has not infrequently been ignored in circumstances where it would seem to have been applicable.[52] However, following the endorsement of Roxburgh J in *Re Astor's Settlement Trusts*,[53] the principle has been given renewed impetus in recent years. So what lies behind the beneficiary principle? Despite the dicta of Sir William Grant MR it is not really concerned with identifying 'somebody in whose favour the court can decree performance' but in identifying *somebody at whose behest the court can enforce performance*.[54] For the principle is not concerned with identifying an owner of the beneficial interest but with locating an enforcer of the trustee's duties as can be seen from the comments of Viscount Simmonds in *Leahy* v. *Attorney General for New South Wales*:

> A gift can be made to persons (including a corporation) but it cannot be made to a purpose or to an object: so, also, a trust may be created for the benefit of persons as [beneficiaries] but not for a purpose or object unless the purpose or object be charitable. *For a purpose or object cannot sue, but, if it be charitable, the Attorney General can sue to enforce it* ...[55]

This is the other side of the coin considered in Part I above. For trustees to be under a duty requires there to be somebody in whom the right to enforce the duty is vested. For a duty without means of enforcing the duty is no duty at all.[56] However, as one can see from Viscount Simmonds' dicta, the uncritical application of this principle would provide severe limitations on the usefulness of the private trust in the context of communal property rights. If the beneficiary principle requires that all trusts be for persons, with the equitable interest necessarily vesting in those persons, the trust model will not provide a means by which communities can own assets and, at best, will only provide a cloak behind which individual members of the community will each own particular shares in the asset.[57] Such a solution is incomplete and antithetical to the notion of communal property in which members' interests are derived from their status as members of the community and not because they own a vested interest.

However, whilst Viscount Simmonds correctly identifies the mischief towards which the beneficiary principle is directed, it does not necessarily follow that every non-charitable trust[58] must be for a person. There has been a retreat from *Leahy* in recent years[59] and in *Re Denley* Goff J added an important gloss to Viscount Simmonds' dicta: 'Where, then, the trust, though expressed as a purpose, is directly or indirectly for the benefit of an individual or individuals, it seems to me that it is in general outside the mischief of the beneficiary principle'.[60]

For the purposes of communal property and common property rights in the environment this is an extremely important observation. For in this sentence lies the roots of what could become a fully-fledged public trust doctrine removed from the constricting embrace of charitable status. Under *Re Denley* Goff J invokes the possibility of a purpose trust in which no one owns the beneficial interest yet which is freed from the threat of invalidity because of the presence of indirect beneficiaries capable of enforcing the trustees' obligations. As a community is a collection of individuals with no legal personality of its own, a structure that does not require there to be an owner offers obvious possibilities. The trust can be held for the purposes of promoting the community's aims whilst the individual members of the community will qualify as persons with sufficient interest to enforce the trustees' obligations. There is, in such an analysis, the potential for such a trust to develop further to create a mechanism for promoting environmental goals by regarding the public in general as the indirect beneficiaries of such a trust with the necessary capacity to enforce the trustees' obligations. This however would require some conception of the public good which might necessarily collapse back into nothing more than a question regarding charitable status, which, after all, is the mechanism which currently exists in respect of purpose trusts deemed to be in the public interest.[61] The real potential of the *Re Denley* purpose trust lies in its capacity to provide communities with a mechanism to promote their aims irrespective of whether or not those aims are regarded as being in the public interest. This has obvious advantages over the current analysis of such communities which tends to deal with them as nothing more than a gathering of individuals each with a vested and, from a proprietary stance at least, alienable interest (see note 57).

The question which needs to be addressed is: what does it take to become an indirect beneficiary with power to enforce the trustees' obligations? This is, in effect, a question about *locus standi* and to whom the court will listen in any dispute concerning the exercise of the trustees' duties. In *Re Denley*, the trust related to a sports ground primarily for the benefit of employees of a company and Goff J had little difficulty in identifying them as the indirect beneficiaries of the trust. However, on the general question of *locus standi*, all he makes is the following comment:

> ... there may be a purpose or object trust, the carrying out of which would benefit an individual or individuals, where that benefit is so indirect or intangible or which is otherwise so framed as not to give those persons any *locus standi* to apply to the court to enforce the trust, in which case the beneficiary principle would, as it seems to me, apply to invalidate the trust ...[62]

This, coupled with his insistence that all the indirect beneficiaries need to be capable of being listed,[63] underlines that the decision is not as radical as one might imagine. Despite its liberal approach to the beneficiary principle there is still a strong conservative element in the judgment which acts as a brake on the potential developments I have outlined above. From the tone of his comments it seems likely that Goff J would not have needed much persuasion that a particular purpose was too abstract. This has necessarily led commentators to downplay its significance. For example, despite flirting with the *Re Denley* type trust as a form of purpose trust, Hayton seems to have settled upon describing it, more conventionally, as a trust for people (Hayton and Marshall 1996: 191, but compare with earlier editions of this text). Even Cotterrell (1992), who can normally be relied upon to offer interesting and illuminating insights in this field, has contented himself with the rather tame (but no doubt accurate) observation that 'the scope and long-term influence of this decision remains unclear'. Likewise the response in the case law has been somewhat muted and, despite the odd appeal to its underlying principle,[64] this has often either been overlooked[65] or actively ignored.[66]

It would consequently be over-optimistic to see in *Re Denley* anything more than the potential to give new impetus to the ownership aspirations of communities within our society. However it stands as a judgment which offers the possibility of such development which, with its reliance on a test of *locus standi*, empowers the community, by making their rules as to membership the litmus test of standing. In the public law arena, of course, the question of *locus standi* is still a matter of debate and argument.[67] Yet, in the context of *Re Denley*, such issues seem less problematic for here the court is relieved of the task of formulating a test of standing because the community, by reason of its status as a community, must necessarily have provided one.[68] Of course, the test might not be referred to as such and in many instances will be implicit rather than explicit. However, some form of test must exist for otherwise it would be meaningless to talk of a community if there is no method of identifying to whom it applies.[69] Thus, under a liberal interpretation of *Re Denley*, a community possesses a means by which legal title can be held on behalf of its members each of whom hold the common property right not to be excluded from the resource so held, provided they retain their status as members of the community.

Conclusion

As I stated at the outset my primary aim in this chapter was to offer a description of the present, rather than a vision of a brave new tomorrow.

Common Property and Private Trusts 243

Common property is all around us and it has always been thus. We devalue our jurisprudence by failing to recognise this essential truth and caricature the Common Law with our preoccupation with private property. As I hope I have shown, the Commons exist in numerous forms and are protected by various legal mechanisms many outside the narrow confines of the Chancery lawyer's arsenal. However it is to the quintessential creation of the Court of Chancery, the express private trust, that I have turned to provide a mechanism to give renewed impetus to the ownership aspirations of communities: at least those not feted with charitable status. Such groups will often meet with the displeasure of the majority but that, in a sense, is the point. *Re Denley* would empower communities irrespective of society's views on their worth and only time will tell whether society is willing to allow such latitude to those in whom, almost by definition,[70] it does not approve.

Notes

1 Which, in respect of customary rights, requires them to have existed 'from time immemorial'.
2 See *New Windsor Corporation v. Mellor* [1975] 3 All ER 44.
3 Rights of Way Act 1990.
4 A government Access to the Countryside Bill was introduced to Parliament in 1998 but later withdrawn in favour of pursuing change under voluntary agreements. A stronger private member's Right to Roam Bill was introduced in January 1999 which seeks to give a general right 'to enter on to, roam on and pass over open country on foot for the purposes of open air recreation'.
5 K. Gray (1991: 268). But note the qualifications made in n.4 on that page.
6 It is, perhaps, not without significance that Reich was able to make the same arguments a few years later (Reich 1965) without at any point using the term 'property'. But see also Reich (1990–1).
7 For a compelling defence of Hohfeldian analysis in the context of property rights see Eleftheriadis (1996).
8 Of which property rights form a sub-set.
9 Of which contractual rights likewise form a sub-set.
10 It is perhaps a little more complex than this as Hohfeld indicates when he points out 'that instead of there being a single right with a single correlative duty resting on all the persons against whom the right avails, there are many separate and distinct rights, actual and potential, each one of which has a correlative duty resting upon some one person'; Hohfeld (1978: 92).
11 But see Sykes and Walker (1993: 6–10).
12 For example, since the abolition of slavery, it is no longer possible to have property rights in living human beings, whilst, in respect of non-renewable body parts, the ambit of property is much restricted. See the policy orientated decision of the Criminal Division of the Court of Appeal in *Regina v. Kelly* (1998) *The Times* 21 May and the obiter comments of Rose LJ speculating on the possibility of the Common Law, in time, recognising property in body parts required for organ transplant. See also the musings of the ethics committee, comprising such luminaries as Professor Ian Kennedy

of the UCL School of Public Policy, reported in *The Independent* on 24 June 1998 which proposed the legalisation of the sale of kidneys from living donors.
13 2 PH 774 (41 ER 1143), 11 Beav 571 (50 ER 937).
14 Case C-361/88, *Commission of the European Communities* v. *Federal Republic of Germany* [1991] ECR I-2567 and Case C-59/89, *Commission of the European Communities* v. *Federal Republic of Germany* [1991] ECR I-2607.
15 In the succinct words of Melinda Kimble, a United States government spokesmen discussing the emerging market in sulphur and carbon dioxide permits, 'we can trade anything' (*Newsnight*, BBC2, 28 May 1998).
16 See, for example, the views of Auberon Waugh in a discussion on the merits and demerits of virtual publishing via the Net (*Newsnight*, 1 July 1998).
17 See, for example, the discussion on this point (*Newsnight*, 5 January 1998). It is testament to the fundamental importance and dynamic nature of property rights that such discussion features so often in current affairs programming.
18 It is commonly accepted that there are three types of property: private, common and state. See for example Demsetz (1967) and Grunebaum (1987). It is not proposed to consider the third form of property right here although it is perhaps worth laying down a marker as to whether this really is a third form of property right or simply a specialised sub-category of private property.
19 I am grateful to Kevin Gray for drawing my attention to this article.
20 For a partial recognition of this point see Lawson and Rudden (1982: 116).
21 For an examination of the various property rights that might be the subject of ownership (albeit in a private property context) see Honore (1961) Ch. 5.
22 This is as true in a joint tenancy as it is in a tenancy in common although in the former a severance must first occur (although – to the logician's dismay – this might be effected by the logically subsequent act of alienation itself).
23 [1895] AC 587.
24 However, as we saw when we considered the ultra-communist society, every common property system must at some point interface with private property. It then becomes a question of determining the most practicable point for that interface to occur.
25 Admittedly this form of land tenure became increasingly inappropriate in the light of progress in the arts of agriculture. But this was not a problem concerning negative externalities as identified by Hardin but one of positive externalities associated with free riders and lack of incentive. See Cole and Postgate (1971: 121–123).
26 Where a common property system of grazing has lasted for more than a thousand years. See Stevenson (1991).
27 As to the point at which a whale swimming in the ocean is deemed to be reduced to private property see *Littledale* v. *Scaith* (1778) 1 Taunt 243, 127 ER 826. On the special provisions regarding ownership of 'royal fish' (sturgeon, porpoise and whale) see *De Prerogativa Regis* (1324).
28 There are also civil remedies available to protect such resources. See, for example, *Secretary of Defence* v. *Percy* (1998) *The Times* 11 May, where a member of the public who had entered upon a public footpath not to 'pass and re-pass' but to remove unlawful notices was held to be a trespasser.
29 Although it should not be overlooked that, in the next line, he adds the caveat that '[i]t consists in the free use, enjoyment, and disposal of all a person's acquisitions, without any control or diminution *save only by the laws of the land*' (emphasis added).
30 (1934) 291 US 502, 523.
31 But see my earlier comments on the use (or misuse) of this term.
32 However as the user of the thing will always have a limited property in it arising from

his possession it is at least arguable that these are restrictions affecting the possessory title and thus within the ambit of property.
33 See, for example, the judgment of Birkett J in *Constantine* v. *Imperial Hotels* [1944] 1 KB 693.
34 At about the same period in its development the Common Law extended control over *de facto* monopoly providers of services to the public by means of a doctrine regulating businesses 'affected with a public interest'. See Taggart (1990: 29).
35 This is an area where the natural acquisitiveness of public law is casting a hungry eye. See for example Oliver (1997).
36 [1975] 3 All ER 44.
37 [1975] 3 All ER 44, 52.
38 Cf. *The Wik Case* (1996) 71 ALJR 173 where, in an inversion of this approach, the Australian High Court held that the granting of private pastoral leases to individual farmers did not, of itself, extinguish communal native title already subsisting in the leased land.
39 (1813) 2 M&S 175, 184; 105 ER 348, 352.
40 (1671) 1 Mod 74, 74; 86 ER 742, 743.
41 [1995] 4 All ER 931, 937.
42 But as the law relating to unincorporated associations indicates the law is very resourceful when it comes to defining form. See *Conservative Central Office* v. *Burrell* [1982] 1 WLR 522.
43 See Commons Registration Act 1965, ss.1(3), 8(3).
44 In the context of private property rights in chattels there are only two forms of title and the term ownership is used in contrast with the less extensive rights derived from possessory title. See generally Goode (1995).
45 *Paepcke* v. *Public Buildings Commission of Chicago* (1970) 263 NE 2d 11.
46 *Wade* v. *Kramer* (1984) 459 NE 2d 1025.
47 (1972) 405 US 727. See also Chapter 1.
48 Normally both community associations and development trusts achieve their principal aims by adopting charitable status. However there is a growing trend whereby companies limited by guarantee are established as non-profit-making bodies which provides the advantage (or disadvantage depending upon one's standpoint) of an absence of Charity Commission supervision. See, for example, 'Doing the Coin Street flip', *The Observer*, 7 June 1998. Although outside the remit of this chapter such developments merit further research into the adequacy of the safeguards to prevent abuse of this mechanism. Cf. charities where the Charity Commission is required to fulfil such a function and *Re Denley*-type purpose trusts where the indirect beneficiaries have *locus standi* to enforce the trustee's obligations (see text at n.59 onwards).
49 [1929] 1 Ch 557.
50 See for example *National Anti-Vivisection Society* v. *IRC* [1948] AC 31 where a trust to promote anti-vivisection was held not to be charitable because (i) on balance the House of Lords was not convinced its aims were in the public interest and (ii) it was deemed to be too political because it advocated a change in the law. Cf. the American *Restatement on the Law of Trusts*, 374 which states that: '[t]he courts do not take sides or attempt to decide which of two conflicting views of promoting the social interests of the community is the better adapted for the purpose, even though the views are opposed to each other. Thus a trust to promote peace by disarmament, as well as a trust to promote peace by preparedness for war, is charitable.'
51 (1804) 9 Ves 399, 405.

52 Both consciously as in *Re Dean* (1889) 41 Ch D 552, 556 and unconsciously as in *Re Trusts of the Abbott Fund* [1990] 2 Ch 326.
53 [1952] Ch 534.
54 Cf *Re Endacott* [1960] Ch 232.
55 [1959] AC 457, emphasis added.
56 Hence the somewhat antiquated term *trusts of imperfect obligation* used to describe those anomalous purpose trusts which are valid despite offending the beneficiary principle.
57 This is admittedly the solution embraced in the context of unincorporated associations (see *Re Recher's Wills Trust* [1972] Ch 526) but this is the result of applying private property thinking to the essentially communal property scenario one is confronted with in such associations. Needless to say it produces a wholly unconvincing fudge which, against all the wishes of the donor, gives current members a vested interest in the gift whilst failing to explain how those interests pass, absent compliance with s.53(1)(c) of the Law of Property Act 1925, when new members join or old ones leave.
58 With the exception of the anomalous purpose trust where, in the memorable phrase of Harman LJ in *Re Endacott* [1960] Ch 232, 250, 'Homer has nodded'.
59 Particularly in the context of discretionary trusts. See *McPhail* v. *Doulton* [1971] AC 424 and the discussion of its import by Grbich (1974: 655–656).
60 [1968] 3 All ER 65, 69.
61 On the question of the public interest in the context of stewardship see Lucy and Mitchell (1996: 586–598).
62 [1968] 3 All ER 65, 69.
63 Admittedly prior to the liberalising effect of *McPhail* v. *Doulton* [1971] AC 424 the effect of which has led many commentators to suppose that a conceptual certainty test is now applicable to *Re Denley*-type trusts. See Hanbury and Martin (1997: 101). However it is surely possible to argue that, because no beneficiary can even hope to take a share in the beneficial interest, it is possible to embrace the even less stringent one person test as applied in *Re Gibbard* [1967] 1 WLR 42 in order to establish whether an applicant has the necessary *locus standi* to enforce the trust. This is arguably a more apposite application of the flawed argument raised by Browne-Wilkinson J in *Re Barlow's Will Trust* [1979] 1 WLR 287.
64 *Re Lipinski* [1977] 1 All ER 33.
65 *Barclays Bank* v. *Quistclose* [1970] AC 567.
66 *Re Grant's Will Trusts* [1979] 3 All ER 359 where Vinelott J, surely incorrectly, interpreted *Re Denley* as a trust for people and not a purpose trust at all.
67 See generally Le Sueur and Sunkin (1997: 490–498) and, more recently, *R.* v. *Somerset County Council & ARC ex parte Dixon* [1997] JPL 1030 where Sedley J at first instance took a very liberal approach to the question of standing, though see also the restrictive view of Popplewell J in *R.* v. *North Somerset District Council and Pioneer Aggregates (UK) Ltd ex parte Garnett and Pierssene* [1997] JPL 1015.
68 There is a parallel here with the approach in *R.* v. *Somerset County Council & ARC ex parte Dixon* [1997] JPL 1030 where the court paid particular regard to the applicant's own criteria in determining whether or not he possessed *locus standi*.
69 Which is, perhaps, the point that Harman J is seeking to make in the already quoted extract from his judgment in *Ministry of Defence* v. *Wiltshire County Council* [1995] 4 All ER 931, 937 (and accompanying text).
70 For otherwise, at least arguably, they would possess charitable status.

References

Ackerman, B. (1977) *Private Property and the Constitution* (London: Yale University Press).
Ausness, R. (1986) 'Water Right, The Public Trust Doctrine and the Protection of Instream Uses', *University of Illinois Law Review* 407–437.
Austin, J. (1885) *Lectures on Jurisprudence* 5th edn (London: Murray).
Bentham, J. (1948) *An Introduction to the Principles of Morals and Legislation* (ed. Harrison, W.) (Oxford: Blackwell).
Bentham, J. (1970) *Of Laws in General* (ed. Hart, H.L.A.) (London: Athlone).
Blackstone, W. (1787) *Commentaries on the Laws of England*, 10th edn (London: printed for A. Strahan, T. Cadell and D. Prince).
Borkowski, A. (1997) *Textbook on Roman Law*, 2nd edn (London: Blackstone Press).
Bryl, Yanka (1976) *An Anthology of Soviet Short Stories*, Vol. 2 (USSR: Progress).
Cohen, F. (1954) 'Dialogue on Private Property', *Rutgers Law Review*, 9: 357.
Cole, G.D.H. and Postgate, R. (1971) *The Common People* (London: Methuen).
Cotterrell, R. (1992) 'Some Sociological Aspects of the Controversy Around the Legal Validity of Private Purpose Trusts', in Goldstein, S. (ed.) *Equity and Contemporary Legal Developments* (Jerusalem: H&M Sacher Institute).
Craig, P.P. (1991) 'Constitutions, Property and Regulation', *Public Law*: 538–554.
Demsetz, H. (1967) 'Towards a Theory of Property Rights', *American Economic Review*, 57: 347–373.
Eleftheriadis, P. (1996) 'The Analysis of Property Rights', *Oxford Journal of Legal Studies*, 16 (1): 31–54.
Ellickson, R.C. (1993) 'Property in Land', *Yale Law Journal* 102: 1315–1400.
Field, S. (1990) 'The Economics of Common Property: A Review of Two Recent Books', *Natural Resources Journal* 30.
Gadsden, G.D. (1988) *The Law of Commons* (London: Sweet & Maxwell).
Goode, R.M. (1995) *Commercial Law* (Harmondsworth: Penguin).
Gray, K. (1991) 'Property in Thin Air', *Cambridge Law Journal* 50(2): 252–307.
Gray, K. (1994) 'Equitable Property', *Current Legal Problems* 47(2): 157–214.
Grbich, Y. (1974) 'Baden: Awakening the Conceptually Moribund Trust', *Modern Law Review* 37: 643–656.
Grunebaum, J. (1987) *Private Ownership* (London: Routledge).
Halsbury, *Laws of England*, 4th edn (London: Butterworths).
Hanbury and Martin (1997) *Modern Equity*, 15th edn (London: Sweet & Maxwell).
Hardin, G. (1968) 'The Tragedy of the Commons', *Science* 162: 1243–1248.
Harris, J.W. (1995) 'Private and Non-Private Property: What is the Difference?', *Law Quarterly Review* 111: 421–444.
Hayton, D.J., (1996) *Hayton and Marshall: Commentary and Cases on the Law of Trusts and Equitable Remedies*, 10th edn (London: Sweet & Maxwell).
Hegel, G. (1952) *The Philosophy of Right* (Oxford: Oxford University Press).
Hohfeld, W.N. (1978) *Fundamental Legal Conceptions As Applied In Judicial Reasoning* (Westport: CT: Greenwood Press).

Honore, A.M. (1961) 'Ownership', in Guest, A.G. (ed.) *Essays in Jurisprudence*, First Series (Oxford: Oxford University Press).

Jhering, R. von (1878) *Der Geist Des Romischen Rechts auf den Verschiedenen Stuffen Seiner Entwicklung*, 4th edn (Leipzig: Briettkopf und Hartel).

Kelsen, H. (1970) *Pure Theory of Law* (Berkeley: University of California Press).

Large, D.W. (1973) 'This Land is Whose Land? Changing Concepts of Land as Property', *Wisconsin Law Review*.

Lawson, F.H. and Rudden, B. (1982) *The Law of Property*, 2nd edn (Oxford: Clarendon).

Le Sueur, A. and Sunkin, M. (1997) *Public Law* (London and New York: Longman).

Lester, A. and Bindman, G. (1972) *Race and the Law* (Harmondsworth: Penguin).

Lucy, W.N.R. and Mitchell, C. (1996) 'Replacing Private Property: The Case for Stewardship', *Cambridge Law Journal* 55(3): 566–600.

McCay, B.J. (1995) 'The Making of an Environmental Doctrine' in Milton, K. (ed.) *Environmentalism: The View from Anthropology* (London: Routledge).

Macpherson, C.B. (1975) 'Capitalism and the Changing Concept of Property' in Kamenka, E. and Neale, R.S. (eds) *Feudalism, Capitalism and Beyond* (London: Edward Arnold).

Macpherson, C.B. (1977) 'Human Rights as Property Rights', *Dissent* 24: 72.

Oliver, D. (1997) 'Common Values in Private and Public Law', *Public Law*.

Powell, R.R.B. (1968) 'The Relationship between Property Rights and Civil Rights', *Hastings Law Journal* 15: 135.

Rawls, J. (1971) *A Theory of Justice* (Oxford: Clarendon).

Reich, C. (1964) 'The New Property', *Yale Law Journal* 73: 733–787.

Reich, C. (1965) 'Individual Rights and Social Welfare: The Emerging Legal Issues', *Yale Law Journal* 74: 1245–1257.

Reich, C. (1990–1) 'Beyond the New Property: An Ecological View of Due Process', *Brooklyn Law Review* 56: 73.

Reisner, A. (1991) 'Ecological Preservation as a Public Property Right: An Emerging Doctrine in Search of a Theory', *Harvard Environmental Law Review* 15: 393.

Rose, C. (1986) 'The Comedy of the Commons', *University of California Law Review* 53: 711–781.

Russell, B. (1961) *A History of Western Philosophy*, 2nd edn (London: Allen & Unwin).

Sackville, R. (1978) 'Property, Rights and Social Security', *University of New South Wales Law Journal* 2.

Sax, J.L. (1969–70) 'The Public Trust Doctrine in Natural Resources Law: Effective Judicial Intervention', *Michigan Law Review* 68: 471–566.

Seipp, D. (1994) 'The Concept of Property in the Early Common Law', *Law & History Review* 12: 29–91.

Simpson, A.W.B. (1986) *A History of Land Law*, 2nd edn (Oxford: Clarendon Press).

Sokol, M. (1994) 'Bentham and Blackstone on Incorporeal Hereditaments', *Legal History* 15(3); 287–305.

Stevenson, G.G. (1991) *Common Property Economics: A General Theory and Land Use Applications* (Cambridge: Cambridge University Press).

Stone, C. (1972) 'Should Trees have Standing? – Towards Legal Rights for Natural Objects', *Southern Californian Law Review* 45: 450–501.

Sykes, E. and Walker, S. (1993) *The Law of Securities*, 5th edn (Sydney: Law Book Co.).

Taggart, M. (1990) *Corporatisation, Privatisation, and Public Law* (Auckland, NZ: Legal Research Foundation).

Thomas, J.T. (1976) *Textbook on Roman Law* (Oxford: North Holland Publishing Co.).

Waldron, J. (1988) *The Right to Private Property* (Oxford: Clarendon Press).

Weiss, E.B. (1983–4) 'The Planetary Trust: Conservation and Intergenerational Equity', *Ecology Law Quarterly* 11:495–581.